D0906701

Soviet Economic Thought and Political Power in the USSR

Pergamon Policy Studies on the Soviet Union and Eastern Europe

Abouchar ECONOMIC EVALUATION OF SOVIET SOCIALISM
Allworth ETHNIC RUSSIA IN THE USSR
Blazynski FLASHPOINT POLAND
Dismukes & McConnell SOVIET NAVAL DIPLOMACY
Douglass SOVIET MILITARY STRATEGY IN EUROPE
Duncan SOVIET POLICY IN THE THIRD WORLD
Fallenbuchl & McMillan PARTNERS IN EAST-WEST ECONOMIC RELATIONS
Francisco, Laird & Laird THE POLITICAL ECONOMY OF COLLECTIVIZED AGRICULTURE
Kahan & Ruble INDUSTRIAL LABOR IN THE USSR
Koropeckyj & Schroeder ECONOMICS OF SOVIET REGIONS
McCagg & Silver SOVIET ASIAN ETHNIC FRONTIERS
Neuberger & Tyson THE IMPACT OF INTERNATIONAL ECONOMIC DISTURBANCES ON THE SOVIET UNION AND EASTERN EUROPE
Schulz & Adams POLITICAL PARTICIPATION IN COMMUNIST SYSTEMS

Related Titles

Brezhnev L.I. BREZHNEV — SELECTED SPEECHES AND WRITINGS ON FOREIGN AFFAIRS
Close EUROPE WITHOUT DEFENSE?
Gorshkov SEA POWER OF THE STATE
Laszlo & Kurtzman EASTERN EUROPE AND THE NEW INTERNATIONAL ECONOMIC ORDER
Strickland SOVIET AND WESTERN PERSPECTIVES IN SOCIAL PSYCHOLOGY

PERGAMON
POLICY
STUDIES

ON THE SOVIET UNION
AND EASTERN EUROPE

Soviet Economic Thought and Political Power in the USSR

Aron Katsenelinboigen

Pergamon Press

NEW YORK • OXFORD • TORONTO • SYDNEY • FRANKFURT • PARIS

Pergamon Press Offices:

U.S.A. Pergamon Press Inc., Maxwell House, Fairview Park, Elmsford, New York 10523, U.S.A.

U.K. Pergamon Press Ltd., Headington Hill Hall, Oxford OX3 0BW, England

CANADA Pergamon of Canada Ltd., 150 Consumers Road, Willowdale, Ontario M2J 1P9, Canada

AUSTRALIA Pergamon Press (Aust) Pty. Ltd., P O Box 544, Potts Point, NSW 2011, Australia

FRANCE Pergamon Press SARL, 24 rue des Ecoles, 75240 Paris, Cedex 05, France

FEDERAL REPUBLIC OF GERMANY Pergamon Press GmbH, 6242 Kronberg/Taunus, Pferdstrasse 1, Federal Republic of Germany

Library of Congress Cataloging in Publication Data

Katsenelinboigen, Aron Iosifovich.
  Soviet economic thought and political power in the USSR.

  (Pergamon policy studies)
  Includes bibliographical references and index.
  1. Economics, Mathematical—Russia—History.
I. Title.
HB135.K375 1979   330'.0947   78-17552
ISBN 0-08-022467-9

Printed in the United States of America

In memory of my

grandparents,

Yitshak and Rebecca

Katsenelinboigen

and

Gersh and Sara

Feldman

Contents

Preface

This book attempts to demonstrate the process of the evolution of economic theory in the Soviet Union from uniformity under Stalin to diversity in the post-Stalin period. The investigation of this process has a general significance for Soviet studies because economics has taken first place among Soviet humanities and social science to the degree that a variety of opinions has been permitted. In the USSR diversity of opinion has not yet developed in the fields of history, law, and philosophy, for example, as rapidly as in economics. At the same time, the tolerated diversity of opinions in economics is limited, and not only by the traditional use of Marxist terminology. For example, a taboo is still placed on the discussion of many of the major economic problems, such as the introduction of private property.

As well as attempting to explain the reasons for the uniformity of economics under Stalin and for the appearance of diversity in this science during the post-Stalin period, in this book I am also trying to clarify the structure of this diversity, the paradoxes in its development, and the conditions under which it will continue. The connection between leaders of Soviet economics and the Party rulers is also examined. This examination includes the attitudes of various factions of economists, e.g., reactionaries, conservatives, and modernizers, toward the question of the limitation of the leaders' power, toward some areas of economics, such as problems of mathematical modeling and institutional economics, and toward the Marxist ideology. Such dual analyses allow for a deeper understanding of how progressive and reactionary traits can be neighbors, occupying the same general trend of thought in Soviet economics. It becomes clear, for example, why reactionary Party circles can support economic trends which contain some significant progressive theoretical ideas.

In trying to paint several pictures of the evolution of Soviet economics in the post-Stalin period, I have concentrated on the analysis
of one of its new leading trends--mathematical economics. It is well
known that in the West, every economist makes use of mathematical
methods to one degree or another. These individuals, called math-
matical economists, deal with proving theorems related to mathematical models of economic systems. The elaboration of algorithms for
resolving economics problems, on the other hand, is the domain of
operations research. A related group of economists, econometricians,
specialize in statistical analyses of economic processes.

In the Soviet Union, however, all economists who make any use
of mathematical symbols at all are called mathematical economists, a
direct result of the fact that the overwhelming majority of Soviet economists are scarcely familiar with mathematics. The variety of trends
in mathematical economics in the Soviet Union is very much the same
as that in the West. The number of economists behind each trend in
the Soviet Union, however, is too small to warrant separate grouping.

Though I will not give a general evaluation of the role of economic-
mathematical methods in the USSR, the development of the economic-
mathematical trend seems to promise a partial deliverance of Soviet
economics from the fetters of Marxist dogmatism and an increase in
communication with Western economics. Keep in mind, however, that
with the help of the computers this trend threatens the potential preservation and intensification of the rigid centralization of the political
system.

The analysis of the development of the economic-mathematical
trend in the USSR is divided into three parts. In Chapter 1, I examine
the social environment in the Soviet Union in macro terms because this
determines above all the conditions for the development of economics.
Chapters 2-5 consider the role of various mutations among the economists, the flexibility of the society in allowing the formation of diverse
groups around these mutations, and their institutionalization, especially
in the framework of the existing research institutes and universities.
Finally, Chapter 6 illustrates the confusing struggle among the various
trends in Soviet economics and the ways in which this struggle is supported by the political leaders of the country.

Of course, one must not expect a systematic exposition of the development of Soviet mathematical economics from this book, since on
the whole the methodology for studying socioeconomic life in the USSR
is undeveloped. It is possible that this work, however, will help in the
creation of such a methodology.

In Western literature, there are a certain number of books devoted
to the development of Soviet mathematical economics. Among these

are A. Zauberman's remarkable books, particularly one of his latest
works: Mathematical Theory in Soviet Planning (London: Oxford
University Press, 1976). Another work of interest is M. Ellman's
Planning Problems in the USSR: The Contribution of Mathematical
Economics to Their Solution 1960-1971 (Cambridge: Cambridge Uni-
versity Press, 1973). A group of American economists, J. Hardt,
M. Hoffenberg, N. Kaplan and H. Levine edited Mathematics and
Computers in Soviet Economic Planning (New Haven and London: Yale
University Press, 1967). This book is a collection of excellent articles
including: "Information, Control, and Soviet Economic Planning" by
R. Judy, "Soviet Optimizing Models for Multiperiod Planning" by J.
Montias, "Input-Output Analysis and Soviet Planning" by V. Treml,
and "Linear Programming and Soviet Planning" by B. Ward.

As with all Western analyses, both these works are based primarily on external sources and observations. The limited access for
Western scholars to the informal aspects of Soviet economic life must
also limit to a certain degree the group of problems examined in these
works. The basic distinction of this book is its reliance on informal,
first-hand sources gathered between 1956-73 when I worked in the
USSR Academy of Sciences, first as a junior scientist and later as the
head of a section, as well as from 1970-73 when I was also a Professor
of Economics at Moscow State University.

I have talked with the people who began the trends in economics
and those who assisted or obviously impeded their development. At
times my characterizations of these people may contain too many personal remarks because I attempt to show as concretely as possible the
development of these scholars. To help the reader better sense the
atmosphere in which Soviet economics has developed, I have put into
footnotes a number of remarks which support and explain to some
degree the development of differing economic schools of thought. For
the same reason, I also prepared an appendix where some general
problems of economics and sociology are discussed.

Some of the ideas discussed in this book were published in the
articles: "Conflicting Trends in Soviet Economics in the Post-Stalin
Era," The Russian Review, vol. 35, no. 4, 1976, pp. 373-99; "Soviet
Science and the Economist/Planners," Soviet Science and Technology:
Domestic and Foreign Perspectives, published for the National Science
Foundation by the George Washington University, Washington, D.C.,
1977, pp. 230-42; "L.V. Kantorovich: Political Dilemma in Scientific c
Creativity," Journal of Post-Keynesian Economics, vol. I, no. 2, 1978,
pp. 129-47; and in Studies of Soviet Economic Planning, White Plains,
N.Y.: M.E. Sharp Publisher, 1978, pp. 1-229.

Acknowledgments

At the end of 1973, I emigrated from the USSR. In the United States I met a number of American specialists on the economics and history of the USSR, among whom were Professors M. Adams, V. Bandera, S. Cohen, G. Grossman, M. Feshbach, I. Koropeckyj, H. Levine, A. Riasanovisky, A. Rieber, V. Treml and R. Tucker. I often spoke with them about the routes along which Soviet economics was developing. Their interest convinced me to write down my thoughts on the subject. Although they are not responsible for my thoughts--and my errors--I appreciate their encouragement.

I also would like to take this opportunity to thank Alexander Yanov for the conversations in which he shared with me his methodology for the investigation of social life in Russia. During these conversations we discovered new aspects of the problems and better understood the process of examination. These conversations had a tremendous influence and aided me in systematizing the diversity of trends in Soviet economics.

I am grateful, too, for the discussions with Professor S. Gale, which alerted me to possible American misunderstandings.

I would like especially to thank Professor Grossman, on whose initiative I was given the opportunity to prepare the first draft of this book at the University of California at Berkeley.

Dr. T. Emmons, editor of the journal, The Russian Review, and Dr. S. Weintraub, editor of the journal, The Post-Keynesian Economics, personally helped me in the preparation of two articles for their respective journals concerning the problems which are discussed in the present book. Many thanks to them. I am thankful to the National Science Foundation and especially Dr. J. Thomas, to the University of Pennsylvania and especially Professor V. Gregorian and Mr. M.

Doxer, to the Ford Foundation, and the Institute of International Relations of the University of California at Berkeley, which financially supported the writing of this book, its translation into English, and the editing.

In addition, I would like to gratefully acknowledge the assistance of: L. Visson, translator; S. Dechert and B. Gale, editors; my wife, Gena, and M. McCutcheon who typed the manuscript. Also, special thanks to my sons, Alex and Gregory, and my friends, A. Ackoff and M. Brodskaya, for their help in preparing the manuscript for the publisher.

Ideology, Pragmatism, and the Development of Mathematical Economics in the USSR

IDEOLOGY AND PRAGMATISM IN SOVIET SOCIETY

The activities of Communists throughout the world serve the ideology of constructing a Communist society on the basis of Marxist theory; however, this service is performed by varied means, sometimes by deviating from orthodox Marxian doctrine. In such cases the result may be either the elaboration of creative but genuinely Marxian concepts or a fundamental revision of the theory. But how does one differentiate between a Communist who has developed Marxism in a creative fashion from a revisionist? In both cases there are deviations from the doctrine. On the other hand, how does one distinguish when a Communist is a genuine Marxist and when he is a dogmatic Marxist, since both adhere to the original tenets of the doctrine. Perhaps in this respect the situation of Marxism parallels that of organized religion. In the history of the Christian Church, for example, in struggles between orthodoxy and heresy, a heretic ultimately came to be defined as a person who had less power. The usage of power as a tool for the solution of complex problems inevitably increases the role of the pragmatic aspect of the doctrine, i.e., the inclination on the part of those in power to sacrifice doctrinal purity in order to increase their power.

Marxist Ideology

All of the above applies to the situation of Marxist ideology in the Soviet Union. Like every doctrine claiming to be absolute and infallible, Marxism-Leninism was proclaimed sacred by the Russian Communists and its creators have been canonized. In the USSR deviations from Marxism cannot be subjected to any discussion which would cast un-

1

favorable light upon Marx. Criticisms, which take place rarely, are
stated with no mention of Marx. A position must be presented non-
polemically and strictly in a constructive frame. However, in the
USSR the pressure of scientists upon Marxism is sometimes so powerful that it breaks through the barbed wire of censorship. I know of one
published instance of such a breakthrough. In 1967, the Soviet mathematician Michail Bongard published a book, Pattern Recognition, in
one of the central publishing companies, in which he wrote: "The fact
that inexactness in work distinguishes man from other animals was
noted by Karl Marx when he wrote: 'The bee puts some people--the
architects--to shame in the construction of his wax cells. But the
worst architect is distinguished from the best bee by the fact that before building a cell from wax, the man has already built it in his head.'"

The quotation cited from Marx comes with a sign for a footnote. In
the footnote, one would normally expect the title, the year of publication
and the page number of the corresponding work of Marx. Instead of this,
the footnote read as follows:

> Marx, it is true, was mistaken (emphasis added) in thinking
> that the bee could be distinguished from the architect by the
> fact that the architect has a preliminary plan for the future
> construction and the bee does not. In the organism of the bee,
> there must of necessity be a precise plan for the six-sided
> cell. Without this, he could not create honeycombs. The
> difference is something else--the bee has a plan for only one
> type of construction, while the worst architect can build a
> house, a theater, an underground passageway, a fountain,
> etc. It is precisely the degree of versatility that distinguishes
> the work of the human brain from the activity of the nervous
> system of the bee. (1)

Something truly unprecedented is happening on the ideological
front in the USSR if such an expression as "Marx, it is true, was mistaken" is allowed! Was it possible in the literature published in the
theocratic state which the Jesuits organized in Paraguay or in the works
of the Vatican Academy of Sciences to remark that, "Christ, it is true,
was mistaken," no matter what was concerned?

Like every other canonized scholar, Marx provoked in the USSR
either slavish worship or the desire to destroy his image and denigrate
his role. (2) The latter desire appeared especially among the neophytes
who have been able to understand the achievements of post-Marxian
Western thought. While they could not express their opinions in print,
they did express them in conversation. However, Karl Marx was an

important scholar, and his name will remain in history on the list of important thinkers. Of course, the acknowledgement of Marx presupposes an historical approach to his works, the recognition of their strengths and weaknesses, and precludes canonization.

The matter of criticizing Frederick Engels is somewhat simpler r in the USSR. It is easier to publish careful criticism of him because Stalin created a tradition of direct criticism of Engels, notably discrediting some of his theories about the role of the state under socialism. (3)

In an effort at achievement and consolidation of political power, the Communist leaders are ready to waive even the official Marxist ideology. It is well known that Lenin overlooked one of the basic tenets of Marxism concerning the necessity for a simultaneous victory of the revolution in the developed countries. Lenin theorized the victory of socialism in one individual underdeveloped country. Of course, this revision of Marxism was made by Lenin in conformity with his advocacy of the creative elaboration of the doctrine without the sacrifice of its fundamental truths. Lenin, like Trotsky, maintained that in the beginning it was necessary to organize a revolution in the weak link of the imperialist chain and only later to use the power of this country to help the proletariat in developed countries organize revolutions. It might even be argued that Lenin after his successes in taking power in October 1917 and in the Civil War feared the victory of socialsim in the developed countries, especially in Germany, because this would have threatened him with a loss of leadership.

Stalin's Effects

At the end of the 20s Stalin saw that the promised communism could not be achieved in the forseen future and moreover the people would have to make many severe sacrifices to industrialize the country. Under these conditions one of the factors guaranteeing Stalin his political power was his effort to consolidate the Marxist and the old Russian ideologies. (4) Marx and Engels had downplayed the excessive roles of the rulers, patriotism ("Workers of the world--unite!"), and religion ("Religion is the opiate of the masses"). Stalin quite successfully combined Marxist phraseology with the old tried-and-true ideology of the Russian tsars, who had ruled on the principle of faith in the tsar, the motherland, and God. In the early 1930s, Stalin summoned Kosarev, the Secretary of the Central Committee of the Communist Youngsters League and told him that it was necessary to exalt the leader's name; the people needed this expression of faith. It was not by chance that in one of Stalin's orders at the beginning of the Great Patriotic War, the

Commander-in-Chief himself mentioned the banner of Lenin-Stalin.

In 1934, after the famous letter of J. Stalin, A. Zhdanov, and S. Kirov about the mistakes in the interpretation of the history of the USSR,the school of the old Russian monarchist historians was glorified. Just think, such non-Party historians as E. Tarle, M. Tikhomirov, S. Bakhrushin, B. Grekov, and others known for their non-Marxist conservative views headed Soviet history! The historian I. Vipper, a fiery champion of the views of Ivan the Terrible, was invited up from the Baltic. The 1930s also marked the showing of films about Peter the Great, Aleksandr Nevskii, and Ivan the Terrible. The education of people in the spirit of Russian patriotism, combined with phrase- ology about Soviet patriotism, commenced, together with an exaltation of the Russian tsars and the glorification of Russia as the motherland. Stalin's famous toast in 1945 at a dinner in honor of the Victory Parade, incessantly glorifying the Russian people, may be considered its apogee.

Stalin's attitude toward the Russian Orthodox Church also changed in the mid-1930s. After he met officially in 1942 with the head of the Russian Orthodox Church, significant indulgences were allowed for believers. The Russian Orthodox Church has had a long tradition as a state puppet. The Communist Party also controls the Church (e.g. through unofficial communist youngsters league, some young people are sent to study at the Zagorsk Orthodox Academy). The fact that the Church as an institution exists legally, however, is a deviation from Marxist ideology. It was precisely in opposition to established religion that Marxism promised the building of heaven on earth. Let us note, by the way, that this revealed the particular weakness of Communist ideology in the USSR. The possibility of building heaven on earth is not beyond practical verification. Lenin's and Khrushchev's promises to create Communism for the present generation obviously were not fulfilled. On the other hand, the Church's idea of heaven cannot be verified, and this proves to be its strength.

Atheistic ideology is dear to the leaders of despotic regimes which are based on radical ideologies. Such leaders do not want to share their power over people's minds, even with God; they want absolute power in every respect. In this sense, atheistic despots are more rigid than theocratic ones. And the fact that Stalin legally permitted the acknowledgement of God by members of a socialist society and that the Soviet leader shared power with Him was a concession of the regime.

Post-Stalin Era

Open deviations from Marxist dogma also had a place in the years following Stalin's death. During the 1960s, the leaders of the Communist Party of the Soviet Union (CPSU) overlooked Karl Marx's universal law of capitalist accumulation. In the program the CPSU adopted at the 21st Congress, the process of the total impoverishment of the working class in the developed capitalist countries was in fact denied. Such a correction of Marxism was seemingly made under the pressure of the Western Communist parties, who were afraid of losing their position in trade unions. In the meantime, it must be noted that a number of reactionary economists, Kuzminov, for example, continued to insist that under capitalism the process of the absolute impoverishment of the workers was continuing. One of these conservative economists, Adolf Kats, even devised, for the salvation of Marxism, a theory about the absolute relative impoverishment of the workers under capitalism, which is not to be confused with the Marxist theory of absolute and relative impoverishment. The essence of this theory was as follows: under capitalism, the absolute needs of the workers increase and the relative level of their satisfaction decreases. Amid all this criticism, it remained unclear whether such a tenet was in general a law of social development true for dynamic systems or really only for the capitalist system.

The development of basic trends can come into conflict with the official Marxist ideology not only in politics, but in other spheres as well. New ideas in physics and chemistry, the formation of cybernetics, genetics, and general systems theory entailed certain ideological losses. Even the development of mathematics undermines the ideological bases to a certain extent. (5)

The introduction of the new in all societies is connected with noticeable difficulties. First among these problems is the risk of failure. Second, the new devalues the old. It not only challenges available techniques, but also the knowledge of people who have adapted to the old and no longer can master the new, if only because of old age. In the Western countries, however, the structure of society as a whole furthers the introduction of the new in overcoming the conflicts arising here, but also with tremendous difficulty. If the practical realization of ideas begins to dawn in the Western countries, there are usually forces which begin to develop the ideas.

Soviet pragmatism is of a different sort. Using the available ideological monopoly, people who are accustomed to the past rush to kill a new idea and if possible, to slaughter the people standing behind it. But when an idea has already obtained practical embodiment in the West,

particularly when it is used for military ends, then the Soviet forces
begin to beat a gradual retreat. As one of my acquaintances in the
USSR put it, the Western complex is functioning; i.e., the capitalists
would not spend money in vain, so therefore they must have done something useful. Driven with a fear of falling behind the West, especially
in military power, the Soviet leaders then begin feverish attempts to
make up for the omission.

Physics

So it was in its time with atomic energy. In 1937, many physicists
working on atomic problems were eliminated, in particular, the Kharkov
group. In 1940, a group of students of atomic energy at Moscow State
University (MGU) was liquidated because of the "nonactuality of the
problems." In 1948, the eradication of physics began under the banner
of a battle against idealism, similar to the destruction in the field of
biology. To save physics from utter destruction, I. Kurchatov seemingly considered himself justified in accepting the scientific leadership
of the elaboration of atomic weapons. It seems that physics was saved
primarily by the military significance of atomic problems. Yet a certain amount of destruction of physics took place all the same, although
it was not as great as had been intended. At the Physics Faculty of
MGU many professors were fired, especially Jews, and courses on
quantum mechanics and the theory of relativity were curtailed because
they connoted idealism.

Pure Mathematics

In the mid-1940s, destruction of pure mathematics was imminent.
This threat impinged on the interests of a great number of famous
mathematicians who were working on pure mathematics. The organizer
of the debacle was a Leningrad mathematician. An All-Union meeting
was to be called and at it the mathematicians were to be accused of not
contributing to socialist construction and of wandering off into useless
abstract problems. A handful of mathematicians, however, succeeded
in forestalling the event by demonstrating that they were helping the
military. I was told that several works of the academician Andrei Kolmogorov, figured in arguments for the utility of pure mathematics.
It is well known that Kolmogorov was working on pure mathematics,
but at the same time he was also interested in applied military problems.
He presented the idea, for example, that antiaircraft guns must be in-
stalled on a base and be permitted a high degree of flexibility to insure
successful results in firing. A number of dissertations were prepared
on the basis of this idea.

But while the destruction of pure mathematics was successfully avoided, the circumstances of isolation of the Soviet mathematicians from their Western colleagues slowed down the development of new trends. This primarily concerned new branches of mathematics on whose basis the reconstruction of the entire edifice of mathematics began. In the Soviet Union there were mathematicians who were working on similar trends: L. Pontriagin, V. Rokhlin, and D. Fadeev, but their insufficient knowledge of what was going on in the world essentially set back the development of these trends in the USSR. Although more active work began on the new trends in mathematics in the mid-1950s, the number of scholars in the field is limited. In the 1960s, young mathematicians were still defending doctoral dissertations in which the old, bulky apparatus of mathematical analysis was used, because they did not possess more modern methods of investigation. Furthermore, the development of new trends is still very risky because the leading scholars teaching in this area at MGU are seen as dissidents and could be dismissed; one famous professor, I. Shafiravich, was dismissed. In the meantime, the first results of the applications of the new trends in mathematics to physics are evident.

Cybernetics and the General Systems Theory

In the post-Stalin period, cybernetics, previously trampled, has been developed. In the West at around this time, it was receiving practical embodiment for military ends. The general systems theory, developed and investigated during the 1960s, greatly irritated the official philosophers because they understood that this method weakened their position. On several occasions attacks were made on these methods, particularly by the Philosophy Department of the Academy of Sciences, but a powerful defense succeeded in opposing these attacks. As in other sciences, the situation was saved by the use of general system theory for practical goals. In particular, in the beginning of the 1970s in the Presidium of the Academy of Sciences the question of the status of general systems theory in the West was discussed. The representative of the Institute on the United States gave a speech describing the development of this trend in the United States as well as the paths for the practical application of these ideas in the development of space programs and other prominent projects.

Biology

New trends in science and humanities which do not promise practical utility, but do impinge upon the interests of the ruling group, are ostracized even now.

The position in biology is interesting in this respect. It seems that the military played a decisive role in the ultimate downfall of T. Lysenko by turning attention to the fact that he was preventing the development of genetics and thus the creation of new forms of bacteriological weapons which the West possessed. But the development of the new trends in biology which do not have pragmatic implications are very limited. I happened to meet biologists in the USSR in connection with my interest in the sphere of general systems theory, in particular in the investigation of the problem of potential formation. This problem directly suggests the theory of evolution. The prevalent opinion is that evolution is a chance mutational process, and in the course of natural selection the fittest survive. In the meantime, it is difficult from such an approach to obtain direct answers to a number of questions about the development of an animal, in particular about the formation of complex organs such as the brain. It is thought that there are internal natural laws for the development of living beings. I will not expound this point of view; I will only note that it is remarkably difficult for its advocates to develop their position. Even many geneticists, who not so long ago were pursued, are up in arms against this opinion. Scholars who are proponents of the minority theory of evolution are obliged at times to work in applied spheres in order to defend themselves against the attacks of the ruling group of biologists who control the press, the awarding of academic degrees, and other official forms of recognition.

Law and History

The development of new ideas in law is frozen.

The attempt of a group of young scholars to use the structural method of analysis of history was suppressed. An accusatory article appeared against this group at the end of the 1960s in the journal Kommunist. One of the leading historians in this group, Aron Gurevich, was removed from the Philosophy Institute where he had been working on methodological problems in history. It is true that Gurevich was subsequently told by the editors of Kommunist that there had been a misunderstanding, but they did not publish a retraction. Gurevich was hired at one of the history institutes, but the new trend on which he had been working is not being developed.

Sociology

It is well known that sociology was not acknowledged in the USSR for a long time, but the significant results obtained by sociologists in the West stimulated the creation of a sociological trend in Russia. The trend could be seen through the various inquiries by newspaper readers about social opinion, the composition of plans for the social development of enterprises, etc. I will not evaluate the practicality of such works, but the difficulties in their utilization in the Soviet Union are very great.

The development of theory parallels the development of applied sociological investigations. Investigations into sociological theory were motivated by the necessity to form an intermediate discipline between concrete sociological investigations and the basis of Marxist sociology--historical materialism. In the mid-1960s, the Institute of Concrete Social Research (IKSI) was established, headed by academician, Alexei Rumiantsev. Almost all the best forces in sociology in the country were collected at the institute. Furthermore, the presence of an academic institute for sociology created still another channel for information on the social processes taking place in the country. As distinguished from the Party organs and the KGB (Soviet Secret Police), i.e., the secret "sociological" organizations presenting materials in a secret form, this institute was open at least in principle. It was not by chance that there were various rumors about the transfer of the Institute to the authority of the Central Committee of the CPSU, which would have made it secret.

An aggravated conflict between the historical materialists and the sociologists flared up on the eve of the International Sociological Congress in Varnais in 1970. The argument concerned the proportions of historical materialsts and sociologists representing Soviet sociology. It is interesting that in terms of age and national origin the warring sides were as follows: the overwhelming majority of the historical materialists were people around 60 years old, many of them Jews. The sociologists as a rule were aged 40-45, with a smaller percentage of Jews, the result of the longstanding discrimination against the Jews which prevented their admission to the philosophical and historical faculties of the universities.

The Congress had been preceded by a stormy discussion in the Academy of Social Sciences under the Central Committee of the CPSU about the published course of lectures on sociology by Iuri Levada Before this, Levada had been dismissed from MGU where he had given these lectures and a decision by the Ministry of Higher and Secondary Specialized Education to award Levada the title of Professor was subsequently reversed.

It was in this atmosphere that the Sociological Congress took place. Although the Congress brought the sociologists greater recognition, experienced philosophers and historical materialsts saw sociology as a threat and threw their tremendous experience in ideological conflict

into liquidating sociology. Among these fighters were academicians
F. Konstantinov and M. Mitin, famous veterans of the ideological
battles of the 1930s. They accurately took advantage of the fact that
developed Western sociological theories could not be directly applied
in practice to the entire USSR. Lacking such a basis and clearly im-
pinging upon the ideological foundations and the steadfast ideological
personnel, sociology as a science was condemned to death.

In the beginning of the 1970s, the Institute of Concrete Social Research was eliminated. The overwhelming majority of the leading
workers in the institute were dismissed for various reasons, primarily
for espousing liberal principles. The historical materialists celebrated
their victory. From then on, the basic task of the institute was reduced to the illustration of the positions of historical materialsm, thus
demonstrating the pragmatic attitudes of the central powers toward new
trends in science. In the last several years attempts have been made
to return sociology to its previous state. The director of the institute
has been replaced. However, it is difficult to predict the extent to
which sociology will develop in the USSR.

THE STALINIST HERITAGE IN ECONOMICS

All that has been said previously regarding the relationship between ideology and pragmatism in Soviet society applies as well to the
science of economics as a whole and to mathematical economics in
particular.

The present Soviet system of rigidly centralized planning was
created at the end of the 1920s and the beginning of the 1930s. Its
creation resulted from a number of causes: those engendered by the
absence of a developed theory for the functioning of a planned economic
system, and those based on the introduction of planning into a poorly
developed country attempting to reach a high level of military power
in the shortest time possible.

The second set of causes initially overshadowed the first. Indeed,
under conditions in which a poorly developed country is trying to build
up military power rapidly, political problems and an administrative
orientation toward leadership predominate. The highest levels of the
hierarchy are especially clear regarding what must be produced in
such a situation. In enlisting people to work, administrative methods,
even including labor camps, play the decisive role. The general point
is that in large economic systems the central authority cannot decide
directly on all questions. Although a hierarchical system of management of the economy solves this problem in part, there still remains
the question of how the economic units will function independently in
the framework of the overall hierarchy.

Administrative Management

In the early days of the USSR, the problem of administrative organization became particularly evident on the level of the factories and Research and Development(R & D) organizations. The system of management within Gosplan, between Gosplan and the Ministries, within the Ministries seemed quite simple because all these organizations were in the same geographical location and their numbers were comparatively small. The system of management within an enterprise is similar. The enterprise was, in fact, singled out in the management hierarchy as the unit which must have a greater degree of freedom, since there was no possibility of controlling its activity as effectively as the previously mentioned organizations because of its territorial isolation. The importance of granting enterprises freedom in making decisions, which became necessary in the course of the fulfillment of a plan, demanded the creation of something on the order of a price mechanism. The self-acting R & D organizations also were in need of evaluation procedures for making decisions because the competing designs which they offer could not be compared in terms of their physical components.

The problem of the motivation of the economic unit in the framework of a hierarchical structure could not be solved effectively without a developed economic theory. Thus, in the Stalin period it was possible to avoid economic theory with common sense in making decisions on the higher levels of the hierarchy, although it was no longer possible to do this in organizing the mechanism along all levels of the economic system.

In the same period, economics provided no theoretical basis for the organization of the economic mechanism in planned systems. Marxist theory proved totally unprepared for the creation of a planning mechanism connecting centralized actions with the actions of the individual economic units on the basis of the use of prices and money. Marx examined the future society as an extremely simple production system in which resources would be directly allocated according to clear social goals and without any price-money mechanism, prototypes of which are Robinson Crusoe, primitive tribes, and the factory of the nineteenth century.

The inadequate development of economics in the 1920s, together with its inability to connect the physical and value aspects of the functioning of the centralized system of production, precluded the possibility of using economics to organize the economic mechanism in accordance with the adopted political goals for the development of the economy. The development goals projected by the ruling groups were often in

conflict with the demands of the operation of the economy on the basis
of the use of the price-money mechanism. It was necessary either to
improve economics, or to reject it.

While it was possible to improve Soviet economics on the basis of
Western concepts, in particular those of E. Barone, this was rejected.
This rejection was not so much the result of the bad ideological flavor
of these concepts as the necessity of spending a long time to adjust
these ideas to the Soviet economic system. Because there was no time
to wait for economics to be improved, Stalin chose the second method:
to reject the services from economics. Thus, for very pragmatic
reasons, economics was not developed in the USSR. The same occurred
with respect to mathematical economics.

Rebirth of Economic-Mathematical Themes

Recalling the history of the application of economic-mathematical
methods in the postrevolutionary period, we may discover what it was
that predetermined a pragmatic interest in economic-mathematical
themes. It may be assumed that in the 1920s, after a significant in-
terval caused by the revolution and the civil war following it, there
was a quasi renaissance in Russian economic science. On the one hand,
the establishment of ideological unity of thought within the quite rigid
framework of Marxist-Leninist economic doctrine, and on the other,
the development of new economic ideas under the influence of the pressures
of life improved the conditions for such a rebirth. During this quasi-
renaissance, the development of the noted economic-mathematical trends
continued and new ones appeared, but all this was within the framework
of Marxist-Leninist doctrine.

One of the general trends in the development of economics was the
system of the management of economics which would now be called indicative planning. Here the goals for the development of the economy
and the proposed structure of the economy were sought by studying the
statistics of previous development and by offering a corresponding
extrapolation of the tendencies found. Accordingly, the apparatus of
mathematical statistics was used. Such works were developed by V.
Groman, A. Vainshtein and others. For the aggregate plan of the development of the economic system, Feldman developed an original
model at the end of the 1920s. This macroeconomic model of the national economy is methodologically interesting even today. Microeconomic analysis was primarily reduced to the investigation of consumers'
behavior and the clarification of their demand depending upon prices
and incomes. In those years, Alexander Konius worked actively on
such problems. His works in this sphere received recognition in the
West and even today retain their value. (6)

It thus may be considered that in the USSR of the 1920s there were three basic trends studied by a group of scholars developing economic-mathematical methods: the statistical study of the development of the branch structure of the national economy, macroeconomic models, and models of consumer demand. The basic reason for the destruction of these methods during the 1930s lies in the fact that they either contradicted the practical demands of the politics of that period or proved to be unnecessary. Ideological motives aggravated the situation. In reality the proposed mathematical methods for determining the composition of indicative plans on the basis of the reproduction of past experience were foreign to the goals of the first five-year plan. All sorts of statistical predictions based on the framework of an economy of the market-type were rejected by the Soviet leaders as points of reference for the development. The plan directive, reflecting the demands for forced industrialization, comprised the social order of the Party. It was foreseen that very concrete indicators would reflect the demand for the creation of the military potential of the country and that this demand would be expressed in the production of a definite quantity of steel, iron, tractors, oil, and other capital goods. Under these conditions, it proved useless in practical terms to use macroeconomic models, which are especially important in long-term planning or in the management of a market economy helped by various taxes and other mechanisms. Industrialization and collectivization, the decline in living standards, and the introduction of a ration system made the study of consumer demand useless in the 1930s from a practical point of view. Thus, the Western economic-mathematical trends, which did have practical application, were partially developed even in the USSR of the 1920s. However, in this period they did not succeed in putting down deep roots, and in the 1930s practical demand for them was no longer present.

Stalin's Economic Theory

Stalin, having rejected economics as a powerful tool for solving the problems of the performance of Soviet economy, substituted a so-called theory of super profitability. Because this theory doesn't yield to measurement, it can be used only by intuition and only by the people who are granted--somewhere from the unknown depths of Marxist dogma--the knowledge of the ultimate interests of the working class. Of course, the ideological bases of the Western models were also unacceptable for the majority of Soviet economists, as they were based on the anti-Marxist conception of the Austrian school. However, the pragmatism of the Soviet leaders, the surprising ease with which they could call white "black" and black "white" and then shift in a short time

to still another stand if it seemed to their advantage, leads me to think
that the dominating feature in the destruction of the economic-mathematical trend was its absence of practical necessity. A number of
advocates of economic-mathematical methods were arrested; some of
them perished, and a few survived. For many years, mathematical
methods--as at one time, genes, for biologists--became a taboo for
Soviet economists, a synonym for bourgeois economic theory.

Under such conditions, the instructions of Comrade Stalin served
as landmarks in the development of economics. The primary goal of
the economists lay in commentary on these instructions. It was, of
course, impossible to hold a conversation on equal terms with Stalin.
K. Radek's famous pun about the possibility of discussions with Stalin
comes to mind: "You give him a quotation and he gives you a footnote."
(In Russian, footnote and exile are homonyms.) In commenting on
the works of Stalin, one had to be very careful. Carelessness threatened death.

In 1940, at the 18th Congress of the Party, Stalin spoke about the
basic economic goal of the Soviet society: to exceed the Western
countries in the output of industrial goods per capita. After Stalin's
speech, the economist, Kubanin, published an article in the journal,
Problemy Ekonomiki, in which he demonstrated that production of agricultural goods per person in the USSR also has to exceed the Western
level. This article, it seems, was presented to Stalin by N. Voznesenskii. It was regarded as slander on the Stalinist Kolkhoz order,
since it followed from Kubanin's remarks that labor productivity in the
collective farms was lower than that in the farming economy of the
West. Kubanin's article was destructively criticized in Pravda.
In particular, it was explained that the author had confused the concepts
of output per worker and the productivity and intensity of labor. The
indicator of output per worker reflects not only the productivity, but
also the intensity of labor. Under capitalism, where the intensity of
labor is much greater than under socialism, the indicator of greater
output cannot testify to the greater productivity of labor. This point
of view was adopted by Soviet economists for a long time. Kubanin was
arrested soon after the publication of the article. (7) Vasili Nemchinov's attempts to intercede for him were unsuccessful, and Kubanin
perished.

Boris Markus, the director of the Institute of Economics where
Kubanin had worked and the editor-in-chief of Problemy Ekonomiki,
had been among the ideologue economists firmly standing for Stalinist
positions and helping Stalin to destroy any people who thought differently.
Markus' basic book, Labor in a Socialist Society, published in the late
1930s, was profoundly apologetic to the regime. (8) In this book, the

indicators on labor were deliberately chosen in order to show only the great advantages of socialism. The generalizations were of a particularly superficial nature, but in the absence of any other literature in this area, the book was considered a masterpiece. With Kubanin's disgrace, Markus was fired, called a double-dealer, and expelled from the Party. After serving at the front during the war, Markus was restored to Party membership, and in 1946 he was appointed chairman of the Department of Labor Economics at the Moscow State Economics Institute (MGEI). He quickly understood that it was very dangerous to study questions of labor in the postwar period; he, therefore, switched over to a then-fashionable occupation of writing the history of Moscow in connection with the celebration of its 800th anniversary. At the end of 1949, Markus died "in his bed."

Payments for Creativity

Even after Stalin's death, some economists wrote commentaries on his works so carefully that they assumed fantastic forms. In the mid-1950s, discussions took place with the economics faculty at Moscow State University concerning the understanding of the law of "planned proportional development" mentioned by Stalin in the work Economic Problems of Socialism in the USSR. These discussions were reduced to clarifying the grammar in this law. Some thought that the words "planned" and "proportional" should be separated by a comma, others that the second word must be put in parentheses, and still others that the words must be written out without any punctuation marks.

From time to time, appeals were heard from above for economists to "develop Marxism with creativity." These appeals were demagogic and sometimes even deliberately provocative. In 1950 the Central Committee of the CPSU requested one of the leading Soviet economists to give his frank ideas about the development of economics for a future conference of economists. Despite all his carefulness, he expressed himself too freely. The material fell into Stalin's hands. In his work Economic Problems of Socialism in the USSR, Stalin criticized the author of the notes, and taught him some elementary truths. One can easily imagine the feelings of this economist after Stalin's criticism!

Several young economists also were trapped by appeals to develop economics, as my own experience illustrates. From around April 1951-June 1953 I was practically unemployed. I had an insignificant workload in the Moscow Bookselling Vocational School, where I was teaching a course entitled, "An Assortment of Scientific-Technological Literature," this after completing graduate work at the Moscow State Economics Institute in 1949! I also was a supernumerary lecturer at the Moscow

Komsomol Committee (MK VLKSM). Having a lot of time and the
opportunity through the MK VLKSM to visit many enterprises, I wrote
a dissertation early in 1952 about the connection of the new forms of
the organization of labor and wages in Soviet industry. I wanted to
obtain reviews of it from a number of leading enterprises to facilitate
its publication and defense. By no means did this plan represent the
voice of practicality. After the appropriate discussions at workers'
meetings, I received reviews from the "Frezer," the Liuberetskii
Factory for Agricultural Machines, and the Moscow Factory for Small
Cars (MZMA).

I also particularly wanted to obtain reviews from a prominent
enterprise, the Stalin Moscow Automobile Factory (ZIS), because my
work had referred to its experience. I had heard that a group of Jews
had been arrested at the factory and were accused of wanting to "sabotage the factory from within." However, I did not attach the proper
significance to these rumors. My incomprehension seems fortunate,
because had I understood the repercussions of my attempt to develop
economic theory, I could not have remained optimistic and active. It
is not by chance that there is a joke in the USSR that "a pessimist is a
well-informed optimist, and an optimist is a well-instructed pessimist."

In early 1952 with the help of the MK VLKSM I met with one of the
older specialists of the section of labor and wages at ZIS. I gave the
manuscript and abstract of my work and asked that he comment upon it.
Overcrowding of the workers' premises by factory management in the
USSR is well known. It was not surprising, then, that a young worker
sitting nearby had overheard our conversations; he, too, was concerned
with questions of the organization of labor and socialist competition,
and I invited his help in reviewing my work. His name was Valeri
Belkin, and he was a "great Russian." After a couple of days, I was
met in the MK VLKSM by the chairman of the student sector who said
he had heard that I had written an anti-Soviet work. I was accused of
trying to "sabotage the factory from within," an expression used previously in the mid-1940s during the cases of Boris Peltsman, workers
of ZIS, and others. Two professional academic economists invited by
the KGB "demonstrated" that Peltsman, as the head of the planning
department of "Dinamo" factory, created "deliberate" disproportions
in the capacities of the different shops of the factory. Such an accusation could be made against any planner in a factory. Another tale revealed to me in the 1960s by Aron Shuster was as follows: Aron's
wife, nee Kantor, had been arrested in the mid-1940s with a group of
other Jews, who were workers at the ZIS. She was accused of sabotaging political atmosphere at the factory while working in the section
on labor and wages by giving bonus preferences to Jewish heads of the

shops. She provoked anger in the non-Jewish workers. This case was also fabricated by the KGB.

My sabotage consisted in two acts of boldness. In referring to the experience of progressive factories, including ZIS, I had written that some workers achieved higher productivity by combining the functions of the operators with those of the adjusters, and I analyzed the system of payment of these workers. To the specialists at the factory, my proposals for the combined functions of the operators and the adjusters equaled a demand for the termination of the adjusters. Moreover, in a chapter devoted to the payment of the foremen, I wrote that the existing difference between the salaries of the foremen and the wages of the highly qualified workers slows down the enlistment of the best workers as foremen, and I referred to the prewar government resolution to increase the role and payment of the foremen.

Unbeknownst to me Stalin soon after the war had signed a secret resolution in which the increase in pay and tariff rates was forbidden, and I had, thus, unwittingly contradicted Stalin's instructions. Unfortunately, the principle in Roman Law that "lack of knowledge of the law is no excuse" was creatively generalized in the USSR to include secret laws, instructions, and resolutions.

Although my attempts at research had led only to accusations, I was afraid. I confided my fears to one of the workers at the MK VLKSM (let us call him L.), and he, who knew me well and valued me as a lecturer, began to investigate the accusations. That evening I overheard his conversation with Chesnokov, the head of the sector of heavy industry of the Moscow Committee of the Party. L. calmly sought advice from Chesnokov about how one should evaluate, from the standpoint of practicality, the proposals of one of the lecturers of the MK VLKSM--the proposals which had, in fact, occasioned the accusation. Chesnokov answered that these proposals, though reasonable, were not timely.

The following day, in my presence, L. called the Komsomol Organizer of ZIS, Boris Demianov, about the misunderstandings which had arisen over my work. Demianov replied at length, enumerating the accusations made by the specialists. L. said that in looking into this question he obtained advice from the Moscow Committee of the Party. He repeated to Demianov the substance of his conversation with Chesnokov. Then L. told Demianov that apparently the incident with me had been the result of an affront to the pride of the experienced older specialists at the factory: how could they give approval to the work of such a young person who did not have their long work experience? At the end of the conversation, L. advised Demianov himself to judge the work. Fortunately, after this conversation, talk of my sabotaging activity ceased. (9)

In the Stalin period, the theoretical economists were expected to practically elevate Party decisions to the height of wisdom. In bringing Marxist-Leninist doctrine and the works of Stalin to the people, the economists nurtured confidence in the advantages of socialism. Economic theory was the most important component in ideology, and those working on it had to fulfill essentially ritualistic functions. It was not by chance that the teachers of ideological disciplines in the Soviet Union were called priests.

Economic Organization and Economists

The relationships of scholars in economics was organized hierarchically in imitation of Soviet society. Each sphere of this society had a leader-dictator whose power was determined by the degree to which he combined theoretical and practical work. T. Lysenko was powerful because he simultaneously developed theory and gave practical advice.

Economics was fortunate in its leader: the first economist was Stalin himself. As a result, economics was given only a "Fuhrer-curator," although for a time in the mid-1940s, Nikolai Voznesenskii, a member of the Politburo, the Deputy to the Chairman of the Council of Ministers of the USSR and the Chairman of Gosplan, claimed the role of economic leader number two. But this lasted only for a short time, and he was killed by Stalin in the end of the forties. His book on the military economy of the USSR during the World War II was announced as "fallacious." (10)

For a long time the Fuhrer-curator of economics was Konstantin Ostrovitianov. He worked only on commentaries of Stalin, had no opinions of his own, and gave no practical recommendations. For these reasons, Ostrovitianov could not gather the power T. Lysenko had.

I happened to become acquainted with Ostrovitianov in the mid-1950s. Around that time after failing more than once to be elected to the Academy of Sciences, he had finally been elected and had become an acknowledged academician. For several years he had been vice-president of the USSR Academy of Sciences and was already retired. In 1966, when I was the favorite of The Central Economic Mathematical Institute, I was given the opportunity to go to Yugoslavia. I was affirmed as a member of the delegation of economists, apparently the first such delegation after 1948. It was a small group, with Ostrovitianov, who retained his green diplomatic passport, at the head. The other members were Deronic Allakhverdian, the deputy to the director of the Institute of Economics; Gennadi Sorokin, the director of the Institute

of the Socialist System; Mariam Atlas, the chairman of the Department
of Political Economy at the Moscow Financial Institute; Sorokin's wife;
and I, then only a Ph. D. in Economics and the head of a section. For
unknown reasons, Sorokin and Atlas were excluded from the delegation
at the last moment.

We went to Yugoslavia by train, and in four days I succeeded in
talking with Ostrovitianov about many things. After receiving his education in a seminary, Ostrovitianov was taught the art of speechmaking.
He related in detail how he and his fellows had been schooled in the
seminaries for debates with those who thought differently. Ostrovitianov
was a man of extremely conservative views, with little ability in science.
One can judge his sharp rejection of the new trends in economics from
his published speeches, with their criticism of economic-mathematical
methods. His fear of economic-mathematical methods was so great
that in the 1960s he tried in every way to help one of his main adversaries, Jakov Kronrod, to be chosen as a corresponding member of
the USSR Academy of Sciences, only because the latter actively fought
against the new methods. Alas, Ostrovitianov's efforts did not succeed.

During the trip, Ostrovitianov spoke with bliss about his meetings
with Stalin and was regretful that a natural calamity on the road from
Ostrovitianov's country house to the Kremlin had caused one meeting
to be canceled. He talked at length of his battle with Lev Leontiev,
his main rival, and a well-known Soviet economist. At the end of the
1930s, Leontiev was close to Stalin and was fairly often at the leader's
apartment in the Kremlin. Leontiev unofficially was considered the
author of the following formulation: "Under socialism the law of value
functions in a transformed manner." This formulation was used to arm
the Soviet economic theory after Stalin's famous conversation with the
economists in 1940. Even at that time, Stalin was seeking objective
foundations for economic indicators; although his word dominated the
entire Soviet economy, he sought economic laws independent of himself.

Leontiev survived the Stalin period well, working into the 1940s in
foreign policy questions as the editor-in-chief of the magazine, Novoe
vremia (New Times). In creative terms. Leontiev was fairly insignificant. Yet in the 1960s he did encourage the progressive idea of a
transfer to prices based on the principle of production cost. Such encouragement was not entirely inoffensive, because production cost was
viewed by many Soviet economists as a capitalist category, since it is
based on the idea of including the interest of capital in these costs.
Leontiev was moderately inclined toward the application of mathematical methods in economics. Although he considered these methods a
technical means, he did not denigrate their application.

Ostrovitianov conducted himself in Yugoslavia as the acknowledged

head of Soviet economics; in 1966, the Yugoslavians still remembered
him in this role which he had accepted under Stalin. It is well known
that Soviet scholars abroad do not have the right to enter into public
discussions with each other or with their colleagues from the socialist
countries. However, Ostrovitianov, considering himself a power of
the world, broke this commandment. At Belgrade University, Allakhverdian and I made speeches to the teaching staff. During my speech,
as I was talking about the prices in the optimal plan, Ostrovitianov
suddenly interrupted me and tried to initiate a discussion of labor
values as a basis for prices, a topic I had not planned to consider. I
answered that for the examined schemes of optimal planning, there is
no need to use the category of labor value; it is enough to construct the
prices as characteristics of the marginal contribution of each resource
in the realization of society's goals. (11)

As has already been noted, under Stalin there was not any diversity
of opinion; there was a uniform position on all important questions. (12)
This approved point of view was a Marxist one. All other opinions were
anti-Marxist. Such a situation engendered a cruel struggle for survival.
Of course, certain spheres over which Stalin's hand had not passed remained untouched, with no conclusive opinions. Whoever first seized
upon such a sphere, succeeded in acclaiming his position as Marxist,
and consolidated it in print was powerful; his antagonists would be
shamed and in some cases, sent to what Russians call "not so remote
places," i.e., Siberia. Therefore, the present economist had to
denigrate his adversary by any means. Even now many older economists are aggressive; it never occurs to them that now there is no
mortal threat in thinking differently, i.e., within the framework of
current political mores. Moral limitations are incomprehensible to
them because their schooling was in situations which decided survival.
Furthermore, they can neither master new ideas or more precisely,
work actively in the new trends; nor can they occupy their former high
positions, so their aggression is understandable.

The extremely gloomy picture I have painted of the Stalinist state
in economics is, of course, somewhat simplified. There were still
people who tried to develop economics, including economic-mathematical methods, in Stalin's time. There were also economists whose
moral qualities were admirable in spite of reigning moral corruption,
but they were few, and it was extremely difficult for them. However,
it is they who fulfilled the role of "mutants," those who ensure development under altered conditions. I will talk about them in the next chapter,
but now will give one example.

Ostrovitianov, as is apparent from what has been said, played a
very conservative role even after Stalin's death. Another economist

of his rank, academician, Alexsei Rumiantsev, played a progressive role in the post-Stalin period in developing social thought in the Soviet Union, in particular, in the economic-mathematical trend. A. Rumiantsev belonged to the older generation of economists. For a long time he worked in Kharkov. At the end of Stalin's life, Rumiantsev obtained a very high position, heading the section of the Central Committee of the CPSU working on ideology. The fact that in preparing material for the forthcoming economic discussions in 1952 he formulated the basic economic law of socialism, furthered Rumiantsev's successful career. After Stalin's death, Rumiantsev continued to occupy high posts; he was editor-in-chief of the journal Problemy Mira i Sotsializma (The Problems of Peace and Socialism), and the newspaper, Pravda, and then the vice-president of the USSR Academy of Sciences.

Rumiantsev was a progressive in the institutional part of economic theory. He had a conservative point of view on the assumptions of mathematical modeling of economic processes, but he had tremendous respect for innovation in this sphere, tried very hard to understand the new ideas, and supported them actively. At the end of the 1960s, at the All-Union Economic Conference attended by several members of the Politburo, the main speaker was chairman of Gosplan, Nikolai Baibakov, who accused the advocates of the theory of optimal planning of bourgeois ideology. It was hitting below the belt. However, Rumiantsev, who spoke at this meeting, through his authority as a member of the Central Committee of the CPSU and as vice-president of the Academy of Sciences, defended the theory of optimality and consequently, at one of the sections of this conference was accused of protecting foreign views.

I met with Rumiantsev the first time at the All-Union Conference of Sociologists in 1968 in Sukhumi. He accidentally happened to hear my presentation on criteria of optimality and prices in the Soviet economy. After the presentation we talked for more than an hour about the problems concerning my paper. Then several times Rumiantsev called me in Moscow for private discussions, and his assistant, B. Rabbot, was very instrumental in bringing about these meetings. Rumiantsev did not share my views on the nature of the price mechanism in a planned economy, but he was very sincere in trying to understand my opinions.

Rumiantsev supported the new trends in other fields of the humanities as well and was the author of the "old" Novy mir (New World). This magazine, which was directed by A. Tvardovskii in the sixties, was the major liberal magazine in the Soviet Union. I do not want to idealize Rumiantsev, but the fact that a man with such a past can be such an active champion of the new is deserving of every respect.

Rumiantsev's opposition, the head of the science section of the

Central Committee of the CPSU, Sergei Trapenikov, and the members
of the Politburo who supported Trapenikov, proved to be stronger than
Rumiantsev and his allies in the Politburo. A plausible excuse for
Rumiantsev's removal was found, and about a month later, after the
reelection of Rumiantsev as a member of the Central Committee of the
CPSU at the 24th Congress of the Party, his adversaries removed him
from the positions both as vice-president and as director of the Institute of Concrete Social Research. Rumiantsev retained membership
in the Presidium of the USSR Academy of Sciences, but this was just
a sinecure; he had no real duties.

NEW CONDITIONS FOR THE ECONOMIC-MATHEMATICAL TREND
IN THE POST-STALINST ERA

Changes of a general nature in the political direction of the country
contributed to the Soviet revival of economics in the mid-1950s. At
the 19th Communist Party Congress, Georgii Malenkov stated in his
report that if, after World War I, Russia had fallen away from the
capitalist world, and if, after the Second World War, China and other
countries of the People's Democracies had done likewise, then in the
case of a third major confrontation, capitalism would finally succumb
on a world-wide basis. In his short speech at this Congress, Stalin
announced that because the bourgeoisie had thrown down the banners
of freedom, it was now Russia's task to raise them. The statements
of both these leaders manifested an ideological readiness for a new
world war.

Soon after the death of Stalin, the views put forth in Malenkov's
report were changed. Gradually the Soviet Union began to embrace
the Western position that if there were a third world war, it would be
without victors. The new Soviet government renounced the policy of
world domination. A gradual shift began, leading back to the old
Russian aspiration to be a world power. The post-Stalin policy, with
the extraordinary goals removed, now had to substitute new ones. The
rise of military power had to be accompanied by a rise in the living
standard of the people. Moreover, extremist means to reach this
goal were necessarily renounced; for example, it became impossible
to use labor camps as one of the basic sources of manpower. Attainment of these new goals under new conditions necessitated improvement of the economic mechanism. Different points of view in economics were therefore permitted. Among them was mathematical economics.

Economic Theory Changes

As in the case of the other trends in Soviet science, support for this trend became possible toward the mid-1950s, when new methods and means for the solution of economic problems appeared in the West which entirely corresponded to the practical problems of the Soviet economy.

On the level of the national economy, input-output tables were such a method. There is no doubt that the role of the Russian scholars, e. g. , V. Dmitriev, and the experience of the Soviet Union in the composition of national-economic balances played a certain role in the formation of the ideas of input-output tables. But the undoubted service of Vasili Leontiev was in his ability to implement these ideas on the basis of Western economics and create them with numerical results. The appearance of computers created a technical basis for the implementation of ideas of input-output tables, allowing the solution of the equating of systems with several hundred variables. These ideas, while finding practical application in the Western countries and demonstrating their vitality, entirely corresponded to the needs of a socialist planned economy, because they made it possible to improve the practice of planning.

On the microeconomic level, new methods, primarily methods of linear programming, were introduced in the West for the solution of optimization problems of allocation of resources. These methods could, in many cases, be utilized with the help of the now present computers. The solution of such optimization problems entirely corresponds to the practical needs of the Soviet economy. The experience accumulated in the West in many ways furthered the recognition of these methods in the Soviet Union, although even before the war, on the initiative of L. Kantorovich, methods for linear programming for the solution of the economic problems had begun to be used in the USSR. By the end of World War II, input-output and microeconomic optimization methods were allowed to be used, as were ideas of optimal national economic planning coming from Soviet scholars.

It is well known that shortly after the end of World War II, under the stamp of cosmopolitanism in the USSR, a powerful campaign against worship of the West was unleashed. In that period, a pamphlet written, or more precisely, signed Nikolai Rosiiskii was published. In it, Western techniques were recklessly abused. These techniques were described as having reached such a point that men were harnessed into machines, working with hands and legs and everything else one could work with.

Western Literature

After Stalin's death the attitude towards Western technology
changed. The resolutions of the June 1955 Plenum of the Central
Committee of the CPSU--which were devoted to technical progress
and where the necessity for studying foreign experiences was empha-
sized--resounded very sharply. After the opening of this dam, a
torrent of translated Western literature flooded Soviet economics.
Even though the imported literature was not political, nonetheless, it
brought Western concepts into the USSR, tidings of another world, and
there was a definite alghough unintended ideological influence. There
is now great hunger for translated Western economic literature in the
Soviet Union. In fact, the classic works of Western economists, especially after Marx, are inaccessible to Soviet economists who do not
know foreign languages, and they are in the overwhelming majority.
There are no translations of L. Walras, V. Pareto, and A. Marshall
among others.

One fortunate exception is J.M. Keynes' work, The General Theory
of Employment, Interest, and Money. (13) Soon after the war, while
talking with academician Josef Trakhtenberg, Stalin asked him if he
knew about Keynes. Trakhtenberg answered affirmatively. Stalin said
that Winston Churchill had recommended Keynes' work to him and that
he thought the book was worth translating. The translation of the book
was entrusted to Professor N. Lubimov, and in 1948 it was published.
Now this book is a bibliographical rarity.

Since the 1960s, mostly due to the activity of Khabinskaia, who in
fact headed the division of economic literature in the Progress Publishing House, a number of books have been translated, giving the Soviet
reader the opportunity to become acquainted with several theoretical
trends in Western economics. Many of these books, including Paul
Samuelson's Economics and John Kenneth Galbraith's The New Industrial Society, were provided with the stamp "For Scientific libraries."
Such books are usually sold by subscriptions presented to scholarly
institutions. However, I also saw one of these books in open sale--
B. Seligman's Basic Trends in Contemporary Economic Thought.
Protecting the Soviet readers from the decadent influence of the Western ideology, the Soviet editors omitted many parts of these books
which in their mind had a bad ideological flavor. (14) In spite of the
prior limited acquaintance with Western economic thought, the given
books nevertheless proved to be accessible to quite a large group of
readers. Moreover, I saw a photostat of Samuelson's book, made
privately by the lovers of Western literature.

The last book on economics published by the Progress Publishing

House on general theoretical problems apparently was E. Fels' and
G. Tintner's Methods of Economic Investigation. In 1971, in connection
with the measures adopted for an intensified ideological battle against
the West under conditions of detente, the economic editorial board of
this publishing house was fortified. The new editors emphasized the
printing of Western books of an applied nature. However, the publication of valuable translated books on economic theory was continued by
the Statistics Publishing House and on mathematical economics, by the
publishing house Soviet Radio.

Economic-Mathematic Methods

The military also put its weight behind economic-mathematical
methods. These methods are important to the military in its application of operations of research and for the creation of dynamic input-
output tables permitting the clarification of the conversion of a system
from the production of peace-time goods to military, etc. As a measure of the military's interest, consider that in the 1960s, Marshal
Zakharov, the head of the General Staff of the Soviet Army, called P.
Demichev, the Secretary of the Central Committee of the CPSU on
ideology, and personally asked him to further the development of these
methods.

The leaders of the new economic-mathematical trend have promised the powers-that-be a large and rapid effect from its introduction.
If one promises only small results and in the remote future, then one's
proposal will not even be examined. The political leaders need proposals promising a large and rapid effect, proposals which will allow
them to make their wisdom manifest. Thus, for pragmatic reasons,
the mathematical economic trend was granted a lease on life.

Let us finally pay some attention to Michail Iovchuk's article "The
Development of Socialist Ideology and Culture."(15) The author emphasized the pragmatic aspect of the development of science in the Soviet
Union in general and economic-mathematical methods in particular.
He also stressed the ability of decision makers to forego ideology to
attain such goals. This article is even more interesting because it
was presented by the head of the Academy of Social Sciences under the
Central Committe of the CPSU, an experienced political functionary,
who passed through the stern school of rise and fall.

Iovchuk's article was his speech at the impressive ideological conference which took place in 1971. (16) He recalled the mistakes admitted in relation to cybernetics, genetics, economic-mathematical
methods, etc., in relation to the trends concerning the pragmatic
utility of which we have spoken:

In the sphere of social science, the party, the press,
and the scientific community criticized attempts to
justify or use to the detriment of Marxist-Leninist
science the erroneous views admitted in the past by
individual philosophers, economists, and other authors
in relation to several discoveries of science (genetics,
cybernetics, economic-mathematical methods, etc.).
This criticism gave an opportunity to open a still wider
area for scientific research in various spheres of knowledge, for creative discussions and an exchange of opinions on problems of science and culture on the basis
of the principles of Marxism-Leninism. (17)

And then Iovchuk spoke about the correlation of the above-mentioned
pragmatic trends with ideology:

Socialist ideology has always been based and is based
on the firm foundation of the philosophy of dialectical
materialism, of scientific economic theory, of the
theory of scientific communism, on the achievements
of historical and other social sciences. At the modern
stage of development, socialist ideology proposes the
theoretical generalization and recognition not only
of the social and historical experience and the newest
achievements of social science, but also the newest
experience of scientific and technical progress, the
modern achievements of natural science and tech-
nology(such as automated systems of management,
new forms of information, etc.), new methods of
scientific cognition such as system-structural
analysis, the method of modeling, the optimal
variants in planning and management, economic-
mathematical methods, etc.

All these achievements of modern scientific knowledge are by no means some sort of deviation from
socialist ideology, and with their true interpretation
they correspond to the spirit and meaning of Marxist-
Leninist theory which supports the position of Engels
and Lenin about the necessity for a change in the form
of the materialist world view as a result of the epoch-
making discoveries of science. It is impossible, of
course, to agree with the erroneous-opinions to the

effect that the new methods in scientific knowledge
widely applied now in various branches of science
(system-structural analysis, modeling, etc.), which
have arisen in individual sciences, can replace the
universal method of philosophical and scientific
thought--the materialist dialectic--or somehow
limit its sphere.

The application of economic-mathematical methods,
modeling, the optimal variants of planning, the introduction of automated systems of management, etc.,
by no means contradict Marxist-Leninist economic
theory; all this will further the future concrete expression and improvement of economics which are
based on the principles of Marxist theory, on the
laws discovered by Marxism-Leninism for the development of society, and on the generalization of
the great experience of socialist economic management. (18)

I shall add no further comment.

2 The People Who Began the Economic- Mathematical Movement

•

At lease three factors make possible the development of a new variation in the course of the biological evolution: 1) The new growth may already exist as a mutation, even if it is only partly selected by the surrounding environment, i.e., if there is a "direct mutation;" 2) Organisms can help the new mutations to survive, and create a conducive environment for them; 3) The existing organisms may perceive and accept changes and give birth to a new mutation. I find that this serves as a useful analogy for describing the changes in the cast of characters involved in the evolution of the economic mathematical trend in the Soviet economics.

DIRECT ECONOMIC MATHEMATICAL MUTATIONS

Despite the almost complete defeat of a weak economic-mathematical school in the Soviet Union in the 1930s, a small group of scholars continued research in the area. These economists could be compared to "direct mutants," and during the changing conditions of the mid-1950s, they encouraged a faster rate of development of mathematical work in economic research. These economists were of diverse social rank and character. The majority of them--Vasili Nemchinov, Victor Novozhilov, Alexander Lurie, Albert Vainshtein, Jakov Gerchuk--are no longer alive. It is not my task to write their biographies or to present a total analysis of their activities. I would like, however, to add to those published materials, primarily obituaries in the journal, Economika i Matematicheskie Metody (Economics and Mathematical Methods), which gave a general survey of these scholars' works.

Economic Leaders

The most prominent of these men were: 1) Vasili Nemchinov, who, in other conditions, could have been the organizational head of the movement; 2) Leonid Kantorovich, who gave a new scholarly foundation to the school of thought; and 3) Alexander Lurie, who could accurately elucidate the scholarly ideas of the movement. There were others, of course, who also made significant early contributions to the economic-mathematical school.

Nemchinov

Nemchinov, whom I knew slightly, was a man of progressive views, but opposed to harsh methods. By an irony of fate he turned out to be Stalin's accomplice in collectivization; for example, Stalin referred to Nemchinov's work on the distribution of grain among different groups of peasants to support his own position. Konstantin Klimenko, to whom I will return in detail later, was rather close to Nemchinov in those years and told me that Nemchinov was by no means a supporter of collectivization. In his idea of the balance of grain production and consumption, Nemchinov sought to underscore the necessity for leaning on a strong peasantry.

Klimenko told me also about Nemchinov's position as the head of the Department of Agriculture in the Central Statistical Administration. This was an extremely important job; Nemchinov had to produce forecasts on the harvest for the oblasts (provinces). These forecasts were the basis of plans for procurements for which the secretary of the party obkoms (provincial committees) was responsible. During a period of acute grain shortage, Nemchinov forecasted the harvest. Demands were made for an increased harvest forecast. He apparently made some corrections, but not enough to satisfy the country's leaders, and he refused to make any further corrections. As one of my friends, a Soviet economist of the older generation, I. Kvasha put it, an ideological, not biological, harvest was demanded of Nemchinov, and he would not produce it. Although Nemchinov was called to a meeting of the Sovnarkom (Council of Ministers), he still refused to change the forecast. After that, in Stalin's presence at a meeting of the Politburo, Nemchinov was again urged to revise, but he still refused, at which point Stalin allegedly commented, "We'll manage without Nemchinov." Klimenko was at Nemchinov's house in the days which followed this meeting of the Politburo. Nemchinov expected to be arrested, and he prepared a bundle of clothes for prison, but the thunderstorm passed.

Soon after this incident Nemchinov was appointed to the post of

department head for seed growing of the Ministry of Agriculture. This
was a unique post; in the period of grain procurements all the grain
was expropriated, and it was impossible to talk of any serious seed
growing. The destruction of the seed growing process was an inheri-
tance of the period of collectivization, and for many years the country
suffered from it. Even in the1960s, in the period of grain procurements, grains were still expropriated in certain oblasts.

However, Stalin's continued patronage of Nemchinov seemed real.
In 1938, when Stalin was given the lists of statistical administration
workers recommended for medals, in connection with the 20th anniversary of the creation of the administration, he allegedly asked, "And
where is Nemchinov?" Nemchinov received one of the most distinguish -
ed medals in the Soviet Union; the Lenin medal. I do not know why
Stalin gave Nemchinov the medal, but something else is important here.
Even in totalitarian systems the whims of dictators are such that they
sometimes preserve decent people. If the given person--not being a
political figure--behaves in a direct and open way, the dictator is less
afraid of him and knows what can be expected. Sometimes the dictator
must trust and use professional workers if he is assured they have no
great interest in political activity.

On the other hand, one could view Nemchinov as a collaborator
with the Stalinist regime. The refusal of a creative person to collabor-
ate with a totalitarian regime is a moral act of selfless asceticism,
difficult for most people. Activity, with its possibility for creation,
is too important. Moreover, a young person once fallen into the rut
of collaboration finds it difficult to leave. Such is the subjective side
of the behavior of many scholars in totalitarian regimes. However,
this activity has some positive aspects. Since the regime is already
formed, the presence of decent people with power can, in changing
conditions, result in a renewed moral atmosphere and the creation
of new directions in science.

When in the mid-1950s, the atmosphere in the USSR had changed
slightly and the economic-mathematical school had started to develop,
a movement leader was necessary. Nemchinov was that leader. Taking
advantage of the statute of the Academy of Science which permitted an
academician, in certain circumstances, to create an independent
scientific division, Nemchinov organized the Laboratory of Economic-
Mathematical Methods in 1958. Furthermore, largely as a result of
Nemchinov's efforts, the First All-Union Scientific Conference on the
Application of Mathematical Methods to Economics was called in 1960;
for political reasons it was called a scientific meeting. This conference for the first time brought together the disunited efforts of
those scholars who were able to work with mathematical methods in

economics under Stalin. Among those represented was the group of well-known specialists on the organization of machine building production: S. Dumler, A. Konson, Neimark, S. Sokolitsyn, and K. Velikanov. Since the organizational problems in industry are considered to be borderline cases of engineering, it was possible to use mathematical methods in this area even under Stalin. Although the mathematical methods used by this group were rather simple, they were, nevertheless, important as an organic part of their work.

Another group represented were the statisticians who were also allowed within certain limits to use mathematical methods, in particular for determining the procedures of random samplings.

Lev Mints, a well-known Soviet statistician and representative of this group, played an active role in the establishment of new techniques. Although in exile during the Stalin years, in the late 1950s, Mints doggedly worked on the development of input-output tables, for which he received the state prize. Mints also took on the enormous organizational task of preparing the papers of the 1960 conference for publication. After retiring he continued to work as a consultant in TSEMI, and many people marvelled at his youthful energy and organizational ability. A corresponding Member of the Academy of Sciences, statistician, Timot Riabushkin, in the 1960s was often a reader for economics-mathematical dissertations, as well as becoming a member of the editorial staff of the journal Economics and Mathematical Methods. Several times he attempted to create an institute of demography, but with no success; the forces which feared such an institute were too powerful. Now Riabushkin is the Director of the Institute of Concrete Social Research of the USSR Academy of Sciences.

Many other well-known mathematicians were invited to the 1960 conference: B. Gnedenko, Iu. Dobrushin, A. Dorodnitsyn, A. Kolmogorov, L. Liusternik, A. Liapunov, A. Markov. Their participation in the conference and support of the new movement in their speeches were important in stabilizing the fledgling group.

Nemchinov's efforts were also directed toward the publication of economic-mathematical works. The difficulties here were enormous because publishers were frightened of publishing unusual economic literature, particularly from mathematicians. Thanks to Nemchinov, the important book by L. Kantorovich, The Best Use of Economic Resources, was finally published in 1959--after a seventeen-year delay. Nemchinov took responsibility for its publication; he wrote a largely favorable preface in this book. However, certain critical remarks suggest a flaw in his comprehension of the book's main idea--the role of prices which were called objectively conditioned valuations by Kantorovich. These critical remarks were not the result of Nemchinov's

political caution or his fear of criticizing Marxist theory of value, but
were simply the result of his lack of knowledge of Western economic
thought. Other works by Nemchinov on the theory of price formation
and general economic problems also display some confusion, although
they express progressive ideas.

This lack of sophistication, however, was reflected in his personality as well as by his extreme naivete. One might naturally assume
that Nemchinov, as the creator of TSEMI in 1963, would have become
the director of the institute, but something happened which often occurs
in political life. As a member of the Presidium of the Academy of
Sciences of the USSR, a recognized leader of the economic-mathematical movement and other distinctions, Nemchinov did not want to take
on the role of director, with its trivial duties and daily activities such
as selecting a suitable location for the institute. It was easier for
Nemchinov to hire an administrator for these tasks, reward him with
an appropriate title, and retain the intellectual directorship of the institute. Such a situation is reminiscent of that between Stalin and
Zinoviev at the beginning of 1924, and between Khrushchev and Malenkov
in 1953 soon after Stalin's death. Malenkov had considered Khrushchev
his man; in Stalin's time, Khrushchev had gone to Malenkov's house as
to a guru. Great people look for administrators to relieve them of
trivia, but when the administrators receive power, they quickly rid
themselves of their bosses.

Nemchinov hired Nikolai Fedorenko as a director of TSEMI. Previously Fedorenko was the Deputy of the head of the Department of
Economics of the Academy of Sciences. A. Arzumanian, the head of
this Department, playing for high stakes and needing a deputy for his
department, had hired Fedorenko, an energetic man of about forty with
experience in administrative work, as a provost of the Chemical-
Technological Institute. Switching to the Academy gave Fedorenko the
title of Corresponding Member; switching to TSEMI gave him the title
of academician.

In September 1963 I was at one of the first meetings of TSEMI.
Those present sat at a horseshoe-shaped table. Nemchinov walked
back and forth about the room, his hands behind his back, talking
about the tasks of the institute. Then he introduced Fedorenko and
said that he had yielded to Fedorenko's business sense. Nemchinov
asked Fedorenko when the stable would be remodeled. (The stable
actually housed horses during the time of Catherine the Great and
served as the main building of TSEMI; this building is located in the
series of buildings of the Presidium of the Academy of Sciences of
the USSR) After several months, however, Nemchinov had become
merely one of the laboratory heads, because Fedorenko and his deputy

shifted the direction of research out of Nemchinov's chosen field.
Nemchinov had managed in 1963 to hire the mathematician, Iuri Oleinik,
not a Party member at that time, as Deputy Director. Oleinik had
demonstrated great energy in the Computer Center of the Academy of
Sciences, creating the first computer programs for the solution of
optimal transport problems and teaching programming to workers of
various Moscow institutions. Oleinik's role in the institute should
have consisted in the organization of mathematical-computer work,
but Fedorenko quickly realized Oleinik's understanding of political, as
well as professional problems, and he made him his right-hand man,
a position he occupied exclusively for some time.

By the fall of 1963, a group run by Oleinik had been formed to prepare a report to the scientific council of TSEMI on the basic directions
of work at the Institute. The report stressed the development of optimal planning in conjunction with the hierarchical character of the
management of the Soviet economy. Because Nemchinov's economic-
mathematical work dealt basically with input-output tables, the construction of price models on the basis of labor cost, and so on, however,
the founder of the Laboratory found himself on a tangent to the major
direction of the institute's work.

If Nemchinov was primarily an organizer in the field of economic-
mathematical research, Kantorovich, Novozhilov, and Lurie were
truly great scholars. However, unlike Nemchinov, they were not
Communist Party members.

Kantorovich

The Nobel prize laureate, academician Kantorovich, was a real
innovator in the field of economic-mathematical methods. At the age
of nineteen, Kantorovich graduated from Leningrad State University
and at twenty-two was a mathematics professor. His brilliant studies
on the theory of sets were published when he was sixteen years old.
In 1938, using the pure theory of functional analysis, a field then new
for Soviet mathematicians, he solved a practical problem of optimal
allocation of resources for producing veneer. The method which he
used subsequently became widely known as linear programming. (1)

For mathematicians, the method he discovered for problem solving
and its use in solving the problem of Monge would have been sufficient.
However, Kantorovich's unusual talent is evidenced in that once having
solved the given problems and having found a series of other similar
practical problems, he was then able to generalize them for application to the national economy. Furthermore, Kantorovich realized that
the Lagrange multipliers he applied in solving the problem were more

than mathematical parameters; they were extremely important economic categories, i.e., prices. For the majority of Soviet economists, even now the role of prices in constructing and implementing a plan remains unclear.

The desire to combine scientific results with practical applications was characteristic of Kantorovich, both as a mathematician and as an economist. If we remember the conditions of the Stalin era, we must be amazed by Kantorovich's courage in introducing new material. Before the beginning of the war with Germany, Kantorovich sent a letter to Gosplan in the USSR with recommendations for improving the system of price formation. This note found its way to the chief of the Department of Prices of Gosplan, USSR, Shamai Turetskii. Turetskii said to me that Kantorovich's energy could cost him dearly; it was known in Stalinist times that people who offer reforms, insofar as they distracted leading economists from work, could very simply be shipped off to camps; there they would not prevent people from real work. Kantorovich, it seems, was saved by the fact that he already was a very famous mathematician. In the 1940s, Kantorovich's work on mathematical economics could be excused because he was simultaneously working on applied mathematics and participating in the solution of various practical problems, some of which had great military significance.

In the mid-1950s, when a certain diversity in economics became possible, Kantorovich began to propagandize his views. At the beginning of 1957, Kantorovich was given the chance to report on his work to the Institute of Economics of the Academy of Sciences. I attended the presentation of the report, though there were not many people there, and Kantorovich's work conquered me with its logic. At the end of the 1950s, Kantorovich organized courses for economists on methods of mathematical programming at Leningrad State University. Students included not only young Leningrad economists, but also some from Moscow and among them Stanislav Shatalin, now a Corresponding Member of the Academy of Sciences, who did a great deal for the development of the economic-mathematical school.

Kantorovich continued work on practical problems. As a result of research he conducted on the use of taxi fleets, the system of payment for taxis in the Soviet Union was changed. The introduction of a definite fare per ride as well as the fare per kilometer noticeably increased the use of taxis. Kantorovich recounted with pride how he persuaded the employees of the Ministry of Finances that his suggestions were rational.

Kantorovich spent the 1960s in the Institute of Mathematics of the Siberian Division of the Academy of Sciences of the USSR. As Deputy

Director of this institute he organized a division for mathematical economics and encouraged mathematicians to work on economics. At the same time Kantorovich took an active part in the development of the economic-mathematical movement on an all-union scale. At the beginning of the 1970s Kantorovich transferred to Moscow where he was appointed as the head of a laboratory for economic-mathematical methods in the business school which deals with raising the qualifica - tions of managers in the highest levels of the hierarchy; a couple of years ago he moved to the All-Union Institute of Systems (VNIISI).

A very kind and witty person, nothing human is alien from Kan- torovich. Valeri Makarov, Kantorovich's friend from Novosibirsk, was my house guest for a few days. At one point early in the morning the phone rang, and I sleepily heard someone asking me in broken English if Makarov was there. The caller introduced himself as a member of the American Academy from Boston. I tried to answer something in English. The American caller kept repeating his question about Makarov in English. I explained to him that Makarov had already left and that it would be easier to find him through Kantorovich, who was then in Moscow. In answer I heard, "This is Kantorovich speaking." To reward me for my patience and amusement at his practical joke, Kantorovich read me on the phone a fable he had written on how a cook prepares a scientific dish.

Of course, both the strength and the limitations of Kantorovich's work are apparent from the present development of Soviet economics. But it should be noted that the scientific generalizations mentioned were set forth and explained in a 1942 manuscript by a thirty-year-old mathematics teacher cut off from Western economic thought and re- mained unacknowledged for seventeen years. Unfortunately, the book's publication was Kantorovich's last original work, his swan song in the field of mathematical economics.

Novozhilov

As with Kantorovich's influence, Novozhilov's enormous role in the formation of economic-mathematical methods is well known. Novozhilov, whose role will be more thoroughly discussed subsequently, applied an economic sense to mathematical methods for optimal prob- lem solution on a national scale. As a scholar-economist, he was far removed from any serious administrative activity. For many years he worked as a teacher in one of the Leningrad economic institutes. In the mid-1960s, when TSEMI was founded, he went to work heading until his death a small laboratory in its Leningrad branch. Highly ed- ucated in economics, under Soviet conditions, Novozhilov also enjoyed music and played in a family quartet.

Lurie

Lurie followed the stream of well-known ideas in the field of
mathematical economics. His talent lay in making them clearer and
more precise than anyone else. All of Lurie's scholarly work was
steeped in the idea of unifying the newest economic and mathematical
concepts. Already in 1927, in a paper called "The Average Salary
Level," he clarified the economics-mathematics link. Because of his
works researching the "time of recoupment," in 1948 Lurie was
accused of worshipping the West and its bourgeois economic science.
One of the teachers of the transport institute where Lurie worked
wrote an article blasting his work in the journal, The Economics of
Railroad Transportation.

For a few years Lurie did not work on economics; in Stalinist
times this was a small price to pay for free thinking. During this time
Lurie wrote and published a series of articles on the theory of probability which displayed his marvelous mathematical ability. He often said
to me that it was an unfortunate quirk of fate which had caused him to
have an economic rather than mathematical education.

From the mid-1950s on, Lurie again began to work on economics.
Using both his knowledge of economics and his mathematical ability,
Lurie created an algorithm for the solution of the so-called "transport
problem." This algorithm bears his name. Unsatisfied by theoretical
work alone, Lurie tried to implement the results of his research in
practice. At the end of the 1950s, as a worker at the Institute of Complex Transportation Problems, jokingly named by Kantorovich the
Institute of "Real" and "Imagined" Transport Problems, he took an
active part in the work of organizing optimal transportation of freight
in Moscow. In the 1960s, Lurie was primarily a research worker at
the Institute of Economics of the USSR Academy of Sciences, but he
continued to teach a course on optimal planning in the economics
faculty of Moscow State University.

Lurie was an honest and impartial person who fought against cow-
ardice and obscurantism; he was called the "musketeer" not only because of his small beard. His total dedication to science, however,
sometimes led to dangerous incidents. In the early 1960s, Lurie was
the reader for Lipa Smoliar's dissertation on optimal planning. In his
speech to the dissertation committee Lurie mentioned, as was required in such cases, the good points of the dissertation. He touched
on the economic sides of the problems Smoliar had considered. Expenditures involving capital interest were minimized as a criterion of
optimality. Suddenly Lurie turned to Abram Probst, a member of the
dissertation committee and an old adversary on problems of the

effectiveness of investments, and began arguing with him. The student
was forgotten and so was the audience; Lurie and Probst argued the
problem of effectiveness. Although the disputants were separated, the
skirmish nearly cost Smoliar his degree, for several members of the
dissertation committee used Probst's disagreement with Smoliar's
view on the effectiveness of capital investment to vote against the
dissertation, although this issue was of minor importance in the dissertation. I worked together with Lurie for many years, at first in
the Institute of Economics, then in TSEMI. Our friendship helped me
to understand more than just economic problems, although I could not
accept his leftist views on several political issues.

Vainshtein

Among the scholars important to the development of mathematical
economics was Albert Vainshtein, who had a complex fate. Lenin had
once made an unfavorable remark about him, and Vainshtein was constantly being reminded of this. He had occasioned this remark by
"indecent" statistical research on Soviet economics, and so Vainshtein
was sent into exile at the beginning of the 1930s. He returned to Moscow in the 1950s and took an active part in scholarly work, publishing
a book devoted to problems of measurement of Russia's national
wealth. While working in the laboratory headed by Nemchinov and
then in TSEMI, Vainshtein conducted research in the field of financial
flow and wrote an article on the history of linear programming in the
Soviet Union. Even in the 1960s, however, when he was proposed for
the title of "honored scientist," he was not given the title immediately
because of the earlier incident.

Vainshtein's primary activity was the dissemination of economic-
mathematical ideas. As an editor he spent much time editing Kantorovich's book, The Best Use of Economic Resources. The fact that
Vainshtein agreed to be the editor of such a "seditious" book was extremely important in its publication, and Vainshtein's contribution here
is indisputable. He was a most conscientious editor. At the same time,
as someone with a fairly unclear theoretical Weltanschaung and with an
excessive inclination toward Marxist constructs, Vainshtein, in my
opinion, overedited the book in an attempt to make it thoroughly Marxist. Earlier, Kantorovich had given me the manuscript of the book,
and knowing the original Kantorovich manuscript, I was aware of
Vainshtein's efforts to reorient it.

It is particularly important to stress Vainshtein's role in translating economic-mathematical literature. Vainshtein's excellent
translation of R. Allen's book, Mathematical Economics, had and

still has great significance for the continuing development of the
economic-mathematical school. (2) This book contains not only mathematical apparatus for economics, it brings to the Soviet reader a
series of concepts and a mode of thought peculiar to Western economists.

In characterizing Vainshtein's important role in the development of
economic-mathematical methods, I cannot fail to note that the role of a
fighter, which he played from the 1920s on, has left unpleasant traces.
The years of struggle damaged his understanding of the role of means
and the value of means in themselves. On the whole, Vainshtein's
behavior was irreproachable, but he is marred by "birthmarks of
socialism in people's consciousness." (Soviet officials explain all bad
behavior as birthmarks of capitalism in people's consciousness.)
These birthmarks could be identified in the following way.

At the time when the Scholarly Council of TSEMI was debating the
question of Igor Birman's doctoral dissertation defense, no one doubted
that Birman, the author of numerous valuable books and articles on the
theory and practice of optimal planning, deserved the doctoral degree.
(3) At their meeting, Vainshtein actively protested approving Birman's
book for a defense. Then he asked for the floor to read a statement on
Birman's work from Ia. Gerchuk, (4) an economist of the older generation who actively helped develop the economic-mathematical school.
The scientific accuracy of this critique is not at issue here, but as
presented by Vainshtein and in the demagogic tone used for such pro-
nouncements, Birman's work was criticized for divergence from historical and dialectical materialism. To ascribe apostasy to Birman
at the end of the 1960s was an act which, to put it mildly, did not show
its authors in a very good light. Moreover, Birman was accused of
divergence from orthodox philosophical principles in a book devoted to
very concrete problems far removed from philosophy. (5)

Boiarskii

Another economic-mathematical mutation is Professor Aron
Boiarskii, a Communist Party member. In the 1930s, Boiarskii had
worked on mathematical statistics and their applications to economics.
He quickly realized the depravity of the theoretical views of economists
of this school and became one of their most active critics. He was
attacked in the mid-1940s for submitting one of his student's dissertations showing a high rate of population growth in the Baltic countries
under the German occupation during World War II. A note in Pravda
concerning this could have resulted in a tragic ending for Boiarskii,
had influential people not saved him. Among them was the well-known
old Communist, Nikolai Semashko.

Boiarskii, knowledgeable in mathematics and author of a mathematics textbook for economists in the mid-1950s, began to play an important role in the field. He at once came out against the ideas of optimization in economic theory on the basis of the concept of utility; he was against the concept of shadow prices as prices, and even presently he still fulminates against these ideas at every possible opportunity during meetings and conferences. In the economics faculty of MGU, where Boiarskii is head of the statistics department, he is one of the most active economists opposing the mathematical analysis of economics.

However, Boiarskii is also the director of the institute planning the network of computer centers of the Central Statistical Administration of the USSR. His program for a system of planning does include the concept of an optimal plan, but one that is based on the criterion of minimized labor expenditures. In fact, Boiarskii uses Novozhilov's model, but without accepting the interpretation of shadow prices as prices. Boiarskii's position toward the economic-mathematical trend can be roughly summarized as follows: practically speaking, mathematical methods ought to be reduced to a technical tool for solving different economic problems assigned by the Party and the government.

By the end of the 1950s, Boiarskii was justifying his conservatism in private conversations because he feared the destruction of the economic-mathematical school if it dealt with theoretical questions that did not agree with Marxism, ideas, for example, which were clearly connected with the theory of marginal utility. Boiarskii showed himself to be different from the other mutants--Nemchinov, Kantorovich, Novozhilov, and Lurie, who despite the divergences of their views respected each other and never wrote accusations against other economists. Boiarskii was intolerant of other views and would have rid himself of people who disagreed with him by any means, including ideological accusations.

Boiarskii's behavior reflected perhaps the temperament of a fighter: a great ability to get back at people when his conceit was wounded, an anger at being relegated to secondary roles behind Nemchinov, Novozhilov, and Kantorovich, and at being forced to follow them. All these factors aggravated Boiarskii's struggle with the new movement.

Meanwhile, Boiarskii was a tolerant advisor for very good graduate students in mathematical economics. Even if he disagreed with students as scholars, he sometimes helped with personal problems.

THE IDEOLOGICAL MEMBRANE
OF ECONOMIC-MATHEMATICAL
MUTATIONS

The proposed theoretical principles of optimal planning can concern ideological problems at various levels of the hierarchy. The
examination of an economic system as a whole, because it links directly
with ideology, impinges to a greater degree on the interests of the
ruling group. Therefore, a pragmatic basis is especially needed here.

When the problem of optimal planning of a factory is discussed
using shadow prices to solve the problems, the economic meaning of
shadow prices as parameters can be ignored and considered to have
only a technical character useful in figuring calculations. However,
the need to use mathematical methods on a national-economic level
soon becomes apparent. As soon as input-output tables are allowed,
it is entirely natural to allow optimization as well, understandably
under conditions in which the criterion of optimality could be given by
the powers-that-be.

New difficulties arise from this, however, since the optimal plan
engenders the shadow prices of resources. Because these shadow
prices are found at the national-economic level, it is impossible to
reject their economic content, and the presence of shadow prices of
limited resources that cannot be reproduced is difficult to explain
through labor expenses, using the Marxist labor theory of value. It is
here that the necessity for concessions arises (see the earlier discussion on the destruction of the theoretical trends concerning general
sociological problems.) It seems to me that the importance of these
concessions should not be exaggerated from a political viewpoint.
Most advocates of the theory of optimal planning are trying to camouflage their proposals under Marxism, i.e., to unite the ideology of
optimal planning with the labor theory of value.

Any Soviet economist runs into the necessity of imitating Marxism.
It is impossible in practice while working with theoretical problems in
economics to avoid relating to Marxism, but one can get around it in
various ways. I understand that life is impossible without compromises,
especially in authoritarian systems, but the recognition of the compromise is important. One must minimize its negative aspects and try to
revise his position when the circumstances change. The fathers of the
theory of optimal planning--Leonid Kantorovich, Victor Novozhilov,
and Alexander Lurie--worked on an imitation of Marxism. This imitation, in its time, helped these mutations to survive, as did their
research in optimal allocation of resources, and in the concomitant
shadow prices which disagreed with Marxist economic theory.

Unfortunately, bringing into accord the ideas of optimal plannings with Marxism is still not entirely an historical matter; it is a problem even at present in Soviet economics.

Novozhilov

I will begin with Novozhilov, who employed "Marxishness" in his works to the greatest degree. It happened not out of ignorance of world economic thought, as it did for Nemchinov or Kantorovich, but out of the political need to imitate. While the means of imitation he employed in the 1930s-1950s were in many ways justified, when the larger development of economics became possible in the 1960s, the negative aspects of his imitation became apparent. After the stormy discussions of the 1920s and the early 1930s, it became clear to the economists that the elucidation of which final products were to be produced and in what quantity was the task of the Party and its leader. The economists' energies were, therefore, directed at answers to the questions of how to produce and how to fulfill the Party's quotas better. In Novozhilov's mathematical models, just as in those of many other creative economists at that time, the knowledge of the volume of finished production to be produced was axiomatic. As soon as there was a quota of what and how much to produce and it was only necessary to think how to produce it, then the optimal problem, naturally, was to have a minimum of expenses. The available resources were introduced as constraints. The expenses were to be measured in labor. This, of course, brings up the question of the commensurability of various types of labor--the famous Marxist problem of the "reduction of labor," i.e., finding a common denominator for the measurement of labor inputs. Novozhilov passed over it in silence.

Novozhilov concluded that the price of a product is measured in labor units and is equal to the expenditures of labor plus the expenses of the limited resources expressed through their shadow prices. Novozhilov used the term "feedback" for the expenses of the limited resources, when it became fashionable in the mid-1950s to borrow terms from cybernetics.

The indicated concept, it seemed, must satisfy many things in a theoretical sense: 1) everything is measured in labor, and thus, the conversion formula of labor value under socialism is obtained; 2) the quota of what to produce is given, and there is no notorious problem of utility; and 3) both mathematics and cybernetics are used. However, such a model had important theoretical gaps. First, the questions of what to produce and how to produce it were separated, and this cannot be done because the volume of production of various products also

depends on the means of production used. Novozhilov and his supporters
tried to pass over this deficiency by arranging the process of the change
in the limitations on the given volumes of production, but how to change
these volumes remained unclear. Also, the model posed a false problem of "the reduction of labor," which in the framework of the present
model demanded an external solution in principle.

There were two unresolved economic problems at the theoretical
base of Novozhilov's model. One of them, connected with the reduction of labor, does not have a solution outside of the model of the national economy. Unfortunately, Novozhilov quite energetically insisted
on his model as the most preferable. Correctly considering that a
model of national-economic planning according to the criterion of a
minimum of expense had the best chance for practical realization, he
found the development of the optimal trend based on the criterion of
utility unnecessary. In a conversation with me, Novozhilov said directly
that the development of the latter trend was even harmful, because it
distracts from the solution of practical problems. Of course, such
statements by Novozhilov could be made only in personal conversation.
High moral qualities did not allow him to resort publicly to sharp statements about other points of view. I could not agree with Novozhilov at
all. It seemed wrong to me to view practical needs only in terms of
current problems. In order to introduce utility-theory-type models in
the future, it is necessary to begin practical action today, i.e., such
as compiling demand statistics.

It goes without saying that a perfected model would have elucidated
a number of theoretical problems which, in turn, would have affected
the development of science. For example, the problem of reduction,
in the traditional framework, attracted a number of notable scholars
who arranged for a conference on this problem. The understanding of
the problem of reduction on the basis of more developed models could
have saved a considerable effort, which was expended in vain.

Kantorovich

Kantorovich's method of Marxist imitation was somewhat different
than Novozhilov's. Kantorovich had before him the "model of the
Veneer Trust," a model which maximized the planned output under the
resource and assortment constraints. Comparable with Novozhilov's
assumptions, Kantorovich assumes that only the proportions of final
production figures are known; the volume of their production is unknown.

The problem of reduction of labor in Kantorovich's model is solved
in the course of the problem itself through the search for the shadow

prices of various types of labor. Furthermore, Kantorovich investigated problems in which the minimization of expenses for resources
or the time for the achievement of the stated goal appeared as the
criterion. In these problems, not only the structure of the ultimate
demand, but also its volumes were already defined.

Kantorovich thus analyzed problems in which either the maximi-
zation of the output of production in a given assortment, or the minimization of certain expenses was the criterion. As a result of this,
the shadow price of the product, like that of the resources, was obtained from the plan as a dual variable of the corresponding constraint on
the assortment or the minimum output of final production. A comparison of Kantorovich's models with models in which the problem of
elucidation of the conditions for ultimate consumption is reflected--for
example, a model with the criterion of optimality reflecting the degree
of the satisfaction of people's needs--makes clear the reason for the
difficulties in understanding the economic nature of the shadow prices
of finished products in Kantorovich's model. Kantorovich walked away
from the problem of the preference for goods.

Because the shadow prices are not measured through labor costs
in an obvious form in Kantorovich's models, he demonstrated, by
means of a number of conversations of dual ratios, that the shadow
prices can be expressed in average socially necessary labor costs.
I would refer the reader interested in this question in more detail to
the appendices in Kantorovich's The Best Use of Economic Resources.(6)

I had opportunities to speak with Kantorovich many times about the
correlation of shadow prices and labor value, and he always wanted to
reconcile them. As early as 1960 Kantorovich prepared an article, in
which he had written that the shadow prices can be converted into labor
values by multiplying them by a fixed coefficient corresponding to surplus value. This reflected discussions which took place in the Soviet
Union concerning the question of how to include the surplus value in
the expenses. In Kantorovich's later publications, I no longer encountered these above-mentioned proposals about the conversion of
shadow prices into labor values, but other proposals appeared. When-
ever the question of the labor theory of value arose in my conversations
with Kantorovich, he had little to say. Thus, I did not succeed in understanding whether it was out of tactical considerations or from conviction that he wanted to reconcile shadow prices with labor value. It
is also not clear whether the burden of what he had published about the
interrelations of shadow prices and labor value put pressure on him.

In 1972 an episode took place demonstrating that Kantorovich still
adhered to the concept of labor value. Igor Shafarevich, the Chairman
of the Moscow Mathematical Society, invited me to make a speech at

a meeting of the society about the application of mathematical methods
in economics. The society's meetings take place at Moscow State
University and usually attract an audience of several hundred people.
Because those attending are mainly mathematicians, I divided this
speech into two parts: I gave the mathematical aspect of the question
(the models and the theorems accompanying them) to Boris Mitiagin,
and I took the general questions of the interrelationship of economics
and mathematics. In my speech, as is customary in such speeches,
I dwelt especially on Kantorovich's role. This pleased me particularly
because I wanted the mathematicians to hear from the lips of an economist what a prominent role was played in the formulation of the economic-mathematical trend in the USSR by Kantorovich, who was in
the hall.

In the question-and-answer period after the speech, one of the
famous Moscow mathematicians asked me the notorious question,
"What is your attitude toward labor value?" I replied that, as I
attempted to explain in my speech, the price is used in the planning
mechanism on the basis of the analysis of the mathematical procedures
of Dantsig-Wolf. From this algorithm, it is apparent that the prices
can fulfill their function as the parameters of self-action because they
are the Lagrange multiplier. As is evident in the framework of the
examined process of planning, categories such as labor value are not
necessary. It is possible that they may be needed, but I do not know
of such models. Furthermore, I noted that such an attitude toward
prices does not contradict Marxism, because Marx himself wrote
that in the future planned society there will be no labor value, and it
is precisely this society which we were studying. Then Kantorovich
asked for the floor. He said that he could not agree with the speaker's
attitude toward labor value. Kantorovich said that in his own works
he had demonstrated that the shadow prices correspond to labor value,
and so on. Many of those present were astonished that a famous mathematician, at a mature age, protected by world recognition, was trying
to be orthodox, and that a "half-mature," unprotected economist had
abandoned orthodoxy. Fortunately, all this did not prevent us from
conversing after the meeting in the friendliest manner.

Lurie

On the question of Lurie's method of imitation, it is necessary to
note that quotations were found in Marx and Engels from which it became evident that in the future society there would not be labor values,
products would be commensurate with utility, the plan would be directed
at the allocation of resources with the goal of satisfying the people's

needs, and so on. On the basis of these quotations the protection from
criticism was created. The criterion of optimality in the present model
was already expressed through the satisfaction of people's needs. (7)
The constraints were the technological methods and scarcity of
resources.

Unfortunately, Lurie, as a man of the older generation, did not
completely follow these quotations from Marx and Engels and was still
somehow trying to "flirt with labor." Imitating Novozhilov, he called
the shadow prices arising in his model "differential expenses." Moreover, from the model with the criterion of optimality in the form of a
utility function, he found the volumes of output. Then he formed a new
model, having taken the found volumes of production of final goods as
constraints and the minimization of the expenses for any factor as a
criterion of optimality. The results of the solution to the problem
according to the new model, i.e., the intensities of the production
methods and shadow prices, remained the same. As an example, Lurie
cited the model in which the criterion was the minimum expense of
labor, although it could be the minimum of any other resource just as
well. This work later engendered all sorts of speculations, which reflected in the articles of Abel Aganbegian and Kiril Bagrinovskii. (8)

I myself gradually developed the following method of imitation.
At the basis of a scientific work, there must be an exposition of material which is the sincere expression of the scholar's view. Classical
quotations, which the author considers correct, are then added to it.
In principle, the latter demand can be satisfied, although it is necessary
to conduct special work on the investigation of the "canonical texts."
(I once said that a classicist, by definition, is a man in whose works
one can find a positive answer to any question relating to his work.)
It is desirable, of course, that the number of quotations be as small as
possible and without the corresponding epithets.

It stands to reason that there are unpleasant aspects even with this
method of imitation. Although the quotations which I cited in my works
did not contradict my convictions, I cited only positive references to
Marx. I did not cite the corresponding quotations of a general economic
sort from the works of the Austrian or any other Western school. Thus,
I created a distorted idea of Marx and exaggerated his role. I will risk
saying that in my works, and many of them were collective, there was
no "flirting with labor." My coauthors are not responsible for this.
The definition of price was given as a contribution introduced by a small
increase of resources in the realization of the goal posited by society.
At present, this definition of price can be seen quite frequently in
Soviet economic-mathematical literature. I myself later revised this
definition, above all because it seemed incorrect to give a definition

of a general economic category from the point of view of one method
for describing a system--in the present case, an optimal one. I tried
to define price as invariant to the method of description (embracing
what is general in price in various economic mechanisms) and singling
out price as the guideline for a self-acting economic unit. (9)

Soviet Economists

     Some Soviet economists who deal with Western economics and
helped to bring the new western economic deals to the Soviet Union,
also try to find an excuse for using these ideas in a Communist country.
In the mid-1950s, among the Soviet economists supporting the possibility of using economic-mathematical methods based on the positive experience of the West, the following at lease may be named: Israel
Bliumin, Revold Entov, Stanislov Menshikov, Abram Mileikovskii, Irina
Osadchaia, and Vladimir Shliapentokh, all professionally working on
the study of Western economic thought. In their works, these economists
attempted to demonstrate that there are seeds of efficiency in Western
thought, though the Western economists, of course, remain bourgeois
scholars in their theoretical views and class positions. The task of the
Soviet economists was also to clarify the Western ideas which could be
used for the improvement of practice in the Soviet Union.

Bliumin

     I have already mentioned I. Bliumin. (10) I may also point out that
if a man is a scholar (or as the Germans say, Gelernter, i.e., knowledgeable), then most likely he must sooner or later give his colleagues
their due. This Bliumin did in the mid-1950s, although his entire past
prevented him from giving them full recognition. Bliumin's past was
not only one of adherence to Marxist doctrine, it was, in fact, a life
under conditions of incredible fear of the ruling political regime,
sharply aggravated by his Jewish origin. The joint discussions of
Bliumin and Shliapentokh on the problems of econometrics in the West
have been preserved in an article published at the end of the 1950s in
the journal Voprosy Ekonomiki. (11) It was the first article in a Soviet
journal for many years in which the positive aspects of econometrics
were acknowledged.

Shliapentokh

     In the mid-1950s, Shliapentokh belonged to the group of young
scholars. A man with amazing abilities, vitally interested in social

problems, he had entered the history faculty at Kiev State University soon after the war. Not seeing prospects for himself in historical studies after graduation from the University, he decided to train for a new profession, and he graduated from the correspondence Moscow Economic-Statistical Institute in 1952. (12) In 1953 he moved with his family to the Saratov area, where he taught statistics in a technical school. Although his living conditions were unusually bad, Shliapentokh did not cease his scientific work, but studied Western economic thought and econometrics. (Shliapentokh could study this quite seriously because he had learned foreign languages at home as a child.) The results of these investigations were published in a book. (13) On an ideological plane, the book was a continuation of the article on econometrics written with Bliumin. In addition, at the end of the 1950s, while working as a teacher of statistics in the Saratov Agricultural Institute, Shliapentokh published an article on the application of methods of linear programming to agriculture. It was one of the few articles at the time which demonstrated possible practical applications of the new mathematical methods. (14)

Other Soviet Scientific Scholars

Finally, I want to mention that some famous scholars from other spheres of science sided with the economic-mathematical trend and also frequently tried to express their attitude to Marxism, but they often did it in primitive forms. It seems to me that this expression was the result of conformism, a feeling internalized in many members of the intelligentsia, especially of the older generation. And even when there was no urgent need to express their advocacy of Marxism, these scholars did it just in case.

Kolmogorov

The prominent Soviet mathematician, Andrei Kolmogorov, rendered much assistance in the development of the economic-mathematical trend in his initial period. Kolmogorov completely supported the mathematicians conducting investigations in this sphere. One of his graduate students, Iuri Tiurin, defended his dissertation on economic-mathematical methods, the results of which in my mind remained undeservedly in the dark. One of Kolmogorov's closest colleagues, Igor Girsanov, devoted a lot of energy to organizing the teaching of mathematics to economists and to scientific research in the sphere of economic-mathematical modeling. Kolmogorov was a reader of Lurie's doctoral dissertation, one of the first doctoral dissertations on economic-

mathematical methods defended in the early 1960s at Moscow State
University.

Unfortunately, Kolmogorov's interest in the economic-mathematical trend quickly vanished. Furthermore, while he did support the
new trend, in my opinion Kolmogorov placed too much emphasis--to
the detriment of its scientific character--on channeling it into Marxism
and the Marxist labor theory of value, although he was governed in this
by the best intentions. I will cite an excerpt from Kolmogorov's speech
at the First All-Union Scientific Conference in 1960 on the Application
of Mathematical Methods to Economics:

> As concerns the joint work of mathematicians and
> economists on the development of economic theory,
> several comrades have emphasized that new theories
> and ideas are sometimes born from mathematical
> investigations; for example, the electromagnetic
> theory of light arose as a result of the purely math-
> ematical analysis of the equations of the electro-
> magnetic field which, as it turned out, have a
> solution of the wave character. However, in the
> sphere of economics, it is a different story. The
> nature of the phenomena underlying the study are
> well known here; their scientific understanding is
> entirely developed by Marxist political economy,
> and there is no basis for expecting a revolution in
> this sphere. But joint work of economists and
> mathematicians must lead to the improvement of
> the economic theory itself, for in many instances
> the diffuse literary formulations of the economists
> will be made more precise. Linguists, for example,
> willingly acknowledge that joint work with mathema-
> ticians forces them to make many of their concepts
> more precise.
>
> I would like to dwell on the questions of the effectiveness
> of capital investments. In order to bring the mathe-
> matical apparatus of computations into accord with the
> basic concepts of economic theory, it seems most
> natural to measure the labor value in units of labor
> invested in the same computation period (a year, a
> month), when the output is obtained. Under the cir-
> cumstances of a developing, progressing economy,
> such labor value will decrease with the passage of

time. The transfer of labor expenses to an earlier
time allows for an increase in the summary production through a change in the plan (producing an investment of labor in the creation of more improved
equipment). This leads to the appearance of a coefficient evaluating the advantage of the "advance of
labor." Such a coefficient, in my opinion, is the
"standard of effectiveness," of which L. V. Kantorovich spoke. His formal analogy with the capitalist
"rate of interest" must not disturb us. This is an
original category of a socialist economy. Such a
coefficient may be calculated for a capitalist economy
as well, but it by no means will correspond with the
profit obtained by the capitalists, which is defined by
completely different circumstances. (15)

From such a prominent mathematician as Kolmogorov, who is not even
a member of the Party, one expects more independence of spirit. Kolmogorov frequently belied these expectations. When cybernetics was
being defamed in the Soviet Union he came out against it; at a later date,
when it became acceptable, he repented. The note in _Pravda_ in 1974,
therefore, in which Kolmogorov condemned Alexander Solzhenitsyn
did not surprise me. In a word, the coefficient of conformity--the
ratio of acknowledging merits to the independence of behavior--proved
to be too high in Kolmogorov. Such, apparently, is the price for being
considered the top mathematician in the USSR, but we have to keep in
mind that Kolmogorov sometimes used his prestigious position to help
in the development of new things.

THE STRUCTURE OF PERSONNEL FLOW
IN THE ECONOMIC-MATHEMATICAL MOVEMENT

The activity of leading scholars stimulated development of research in the economics-mathematical field. Isolated studies were
consolidated. In fact, after 1956 within some three to four years
there appeared in the country a set of economic-mathematical centers.
One of them, the Laboratory of Economic-Mathematical Methods of the
USSR Academy of Sciences, was completely devoted to economic-
mathematical methods. In some other organizations, such as the
Laboratory of Electronic Machines (Computers), the Institute of Economics, the Institute of Mathematics of the Siberian Division, the
Institute of Economics and Organization of Industrial Production, the
Moscow Plekhanov Institute of the National Economy, and Moscow

State University, were formed divisions/departments which were oriented to investigate economic problems by using mathematical methods.

University Faculty

In principle, institutes of higher education should be the sowers of new ideas. They are supposedly more independent of the government than specialized scientific centers such as the Academy of Sciences. At a Western university a tenured professor is required to teach courses and otherwise guide students. As a rule, he has no rigid plans of theoretical research unless by agreement with an appropriate organization. In addition, if a professor has developed new ideas which are inappropriate for present conditions, he can put them aside for later. The option for a scholar to teach a standard lecture course is often preferable to working on research in which he is uninterested.

The general status of university professors in the Soviet Union is similar, but work conditions are such that creative productivity is complicated. This is due to many factors, including the teacher's large teaching load and his involvement in public work, particularly if he is a Party member. Further, because it is felt by the government that students are the strongest element of fermentation in society, new ideas and new scholarly movements, particularly in the area of humanities, are not encouraged in Soviet higher education. Consequently, in the Soviet Union, most creative work is attempted in the Academy of Sciences, not in the universities. When the development of new directions in economics has come from teachers in educational institutes in my opinion it is often the result of limited staff in the corresponding scholarly economic institutes. As support for my interpretation, I can refer to the fact that as soon as creative economists were given the opportunity to transfer to the Academy of Sciences, they did so; then they engaged in part-time teaching.

Economics-Mathematical Faculty

Personnel was a problem in the formation of economic-mathematical centers. Numerically, "direct economic-mathematical mutations" were few, and a flow of new personnel was necessary. The personnel had to represent two fields--economics and mathematics. A number of forty-to-fifty-year-old economists, who until that time had had no relationship to economic-mathematical methods, began to work actively with these methods. They were, for the most part, creative people moved by a desire to develop new scientific schools of thought.

Obviously, however, they were hindered by their former training and by their ages. After a few years of working in the economic-mathematical field and doing much for its development, many of them were unable to stand the pace set by the younger people and went back to their former occupations, helping the new trend only in an advisory capacity.

Among the recruits to the economic-mathematical school of thought were a group of 30-year-old economists. These scientists, the backbone of the present economics-mathematical school of thought, had experience in conducting economic research and had training in mathematics, but they had no research experience in mathematics. They were mostly graduates of economics institutes and departments, especially statistics departments in which they could study mathematics and computer technology. These young people were interested in applications of contemporary methods to economic research. They now hold more than two-thirds of the important positions, such as heads of divisions and sections and positions as senior research workers.

The selection of young people graduated from economic institutes and departments was difficult, because economics had little prestige in the Soviet Union for a long time. The students in economics were largely untalented people unable to go to an engineering college or a more prestigious natural science faculty. For the same reasons it was difficult to attract young promising scholars from the fields of social sciences which are contiguous to mathematical economics. (16) However, there were capable young engineers and mathematicians who decided to enter economics. Some were interested in social problems and saw the possibility of using their professional knowledge of mathematics in this area. Others went into economics because the mathematical research they were already doing came close to economic research. In addition, for some of these engineers and mathematicians working in military research institutes, economics offered the possibility to openly publish the results of their mathematical work.

Finally, therefore, even pure mathematicians came to economics. Having received freedom for their activities, however, these pure mathematicians were not completely comfortable; they did not see how they were needed in the organizations which supported them because their future contributions to economics seemed remote. They feared immediate dismissal should there be any changes in organizations. Moreover, many young mathematicians who came as junior scientists could not foresee advancement, since in order to become a senior research scientist, it was necessary to work in economic thematics. Furthermore, work on mathematics and on economics were parallel jobs, because pure mathematics could not be quickly utilized in economics. For the overwhelming majority of mathematicians who had considered getting work in Moscow, or who were Jews, the work conditions were preferable to those in other cities or in a high school, but still the drawbacks were considerable. As a consequence, many mathematicians worked in economics only by necessity.

Dynkin

Eugene Dynkin, for example, was an outstanding mathematician of international reputation who went into economics at the end of the 1960s after expulsion from Moscow State University because of personal misunderstandings. TSEMI offered Dynkin a position, and having little choice, he accepted it. Dynkin was able to invite a group of his students to TSEMI and together with them began an intensive study of probability models in economics. The first published results of this work indicated its importance. Dynkin also was able to organize a seminar attractive to all researchers in mathematical economics. In 1976, unable to stand the continuing denigration of his position, he emigrated. Professor Dynkin is presently tenured at Cornell University.

Moishezon

Necessity also spurred Boris Moishezon, a famous young mathematician specializing in algebraic geometry, to accept a position at TSEMI in 1967. Before this, only with great difficulty had Moishezon been able to move out of Tadzhikistan to arrange for work near Moscow in the Orekhovo-Zuevskii Pedagogical Institute. There, he was forced to spend a great deal of time teaching standard courses and he had great difficulty getting to Moscow to communicate with colleagues. However, his participation in the research conducted at TSEMI on socioeconomic modeling increasingly distracted him from his basic work. In 1972, unable to stand the continuing denigration of his position, he emigrated. Professor Moishezon presently is tenured at Columbia University. The same reasons also drove to emigration such brilliant mathematicians as A. Dynin, A. Katok, and B. Mitiagin, who were directly involved in the field of mathematical economics. All of them were accepted for academic work at the leading American universities.

The Compatibility between Economists and Mathematicians

The coexistence of economists and mathematicians in one school has posed problems of compatibility. Arguments arose as to which

group would set the tone. Thinking that mathematics utilized more
sophisticated tools, the mathematicians thought that it was easier for
them to master economics than for the economists to master mathematics. (17) On the other hand, the economists thought it harder for
mathematicians to learn economics, since mathematics involves considerable formalization and economics, in great part, is learned in
the experience of economic activity. These arguments between the
mathematicians and economists were to a certain extent aggravated
by L. Kantorovich who, in his speech at the 1960 conference, said that
like Valentina Gaganova, mathematicians must help economists who
could not cope with their own problems to join a brigade which was
falling behind. (18) The tone was eventually set by those who could
pose and solve new problems, regardless of their original education.

What did these arguments actually reflect? Most applied mathematicians are used to dealing with physicists and engineers with a
mathematical background which enables them to set forth problems and
to understand the methods suggested by mathematicians, including
possible transformations in the formulation of the problem. In other
words, mathematicians as a rule are used to dealing with formalized
problems. For the economist without mastery of mathematics, it
therefore becomes difficult to pose problems for the mathematicians
in the first place. It is easier for the economist to work with researchers who deal with applied problems and at the same time know the
apparatus of mathematics. e.g., engineers who deal with problems of
control, and physicists. P. Mors and G. Kimball refer to a similar
experience in the organization of operations research in the United
States Army during World War II. (19)

Many of the economists, engineers, and mathematicians who entered the field of mathematical economics began to work in its leading
centers. It is also quite interesting to note that some of the talented
young people who found their way into the sphere of mathematical
economics had remained outsiders. Among them I would like to indi-
cate first of all Doctors Lev Dudkin and Anatoli Pervosvanskii. Dudkin
is known for his works in the field of applying the so-called "iterative
aggregation" algorithms to the analysis of large economic systems. In
the recent years Dudkin has also taken a great interest in institutional
economic problems, in particular to those connected with the implementation of new technology. Pervosvanskii is known for his work in
the field of application of the theory of control to the analysis of economic systems. In cooperation with his wife, Tatiana Pervosvanskii,
he has also developed some methods of applying the algorithms of
decomposition to the study of large economic systems. There also
exists a small group of outsiders headed by Doctor Aleksei Makarov.

This group settled down in Irkutsk at the Siberian Institute of Energy.
They carry out some interesting work dealing with the problems of
uncertainty in large economic systems, particularly energy-oriented
ones.

Center Leaders

The feelings of discord among the scholars made the question of
leaders for these new and specialized centers particularly important.
These centers needed as directors people of the older and middle generation with leadership experience. Of such people, only Nemchinov
and Boiarskii could combine knowledge of economics, mathematics,
and leadership with the ability to satisfy the demands of political authorities. Consequently, the leaders were for the most part people with
no previous experience in economic-mathematical methods. They came
to this field primarily as managers and if they were scientists by training, they had not done research for many years. They were, however,
distinguished by a desire to conquer the new environment. Their mo-
tivations were unclear, but the desire for prestige must have been a
factor.

Up until the beginning of the 1960s, scholars primarily were elected
to the Academy of Sciences, but in that decade, when new scientific institutions rapidly arose and made it necessary to find a large number
of leaders, the situation changed radically. In the Soviet Union where
bureaucratic matters take up a great deal of time, a scholar capable
of creative work usually does not agree to take on the administrative
duties in an institute. For others, the most compelling reason to take
on the job of director is the good material compensation. The director,
without the academic title, does not receive maximum compensation.

The base salary of the director of an academic institute is 7200
rubles a year, 20 percent greater than the pay of a section head. Only
academic titles granted by the Academy of Sciences provide a significant lifelong increase in income. Just for his title, a corresponding
member of the USSR Academy of Sciences receives 3000 rubles a year
and an academician 6000 rubles.

Granting academic titles to administrators is by no means good
for science; an academic title is linked with the scholarship of its
bearer. (20) And here confusion arises. In order to keep a title it is
necessary to publish, but the administrator cannot publish because he
does not have time for science. Therefore, he begins to exploit his
coworkers to write works for him. The methods used are quite subtle;
the leader does not simply call someone in and force him to write,
although that sometimes happens. Instead a leader may call in a

subordinate and say, "You're working on such and such a problem. Please write me a twenty to thirty page description of your work." The subordinate is glad to oblige, thereby having the opportunity to show his work to the director. The director repeats his request with half a dozen subordinates and together they bring in enough material for a book. Then a subordinate close to the director, who is not distinguished by great creative abilities, but is a fluent writer, puts this material together and inserts general notes and decisions of the Party and government. The director gives the results for review to some respectable scholar of the insititue as his own work. It may be somewhat awkward to ask the scholar to write anything, but how could such a subordinate refuse to help improve his director's work by correcting his mistakes or improving the composition? He will do it in good faith (professional pride) and it won't be any the worse for him.

Among the older generation of economists, with scholarly academic titles, one rarely encounters institute directors whose works are ghost written, but among the new generation of leaders of economics institutes, those who spend their time receiving titles, it is unusual to meet someone whose colleagues have not written his works for him. This often reflects the fact that the new leaders are not specialists in the disciplines of the insititutes that they direct. Perhaps this is the price that must be paid to allow these leaders to struggle for survival as leaders of these institutes.

In brief, there are varied reasons for the leaders' exploitation of their subordinates. The degree of exploitation varies according to the size of the institute and the appetites of its leadership. In all cases, however, the result is the same: such a system is extremely corrupting. The deputies and division heads begin to imitate the director of the institute, and robbing one's subordinates becomes habitual. And woe to him who refuses to pay; he will not only be disliked by the bosses, but also by his colleagues, insofar as his behavior is a silent reproach to them.

The Role of Jewish Personnel

The system of leader exploitation of subordinates is encouraged by the significant role of Jewish personnel among the active scientists in the economics-mathematical school. (21) Even in post-Stalin times, the government continued to exploit feelings of anti-Semitism, although, of course, not in such radical forms as in the Stalin era. (22) There is usually not active hatred towards Jews by leaders of prominent economics institutes--a notable exception is Olimpiada Kozlova, the director of the Moscow Engineering Economics Institute. In fact,

there is sometimes even unhappiness expressed about the extreme
limitations on the hiring of Jews imposed by Party organs since Jews
are often among the most qualified to carry out the work assigned to
these institutions. Still, on the whole these leaders, the great majority whom are not Jewish, like the government's anti-Semitic policy
because it preserves them from too much additional competition. This
policy also facilitates the exploitation of Jews. When a leader hires a
Jew for scientific work and helps him to get ahead, the latter is very
grateful to him. He is ready to express his gratitude by sharing the
results of his research, which the leader can then publish under his
own name.

It is true that the emigration of the Jews from the Soviet Union in
the past few years has complicated the acceptance of Jews in Soviet
universities and research institutes. The number of Jews that have
emigrated, however, is relatively small, (23) and the chiefs of universities and research institutes have not been dismissed because Jews
left their institutes. All the same, the leader's fear of the possible
departures of the Jews and his own possible punishment is great enough
to stop the acceptance of Jews despite any arguments to the contrary. (24)

Division and Section Supervisors

Not only have significant barriers to the development of new trends
in economics arisen in the attempt to enlist qualified leaders in the
institutes, but they have also arisen in the enlistment of supervisors of
the divisions and sections--the middle level of the institutional hierarchy. In the economic-mathematical trend, such leaders could come
in the beginning mainly from mathematics. In order to become a leader
on the middle level it is extremely desirable to belong to the Party, but
a very low percentage of the mathematicians, especially the qualified
ones, are members of the Party. It is possible to formulate the following law of the disposition of Party membership among the various
groups of specialists: the closer the sphere of the specialist's activity
is to ideology or to leading practical activity, the higher the percentage
of Party members among the given specialists.

In the humanities and social science institutes, the heads of divisions are usually Party members; an exception I know of is the famous
economist, Alexander Notkin, who headed a division in the Institute
of Economics of the USSR Academy of Sciences. For the newly created
institutes where the economic-mathematical trend developed, it was
at first difficult to find Party members who qualified as leaders at the
middle level of the hierarchy. Initially, therefore, in a number of the
new institutes, TSEMI in particular, the percentage of Party members

among middle level leaders was much lower than in other institutes
which dealt with humanities and social sciences, but this gradually
began to change. Non-Party middle level leaders, accustomed to their
positions and not wanting to jeopardize them, joined the Party, and the
opportunity for selecting party members leaders from among the growing number of specialists expanded.

In recent years, it has become quite difficult for a member of the
intelligentsia to join the Party because of the class structure limitations.
Permission for a member of the intelligentsia to join the Party is considered a privilege, and one must wait his turn. Sometimes it seems
as if the institutes are given quotas of workers for Party membership.
For some members of the intelligentsia, however, joining the Party is
important; it heightens individual security in the event of reductions in
staff; facilitates work progress and trips abroad; and most often is a
necessary condition for getting ahead in the official hierarchy, even in
obtaining the first privileged administrative position--the section head
in the institute. (25)

"Fellow-travelers"

The involvement of specialists and leaders in the new trend was a
necessary condition, but not sufficient for its development. A contributing condition was the great role played by "fellow-travelers," i.e.,
scholars who did not participate in the new trend directly, but who
helped in peripheral ways. Many organizational questions have arisen
which cannot be solved without such outside assistance. Representatives
of the new school of thought are needed to read dissertations and to have
their manuscripts reviewed for publications. Among the older generation of economists and mathematicians is a rather large number of
people who have given this type of indispensible support to the new
trend. These scholars were readers for the first doctoral and candidate dissertations in the new field. They agreed to be part of the newly
created scholarly councils which reviewed dissertations on economic-
mathematical methods. They wrote reviews on manuscripts of works
on mathematical economics.

3 Centers of the Economic-Mathematical School: Research Institutes

In the following description of the economic-mathematical school of thought, I will first examine its development in the sections on previously existing institutions (see fig. 3.1). Only one center was completely specialized, the Laboratory of Economic-Mathematical Methods headed by Nemchinov, but I will describe its people in more detail in the discussion of TSEMI, to which they all went.

THE INSTITUTE OF ECONOMICS
OF THE USSR ACADEMY OF SCIENCES

The Institute of Economics of the USSR Academy of Sciences is a citadel of official Soviet economics. I once suggested that the prestige for a scholarly institution should be based on the number of crazy letters it received; by that standard, the Institute of Economics is probably still in first place today. When I worked at the institute from 1956-1963, I had to answer quite a few of these letters. While the contents varied, some of the letters included formulas. One letter from Vol'sk, a small town on the Volga, spent several pages describing a formula whose application would tremendously increase the effectiveness of the socialist economy. (1)

What was the Institute of Economics like in the mid-fifties? It was an institute whose basic task was to praise the works of leaders and the most recent decisions of the Party. The staff of the institute was selected accordingly. Among the personnel were capable people able to maintain the status quo. If these economists deviated, then they deviated with the party line. But during the struggle for power after Stalin's death when it turned out that some Party leaders had deviated the wrong way, the economists of the Institute of Economics found

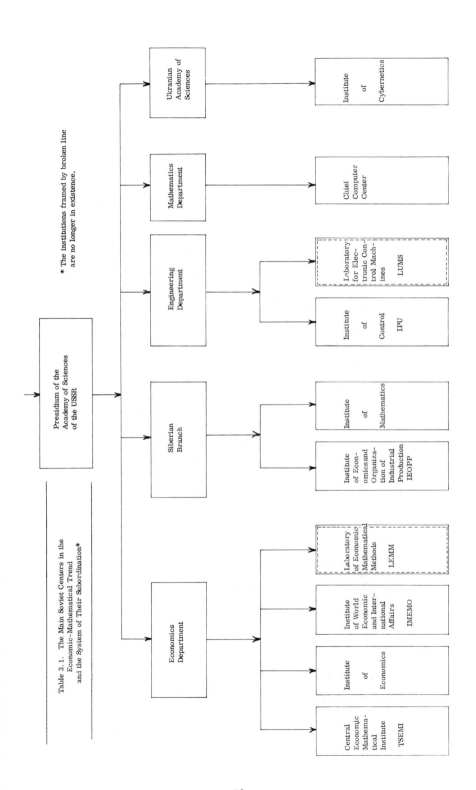

Table 3.1. The Main Soviet Centers in the Economic-Mathematical Trend and the System of Their Subordination*

* The institutions framed by broken line are no longer in existence.

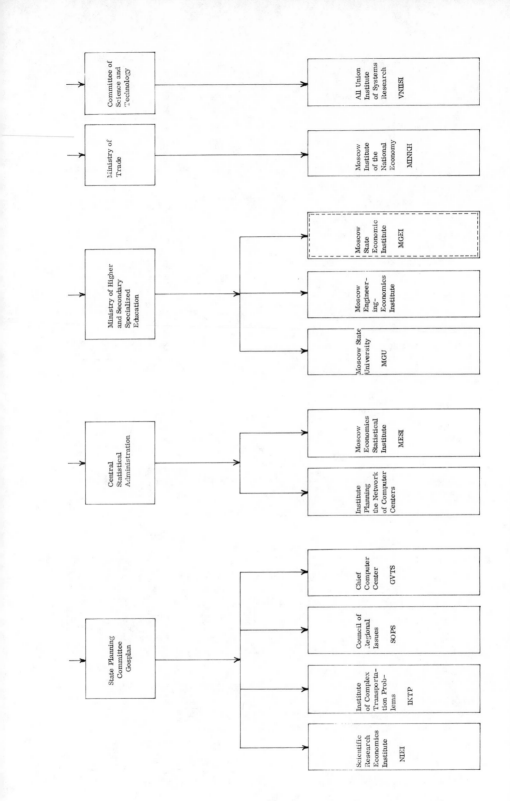

60

themselves in trouble insofar as they, too, had been deviating the wrong way. For example, in 1954 the Chairman of the Council of Ministers of the USSR, G. Malenkov, demanded that the rate of development of light industry exceed the rate of development of heavy industry. The economists quickly responded to this Party call and in their articles showed the wisdom of this latest decision from the Marxist point of view. It soon turned out that Malenkov was leading the Party and the country down the wrong path. Articles quickly appeared in which those economists who had supported the Party line in the period of Malenkov's reign were called "woeful economists." They were punished, not, of course, in the severe Stalinist way, but cruelly enough. One of these economists, previously known for his devotion to Party demands, the venerable P. Mstislavskii, was branded a woeful economist for having deviated with the party line and then for not deviating again fast enough. He was demoted to the status of a junior research worker. This was not only a blow to his pride, but also reduced his salary by one-third.

For many years the majority of scientists at the institute were against the application of mathematical methods in economics, which they considered bourgeois. In the Institute of Economics there were no economists who knew enough mathematics to understand work that used mathematical symbols. However, there were people of another sort working in this institute, well-known economists of the older generation, who, though not knowing mathematics and being professionally uneducated in the economic-mathematical school, were still able to nurture it. These included S. Kheinman, T. Khachaturov, Ia. Kvasha, K. Klimenko, and A. Notkin.

Klimenko

In 1958, when a reader was needed for Kantorovich's book, at the request of Nemchinov, Konstantin Klimenko assumed the job with great pleasure. Klimenko was a reader in those years when there was a particularly great shortage of readers for dissertations on economic-mathematical methods; (2) he was a member of the first Scholarly Council of TSEMI. Klimenko had survived the Stalinist period by chance. His survival was due to not being a Party member and at the beginning of the 1930s, managing to leave the Urals, where he had been a well-known worker in planning agencies. The peaks, as Klimenko was fond of saying, attract lightning. From 1935, Klimenko worked in the Institute of Economics studying the economics of industry and technological progress. As a sign of respect for his knowledge of technology, Klimenko was called the chief engineer of the institute, but was often criticized by the institute's administration for his poor

theoretical work. The criticism, at that time, was based on insufficient
written use of quotations from the Marxist-Leninist classics. (3)
Klimenko was sympathetic to the ideas of socialism and the October
Revolution, but at the same time, he did not entirely accept the mechanism of its realization. The Stalin regime was deeply alien to him. (4)

Kheinman, Kvasha, and Notkin

As well as nurturant scholars like Klimenko, there were such
scholars as Solomon Kheinman, Iakov Kvasha, and Alexander Notkin,
who directly supported the development of the economic-mathematical
school, in particular at a 1960 conference (see pp. 31). Kheinman
gave a speech generally supporting the economic-mathematical trend;
Kvasha presented a report on Marxist schemes of growth; and Notkin
expressed several positive notions concerning the criterion of optimality.
Five years later, a group of workers at the Institute of Economics
wrote a letter to Pravda arguing against awarding Kantorovich, Nemchinov, and Novozhilov the Lenin Prize. At the same time a group of
young workers at the institute, together with economists of the older
generation, sent a letter to Pravda supporting these candidates for the
Lenin Prize. Among those in support, Kvasha and Notkin were prominent. The second letter contradicted the first, which had claimed
uniform protest by the collective of the Institute of Economics against
the anti-Marxist writings of Kantorovich, Nemchinov, and Novozhilov.

Khachaturov

The greatest role, however, in the development of the economic-
mathematical school in the Institute of Economics was played by
academician Tigran Khachaturov. In the 1950s, Khachaturov was a
well-known economist and a corresponding member of the USSR
Academy of Sciences. Reputed to be a man of progressive views,
Khachaturov was among the economists whom P. Mstislavskii criticized
in his 1948 article in Voprosy ekonomiki for using the bourgeois concept of interest on capital. Khachaturov persisted in 1958, however,
in encouraging the discipline. He organized the All-Union Conference
on the Economic Effectiveness of Capital Investments and New Technology. At this conference, various points of view were presented,
including the ideas of Kantorovich, Lurie, and Novozhilov. The conference thus confirmed the right to life of this "bourgeois" concept by
titling it the "recoupment period." Khachaturov made the recoupment
period respectable, even for some of the more traditional economists
and he succeeded in having his chapter, which explained the basis of

this concept, included in a textbook of political economy written in the 1960s at MGU. In 1958, Khachaturov transferred to the Institute of Economics, where he was head of the section for effectiveness of investments. As section head, he soon organized a group for the application of mathematical methods. Khachaturov invited Lurie, whom he had known for many years through their joint work on the implementation of the concept of recoupment period in economic calculations, to join this group. In 1960, Boris Iskakov-Pliukhin, Tiulenev, and Edemskii also joined.

Pliukhin

Iskakov-Pliukhin, known mostly by the second part of his last name, was a young physicist who worked in the Institute of Chemical Physics of the USSR Academy of Science in the 1950s. He dealt with combustion problems and managed to publish several articles on this topic. A very ambitious person, Pliukhin decided to create a new methodology for economic planning using the mathematical methods and computers which had already become fashionable. He set as the groundwork for this methodology the theory of chemical chain processes. The Nobel Prize laureate, Nikolai Semenov, Director of the Institute of Chemical Physics, had offered a great contribution to the development of the theory of chain processes.

I think it is an interesting idea to consider the theoretical relationship between economic and chemical processes since analogies between physical and economic processes have turned out to be very fruitful. But Pliukhin's application of the theory of chain processes to economics was unsatisfactory; he merely used this theory for extrapolating economic development. Moreover, his work was pretentious and filled with jargon. Convinced that it was accepted neither in a scholarly milieu nor in practice at the macro economic level, Pliukhin decided to implement these ideas to solve economic problems in agriculture. Once into this work, he soon had to abandon his former theories and use well-known models of mathematical programming for the description of economic processes. (5)

Personal Experiences

Now a few words about how I landed in Khachaturov's section and about the nature of my work in this section. Research in economic effectiveness of automation, which I had done in the Institute of Economics in 1956-57, led inevitably to general methodological concerns. The works of Kantorovich and Novozhilov convinced me that the measurement of economic effectiveness of capital investments in the automation of processes of production is, in essence, a general economic problem of cost-benefit analysis. I decided to devote my further research to this problem.

Cost-Benefit Analysis

I considered the basic means for studying general economic problems to be the creation of a real micro economic prototype. I wanted to find what would be called in the Soviet Union a "workshop" of some large factory and shift this shop, with the help of computers, to an optimal system of functioning. I found my prototype in the press workshop of the Moscow Factory for Small Cars (MZMA). There was little hope to develop the model within the framework of the section in which I worked at the time. Although Klimenko helped me in all possible ways, my colleagues in charge of the section were too conservative. That is why I presented my idea to Khachaturov who accepted it.

At MZMA, a group was created to implement the automation to management processes. Leonid Grinman, who had experience in management since the 1930s, led the group. In my very first conversation with him, I was amazed at this man's breadth of ideas and his vital mind. He spoke with me about the philosophy of Hegel and started me thinking about the fact that man's real difficulties begin when people satisfy their material needs. In addition, Grinman was quite active in leading this group in spite of his age and chronic illnesses. He did much for the automation of management at the MZMA. At present he is on pension, is very interested in philosophy, writes brilliant epigrams as he did before, and continues his very original thinking.

I put together a small group of people to help me with this project. Turi Ovsienko participated as an economist. He had come to the Institute of Economics in 1960 upon graduation from the Economics Faculty of Moscow State University, and it was suggested that he do scientific work with me. When he revealed that he was interested in mathematics, I agreed to include him in the group working at the factory.

As a preliminary step toward the optimization of the management of the workshop, I considered it necessary to conduct an inventory of the instrumentation and also to clarify the schedules for the maintenance of the equipment. In order to facilitate this labor-consuming stage of the work, a group was created which included young workers from one of the engineering design institutes located at the MZMA. Ovsienko worked with these people on the accumulation of initial information. From his very first days on the job, Ovsienko demonstrated considerable acumen, surprising the workshop engineers in particular with all sorts of questions about the characteristics of the presses.

Thanks to Khachaturov and Grinman, the help of the mathematician Lipa Smoliar was enlisted. He had finished his postgraduate courses in algebra at MGU. For some reason he had not completed his dissertation, and since he had no other plans, I suggested he consider working in mathematical economics. However, to live and work in Moscow, it was still necessary to secure a permit. Here was a vicious circle: without a permit, he could not be accepted for work, and without work a permit was not granted. For the first period of time, Smoliar worked on contract with the Institute of Economics which Khachaturov had helped to organize. With the help of acquaintances and Grinman, who obtained an application form from the factory, Smoliar secured a temporary permit which was sufficient for him to be accepted at the factory. At the same time, I succeeded in connecting Smoliar with the Department of National-Economic Planning at Moscow Institute of the National Economy. There he began to give lectures for teachers and graduate students of mathematics, first and foremost on linear algebra, which was necessary for the understanding of the mathematical aspects of input-output tables. Furthermore, as a mathematician, he took part in the preparation of a book on input-output tables which was subsequently published and became a valuable textbook.

After beginning work at the factory with Smoliar, we attempted to examine scheduling models. Smoliar was also concerned with a mathematical investigation of this problem. The results of our research were presented at the All-Union Scientific Conference of the Application of Mathematical Methods to Economics in 1960. This work defined Smoliar's subsequent interest in the economic-mathematical trend, and for his Ph.D. dissertation in economic sciences he took up more general questions of scheduling. Then he began to teach in the Faculty of Economic Cybernetics in the Moscow Institute of the National Economy.

In order to create a technical basis for my work, I was connected with the Laboratory of Information Storage of the Academy of Sciences of the USSR. The laboratory was headed by Lev Gutenmacher, the creator of the first analog computer in the USSR. A talented engineer, he began the development of the first types of digital computers. He was a difficult person, and there was a joke that he was only a "guten macher" for himself. I hoped that his machines would be especially useful to us because they were capable of both storing and doing preliminary processing of great volumes of statistical information. However, Gutenmacher's machine was not sufficiently developed; it was, of course, difficult to construct a machine to deal with the complexities of the workshop. The possibilities became even less promising when Gutenmacher began to have difficulties at work, ending with his dismissal from the laboratory.

Through joint efforts, led by the group of mathematicians headed
by L. Kantorovich and G. Rubinstein on optimal planning systems of
the primary preparation area of the press workshop was successfully
brought to completion. However, the difficulties in the solution of the
problem of scheduling, the impossibility of introducing an optimal planning system of the primary preparation area of the workshop, and the
absence of a real technological base forced me to admit that the idea I
had thought up was unrealistic for rapid testing.

Production

But, during the work at the factory, an alternative for future research arose. Along with the project at the workshop, I spent quite
a lot of time thinking out general theoretical problems. Influenced by
the workshop-national economy analogy, I began to work on novel
structures of production. (6) Ovsienko, who was very interested in
such schemes, manifested wonderful abilities for theoretical thought
and critical analysis repressed during his studies at MGU. We decided
to work together, but sensed that we needed a mathematician to formal-
ize and strictly analyze the problems to be discussed. Neither of us
knew mathematics, and we decided to study it.

The mathematician, or more precisely the physicist, who entered
our group was Efim Faerman. I met him in 1957, when he was thirty-
three years old. He had graduated with honors from the Physics
Faculty of MGU, but was not accepted for graduate work at this University because he was a Jew. However, he succeeded in entering the
graduate program at the Moscow Pedagogical Institute. Having an
inclination for philosophical thought, he put his dissertation in physics
aside. After finishing his graduate work without defending his dissertation, he went to work as a teacher of physics in a technical school.
His abilities and interest went far beyond the demands of the technical
school, and he was very dissatisfied with his position as a teacher.

I was struck by the philosophical character of Faerman's thought
and by his interest in the new trends in science, especially in cybernetics, (7) but I was also dissatisfied by his straightforwardness, his
attempt to rationalize everything, his desire to create finished systems.

Faerman, Ovsienko, and I began to discuss problems of the formalization of the planning of the national economy. In the beginning, these
discussions concerned the criteria of optimality. I suggested approaching the problem from the established consumption-based norms, and
I formulated the appropriate questions. Faerman introduced mathematical formalism. He also provided a definite economic interpretation for the criterion of optimality. Initially, we accepted the

character of the constraints on the development of the system in
relation to a given criterion as very simple. However, we soon understood that our work could prove to be original if we were to develop a
new way of analyzing constraining functions.

As we knew it then, the accepted method for the analysis of such
constraints was to reduce the structure of the national economy to a
simple line of technological methods. At the same time, we observed
in economic life a developed structural relationship between the participants. This structure was realized either in the form of hierarchies
of management or in a profoundly structured system of contractual
relations.

Faerman, as a physicist, realized the importance of studying
structure to investigate the mechanism of the functioning of systems.
He also understood the limitations of the philosophical thesis of sub-
stantialism, which attempts to substitute for the study of the structural
characteristics of the system. The interest of Ovsienko and myself in
modeling the production processes, together with Faerman's precise
realization of the role of structure in the study of physical systems,
predetermined the subject of our beginning joint work. We began to
devise a structural model of the national economy.

Plotnikov

The general atmosphere in which the work of the above-mentioned
economists and mathematicians has taken place in the Institute of Economics had been quite comfortable. (8) As of 1958, Kirill Plotnikov
became the director of the Institute, replacing Ivan Laptev, with whom
Nikita Khrushchev was dissatisfied. Khrushchev's dissatisfaction was
long-standing, provoked by the fact that Laptev had been manager of
the agricultural section of the newspaper Pravda in the mid-1940s.
In this time an editorial article criticizing Khrushchev's idea of agricultural cities was published, an article clearly published on Stalin's
order.

Plotnikov was quite a decent man for an official of his level (at
one time he was the deputy to the Finance Minister), and he would not
stand for squabbles in the institute. He was a man of conservative
views, but not malicious. He did not fight openly against the new trend;
he wanted to get rid of it peacefully. He once called me, for example,
and said, "Now let's find something for the mathematicians to do so
that they will get absorbed in it and leave us alone." Unfortunately,
I was not able to carry out the director's request.

From time to time, the director organized a review of the leading
works in the institute at a meeting of the board of directors. When the

time came for the review of the work of the mathematicians, as the
economists concerned with economic-mathematical methods were called
at the institute, Khachaturov began with a description of their work.
During his speech, Plotnikov tossed off critical remarks of various
sorts, e.g., that it was impossible to measure the level of the satisfaction of needs by comparing the utilities of the goods. Plotnikov said
it was impossible to compare the utility of boots and butter, that this
comparison could be accomplished only through the labor-time necessary
for their production; nor could he imagine another method of measurement. With its apparent clarity and ease of measurement, he found
the labor theory of value very attractive.

After the conclusion of Khachaturov's speech Plotnikov said that he
had understood nothing of what was being done in the group that was
studying economic-mathematical models. Turning to the members of
the board of directors, he asked them if they understood anything of
what had been said. The director's science deputies must be given
their due; not one of them reacted to the question. As a sign of agreement with the director, only the science secretary of the institute
nodded his head several times. The tension was relieved unexpectedly;
representatives of the trade union and the director's deputy responsible
for the maintaining of the building were also present at the meeting of
the board of directors. The deputy, Nina Kotlova, a woman of fifty
with the face of a komsomolka of the 1920s, screamed, "I don't understand anything either!" Everyone began to laugh. Vera Chernysheva,
the chairman of the local trade union committee and an intelligent
woman, was sitting next to Kotlova. She said, "Nina, perhaps this
matter is not one for your mind."

The director took no organizational measures against the mathematicians, and he soon began to discuss the question of creating a
section on economic-mathematical methods in the institute. He even
mentioned my possible appointment as leader of this section but the
preliminary work which began as early as 1962 on the creation of
TSEMI and the transfer of a group of workers at the Institute of Economics into it put off this appointment. In 1963, all the workers in
Khachaturov's sector who were concerned with economic-mathematical
methods were transferred to work in the newly created TSEMI in
accordance with the resolution of the Presidium of the Academy of
Sciences of the USSR. The departure of the mathematicians from the
Institute of Economics in 1963 interrupted the economic-mathematical
investigations there for several years. However, Khachaturov, who
remained at the institute, continually supported the economic-mathematical trend. In my view, Khachaturov's hostility to this trend which
became apparent in his actions in later years is explained first and

foremost by his personal conflict with Fedorenko, the director of
TSEMI, over the struggle for the position of Academician-Secretary
of the Economics Department of the Academy of Sciences of the USSR.
Fedorenko had wanted to obtain this position for a long time and was
angry at Khachaturov because the latter knew it. Ultimately, Fedorenko
succeeded in forcing Khachaturov out and taking over the coveted position. The selection of Fedorenko for this position was preceded by the
arrival of an alternate member of the Politburo in the Presidium of the
Academy of Sciences of the USSR. This was Petr Demichev, who read
to the assembly the recommendation of the Politburo--the polite recommendation was at that time a new thing--about the top executives
who have to be elected by the Academy of Science.

The Latter Portion of the 1960s

In the second half of the 1960s the Institute of Economics was
essentially the ideological force behind the economic reform. There
were a group of workers in the institute who supported the reform.
Lev Gatovskii, a corresponding member of the Academy of Sciences
of the USSR, was appointed to the position of director of the institute,
and Dmitrii Moskvin was appointed to the position of deputy to the
director in the mid-1960s; both supported the group of workers who
were interested in economic reform. Therefore, it is possible to consider the Institute of Economics during the late 1960s as a center of
innovative thought, however paradoxical this sounds in light of the
traditions of the institute and its personnel, among whom reactionaries
and conservatives were numerous. With a great deal of work and mani-
festing surprising inventiveness, the new leadership of the institute
succeeded in freeing itself from some of the reactionaries and conservatives and enlisting new young workers.

It seems to me that this sort of shift in the institute's work was
also possible because there were a certain number of workers of the
older generation in the institute who were thinking quite progressively
about institutional economics and these investigations into reform were
conducted without the use of mathematics, which these economists did
not know. While this meant that many aspects of the reform directly
connected with mathematical modeling could not be satisfactorily investigated, particularly problems of price formation, a number of
problems concerning the institutional part of economics were skillfully
developed.

The Older Generation

Also, the older generation often understood the socioeconomic
factors better than the younger economist-mathematicians; these older
workers had gone through the period of Stalinist repression and were
more attentive to the disadvantages of a centralized economic mechanism.
Maybe their lack of mathematical knowledge allowed them greater lati-
tude in those areas of economics requiring verbal methodology, such as
the institutional aspects of economic theory. By no means do I wish to
justify these economists' old-fashioned views of mathematical modeling
of economic processes. I only want to point out that concentration on
economic-mathematical methods can seriously detract from the development of the institutional aspect of economics.

In order to characterize the liberal economists of the older generation, I will relate an incident which occurred in 1958. In the corridor
of the Institute of Economics, I was talking with one young economist
who was studying China and had been there. The miracles in Chinese
agriculture were widely touted at that time, and it seemed to me that
the Chinese had been able to achieve significant results, having chosen
the correct and the best agronomy methods. As my colleague and I
stood praising the Chinese methods of farming, the economist Kvasha,
one of the older generation who knew us well, was passing by, stopped,
and began to listen. Finally, he interrupted and stated that every description of Chinese agricultural success was a lie. He explained this
by saying that the social upheavals taking place in the Chinese country-
side simply could not allow such growth in production.

Economic Reforms

Reform investigations in the Institute of Economics concerned more
than such problems as the rights of the leaders of the enterprises and
methods of their stimulation; they concerned the revival of old economic
institutions reminiscent of the capitalistic system. There were a group
of workers in the Institute of Economics who considered the obvious introduction of unemployment advisable as a means to increase the effectiveness of the socialist economy. They developed several mechanisms
directed at the transformation of hidden unemployment into open unemployment. The attempt to transfer workers from industry to agriculture in the mid 1950s provides evidence of hidden unemployment.

The government wanted to provide for growth in agricultural production at this time, and arrived at the idea of transferring people from
industry to agriculture. To achieve this goal, the enterprises were
given smaller plans for the growth of gross output than for the growth

of labor productivity. In the event that the plan for the growth of labor productivity was not fulfilled, the enterprise was to be deprived of a bonus. As a result, a noticeable dismissal of workers from the factories began. Five to eight thousand men (6-9 percent of total personnel) were dismissed from the Gorkii Automobile Factory alone, but they did not move into agricultural positions as expected. The laid-off workers were in no hurry to move to the country, and the resulting unemployment in many industrial cities provoked tremendous anxiety in the government. The government responded to the situation with a resolution accusing some minister or deputy minister of gross mismanagement connected with the dismissal of the workers, and the dismissed workers returned to the enterprises.

The Institute of Economics of the Academy of Sciences of the USSR differed from conservative government circles by supporting various proposals for improving agricultural production. At one time, for example, an author from the outlying districts defended a doctoral dissertation which advocated putting more emphasis on the peasants' private plots. The more conservative workers in the agriculture sector came out against this dissertation, and the institute was put under pressure by the agriculture section of the Central Committee of the CPSU, but even so the Academic Council voted to give the author his doctoral degree. Gradually, a group of young economists actively supporting the economic reform appeared in the Institute of Economics, and Boris Rakitskii was among them. In the late 1960s he wrote a book devoted to economic reform in which he made several statements concerning the role of the Party in economic life. (9)   These statements, while not negating the role of the Party, still were not standard. Sotsialisticheskaia Industriia (Socialist Industry), a reactionary newspaper and the organ of the Central Committe of the CPSU, came out against Rakitskii's book. A special session of the Academic Council of the Institute of Economics of the Academy of Sciences of the USSR was called for the purpose of discussing the reviews of Rakitskii's book in Sotsialisticheskaia Industriia. Several economists of the older generation, including Anatoli Pashkov, a corresponding member of the Academy of Sciences, came out in support of Rakitskii at the meeting of this council. The Academic Council of the Institute of Economics disagreed with the newspaper's opinion and sent its decision which was supported by the majority, to the Central Committe of the CPSU.

Gatovskii

In addition to research in the sphere of economic reform, Gatovskii, the new direct of the Institute of Economics, revitalized the economic-

mathematical trend in the late 1960s. A very colorful figure, Gatovskii
was a man of fantastic flexibility. He survived 1937, at which time he
was a prominent economist and administrator. In the 1940s he not only
survived, but was appointed by Stalin to the staff of the authors' collective for the preparation of a textbook on economic theory. As editor-
in-chief of the journal, Voprosy Ekonomiki, he survived Khrushchev
and became director of the Institute of Economics under the new leadership. In a word, he was a Nutzliche Jude--a useful Jew. Although
Gatovskii was a man with a vital mind and a broad cultural appreciation--
e.g., he spoke French, which is a rarity for economists of the older
generation--one had to be cautious in dealing with him. It was impossible to believe his promises because he was famous for his refined
methods of making promises and not keeping them; he was predisposed
to organize any trends in economic science which promise prestige.
One might well wonder what prompted Gatovskii, an economist of the
older generation who was remote from mathematics, to fall in love
with it so suddenly. In 1969, during Gatovskii's reign, the regular
commission of the Presidium of the Academy of Sciences of the USSR
was working on an examination of the activity of the Institute of Economics and TSEMI. I happened to be at the meeting of the Presidium
at which the results were discussed. The chairman of the commission,
academician Nikolai Inozemtsev, spoke brilliantly. He was able to
detail the development of economic science and to recall the role of the
Institue of Economics and TSEMI in fostering economic thought, even
recalling Stalin's ill-feeling regarding this movement, and such a
recollection was a rarity. Inozemtsev spoke about the government
attention to the experience of the West and the activity of academic
economists as consultants, a subject which provoked the dissatisfaction
of the chairman, Mstislav Keldysh, the President of the Academy of
Sciences of the USSR. Khrushchev had tried to organize an institution
of academic consultants. Under the chairmanship of academician
Lavrentiev, a special academic council was created under the Council
of Ministers of the USSR, which included academicians of various
specialties. I do not know who was on the staff of this council and
have not head of the results of its activity, but in 1964, right after
Khrushchev's removal, this council was liquidated.

    Gatovskii's speech at the same meeting of the Presidium was quite
amusing. He said, for example, that the economic-mathematical trend
would be developed in every way at the Institute of Economics and that
all workers in the institute would therefore study mathematics. This
provoked laughter and remarks from the hall, "So now they're going to
teach the cleaning women mathematics!" Gatovskii's announcement
was funny also because it was impossible to imagine the old guard of

the institute--entrenched conservatives and reactionaries--studying
mathematics. It was also well known how Gatovskii in his time had
felt about mathematical methods in economics. In 1960, Gatovskii had
written a crushing article in Kommunist with M. Sakov, the manager
of the journal's economics department, against economic-mathematical
methods. (10) His article accused the advocates of these methods of
following bourgeois economic theory. There was something Gatovskii
had not anticipated in the situation, although he was famous for his
watchfulness and ability to lean to the side which the Party would eventually adopt. The article later cost him dearly. Gatovskii's cherished
dream was to become an academician, a full member of the Academy
of Science of the USSR, but fate did not favor him. His name came
before the general meeting of the Academy of Science, but was voted
down.

The members of the Academy of Science were highly selective of
candidates from the humanities, social sciences, and biology. During
Khrushchev's government the academy was almost dissolved because
of its refusal to name the biologist, Nuzhdin, an academician,even
though academician A. Sakharov, made a speech concerning the scholar-
liness of Nuzhdin, a follower of Lysenko. After Khrushchev, the academicians voted against the election of Trapenikov, the head of the
science section of the Central Committee of the CPSU who was not
noted for his progressive views, as a full member of the Academy of
Sciences. Although Trapenikov did obtain the title of academician from
the Academy of Pedagogical Sciences, he has not yet been accepted into
the basic organization he controls. The candidacy of Gennadi Sorokin
for academician was also rejected. An economist of the old structure
who was Deputy to the Chairman of the State Planning Committee of the
USSR (Gosplan) during the Stalin years, a man of extremely reactionary
views, and a dull scholar, he was one of those whose articles opposed
decentralization. At the Economic Plenum of the Higher Certifying
Commission, he inveighed against dissertations devoted to decentralization. Also denied as academicians were: Chikvadze, the director
of the Law Institute; the philosopher, M. Iovchuk; and the Ministers of
Higher and Secondary Specialized Education, Eliutin and O. Kozlova.

When a candidacy is marked for failure, one of the academicians
will usually come forward or the speaker will be questioned as to the
credentials of the candidate. Such was the case with Gatovskii as well.
Academician Alexander Aleksandrov, the mathematician, came forward
and read selections from Gatovskii's article in Kommunist. In spite of
the fact that several academicians, even Keldysh, the President of the
Academy of Sciences, came forward in support of Gatovskii, his candidacy was rejected.

After his rejection, Gatovskii wishing to curry favor with the
Academicians and realizing the positive attitude of the powers-that-be
toward economic-mathematical method, decided to develop these
methods in the institute. Gatovskii actually organized a mathematics
course for a group at the institute, but this course offered little to the
economists, and it may even have aggravated their dislike for mathematics. Mathematicians were invited to train the economists, and they
conscientiously began to teach the economists linear algebra and mathematical analysis.

However, the most difficult steps the economist had to overcome
were a fear of mathematics and to learn how to translate problem-
oriented goals into precise mathematical language (see more about this
subject on pp. 103-104).

A more serious measure introduced in the Institute of Economics
under Gatovskii was the creation of three new sections concerned with
economic mathematical methods. Iuri Sukhotin, a young economist
whose views were close to those of TSEMI, headed one of these sections.
In Sukhotin's section, several young economists were working on various
problems; Victor Bogachev was working on the cost-benefit problem;
Oleg Pchelintsev on regional aspects of allocation of resources;
Zaleskii on effectiveness of capital investments; Nikolai Shukhov on the
history of economic thought; and Geli Khovanov on the economic effectiveness of science. The progressiveness of the workers in the section,
their youthful enthusiasm, and their occasional desire to swagger led
to the eventual breakup of the section several years ago.

Before this, a report of the workers in the section devoted to the
cost-benefit problem was heard at a meeting of the Academic Council of
the Institute of Economics. The opponents of the new methods, among
them Ia. Kronrod who was especially prominent, inveighed against the
report. After the section was broken up, Sukhotin and a number of
workers from his section went to work at TSEMI in the early 1970s.

Belkin

Victor Belkin, one of the thirty-year-old economists predisposed
to conduct economic-mathematical investigations and a pioneer in the
sphere of input-output tables in the Soviet Union, directed the second
section. Belkin had gained early experience in the Laboratory for
Electronic Control Machines of the Academy of Sciences of the USSR.
Headed by Isai Bruk, Corresponding Member of the Academy of Sciences
of the USSR, this laboratory built one of the first computers in the
Soviet Union--the M-2. A wonderful group of mathematicians, headed
by Alexander Brudno and including the astute Alexander Kronrod,

worked on it. It was necessary to load the computer with supplements, and economics provided them.

I do not know the details of the invitation, but in 1956 Bruk invited Belkin to work with him. At that time, Belkin was an energetic young person, a graduate of MGEI, who already had experience in the Central Statistical Administration of the USSR. Belkin began to work actively on problems of the methodology of input-output tables, carrying out experimental calculations on the computer. He advocated the idea of using computers for input-output tables and for estimating prices, and an article devoted to computer use in economics prepared by him and signed by Bruk soon appeared in Kommunist. (11) Belkin and Birman also reviewed the American book on input-output tables in the journal, Voprosy Ekonomiki. (12)

As far as I know, Belkin was instrumental in helping the workers at the Scientific Research Economics Institute of Gosplan(NIEI) to begin to study input-output tables, seeking with them the relations for obtaining statistical data. Groups later were created in the Scientific Research Institute of Gosplan (NIEI) and the Council of Regional Issues (SOPS) to study input-output tables. These groups were joined by the young and energetic economists, Eduard Baranov, Felix Klotzvog, and Stanislav Shatalin, the mathematician Emil Ershov, and economists of the older generation, Lev Berri and Lev Mints. In 1968, these people received a state prize for work on input-output tables, but Belkin was not among them. Here, apparently, the mechanism of competition, which is not only cruel in capitalist countries, was working.

Belkin was also a pioneer in the Soviet utilization of input-output tables for the construction of a system for planned price-formation. At the same time, as reflected in his book Prices at a Single Level and the Economic Measurements at Their Foundation, Belkin used the Marxist ideas of labor value as a basis for understanding the nature of prices in a socialist economy. (13) Although there were limitations to this theory, the work conducted by Belkin on the creation of a model of price-formation was very useful. It was the first model in Soviet literature to permit the translation of general theoretical discussions of price-formation methods, which were based on the labor theory of value and its various modifications, into the language of mathematical models. These models facilitated future progress in economic science by revealing the limitations of theoretical premises.

Furthermore, while correctly noting the almost complete absence of quantitative models of price-formation, Belkin in the meantime rejected the application of the concept of optimal planning for these ends because he viewed this concept as abstract and unconnected with existing economic information. However, input-output tables directly allowed

for only one technological mode of production for a given product.
(These ideas are, of course, special cases of John Von Neumann's
models of dynamic equilibrium.) Furthermore, in order to obtain the
prices which would help to realize the plan, it was necessary to take
into account the utility function and natural resources (turnpike theorem).

It was not by chance, then, that Belkin was obliged to supplement
the input-output tables with all sorts of skillful, and at the same time
artificial, methods for the selection of interchangeable technological
methods, the limitations of natural resources. Because of the absence
of a clear theoretical conception, these supplements were incomplete
and omitted some important features, e.g. the price for labor.

Moreover, the information obtained allowed for the use of the idea
of optimal planning. If it is assumed that prices for consumer goods
are close enough to the prices of equilibrium--and such an assumption
is possible--the method of price-formation for consumer goods
considers supply and demand. Consequently, if the set of coefficients
of the input-output tables and the quantity of initial resources are found,
information sufficient for a quantitative definition of the prices appears.
Generally speaking, any available economic information sufficient to
obtain the prices can be interpreted as a special case in the optimal
plan. It is thus possible to use the ideology of optimal planning to understand the nature of the processes of current price-formation in the
Soviet Union. Quantitative models of price-formation based on real information will reflect approximations of the prices in the optimal plan.

At the end of the 1960s, the Laboratory for Electronic Control
Machines, transformed later into the Institute for Electronic Control
Machines, was transferred from the Academy of Sciences to the authority of the Ministry for Instrument Making, Automation Equipment and
Control Systems. Accordingly, there was a change in the theme of the
work in the economics division headed by Belkin. These circumstances
stimulated Belkin to transfer himself with a group of his workers to the
Institute of Economics where he could continue his theoretical research.
The section he headed in this Institute focused on such issues as the
possibility of applying available banking information to the improvement
of planning methods with the help of computers. Albina Tretiakova,
for example, worked on the optimization of the fuel-energy balance.

Postyshev

The third economic-mathematical section in the Institute of Eco-
nomics was headed by Leonid Postyshev, son of a famous Party worker,
P. Postyshev, whose death was order by Stalin at the end of the 1930s.
Leonid Postyshev was arrested and sent to a labor camp in 1942 straight

from the front. He was accused of wanting to flee to the Germans--a laughable accusation considering the nature of the man--and was taken to the camp barely alive. In the camp, he worked as a norm-setter and studied economic theory during his leisure. In the initial rehabilitation of the victims of the Stalin regime, Postyshev was freed from camp, and after returning to Moscow in the mid-1950s, he found work at the Institute of Economics. Taking an active part in scientific work, he studied at one of the economic colleges.

In 1957 I became acquainted with Postyshev at the Institute. He was also interested in the work of Kantorovich, and we had a common topic for discussion. Postyshev tried to develop the labor theory of value, which he had begun to work on even in camp, from quite general natural-philosophic positions. In the following years, Postyshev became very interested in the mathematical formalization of the processes of price-formation on the basis of the labor theory of value. (14) For this reason, he transferred to work at the Institute for Electronic Control Machines. At the end of the 1960s, he again returned to the Institute of Economics and in the beginning of the 1970s transferred to work at the Academy of Social Sciences under the Central Committee of the CPSU.

Postyshev's political opinions were interesting. I was not close to him and did not discuss general political questions, but I do remember his story about Stalin. When Postyshev was living in Moscow during the 1930s, he went to the Bolshoi Theater and sat in a government box. Stalin also sometimes attended the Bolshoi Theater. Postyshev remembered how Stalin approached him during an intermission, patted him on the head, asked him about his studies, and gave him candy. He told me about this event with a tremor in his voice. Postyshev's love for Stalin, evident in this story, surprised me. He defended Stalin's ignorance of many things by blaming G. Malenkov, K. Voroshilov, and the others. He said that these men, wishing to hide their mistakes from Stalin, would not let his father visit Stalin to tell the leader the entire truth about what was happening in the country. All this was told to me in 1957, during the unmasking of Stalin, by a man who had suffered tremendously from the Stalin regime. (15) Furthermore, Postyshev never changed his political convictions, even by the beginning of the 1970s. His attitude was clearly revealed in his reaction to a speech by Vladimir Mash.

Mash

Mash, after graduating from the institute, worked for several years as the head of the planning section in the fish industry in the Far

East and became very interested in economic-mathematical methods
at the beginning of the 1960s. (16) After returning to Moscow, Mash
worked for a short time in the Laboratory for Electronic Control
Machines, and then when TSEMI opened, he went there. Mash called
attention to computer methods, and he worked a good deal with calculations of concrete goals on various levels of the hierarchy.

At the beginning of the 1970s, Mash gave a speech to the directors'
seminar led by Fedorenko. During this seminar, speeches on the results of conducted investigations were given, and scientists from other
institutes were also invited to attend. In his speech, Mash tried to
point out new approaches to the development of the economic-mathematical trend. His critique of the theory of optimal planning, although
it was correct in some respects, was tremendously overdone, and the
speech provoked many critical remarks. However, among those who
came forward to support Mash was Postyshev, with a very original
approach. Postyshev offered consolation, pointing out that Stalin,
who had done so much for the USSR had been removed from the mauso-
leum, but that this mistake would come to be understood, and Stalin
would one day be returned to his earlier veneration. (Who knows?
Perhaps Postyshev will prove to be correct; the grandeur of Ivan the
Terrible and Peter the First has been preserved in Russia!) So it will
be, said Postyshev, with the evaluation of Mash's work; now Mash was
being attacked, but later he would be understood and esteemed. Postyshev's speech was unusual in such company. It seemed absurd coming,
as they say, "quite out of the blue." For the majority of those sitting
in the hall, the ideas of Stalinism were unacceptable; these scientists
remembered the price which Russia had paid for the Stalinist successes.

The Early 1970s

In the early 1970s, the Institute of Economics began to change its
main direction against support of the economic reform; this was apparently the result of the defeat of the advocates of reform in the Politburo.
Gatovskii, Moskvin, and Nikiforov (the secretary of the board of the
Communist Party of this institute who also supported the general policy
of the institute) were removed from leadership.

Kapustin and Skipertrov

Eugeni Kapustin, an unremarkable middle-aged economist and the
former director of the absolutely colorless scientific research Institute
of Labor of the State Committee on Labor and Wages, was appointed
director of the institute.

Kapustin's appointment helped to intensify the influence of the group of conservative economists headed by Skipetrov, the head of the economics subsection in the science section of the Central Committee of the CPSU. Skipetrov and Kapustin, alumni of the economics faculty of MGU had known each other during their student years. Skipetrov's basic idea was the suppression of those who thought differently about economic science. His first inclinations were to make the Institute of Economics an ideological outpost of conservative thought to counterbalance its previous policy of economic modernization and to convert the other center of economic thought, TSEMI, to a center of applied research.

These changes in direction became apparent in Skipetrov's speech on the assets of TSEMI at the end of 1971. It must be said that the very fact that Skipetrov made a speech was unusual. I worked for many years in the Academy of Sciences of the USSR, and I don't recall a time when even an instructor of the Central Committee of the CPSU made a speech at a meeting of the institute where he supervised. But Skipetrov was generally very active and ambitious. His power was notable enough that at a meeting in the Institute of Economics he was quoted with reverence; one of the workers remarked, "As Comrad Skipetrov said...."
In his speech on TSEMI, Skipetrov presented the notion that it was necessary to strengthen the ideological front of Soviet economics. In order to do this, it would be necessary to investigate "Czechism," to understand the reasons for the ideological mistakes of the Czech economists, errors which the Soviet economists had not yet investigated. This barb was thrust at the scholars from the Institue of Economics who had failed to critize the Czechs. Furthermore, Skipetrov noted, it was necessary to intensify the struggle against the bourgeois theories connected with mathematical methods. He clearly stated that TSEMI, through its journal, Ekonomika i Matematicheskie Metody (Economics and Mathematical Methods) had been little concerned with the unmasking of the bourgeois ideology disseminated under the stamp of mathematical models.

In his speech Skipetrov outlined precisely how the Institute of Economics would differ from TSEMI in practical and theoretical functions. TSEMI, he said, should be more concerned with practical goals and be more tightly joined to Gosplan: "Gosplan is a state organization and TSEMI cannot be on an equal footing with it." This was a reaction to criticism of Gosplan by TSEMI. If such differentiation between the Institute of Economics and TSEMI took place, then it would be easy to eliminate TSEMI as a theoretical center and transform it into a purely applied institute subordinate to Gosplan. In the Academy of Sciences, there were already precedents of institutes with applied themes being transferred to the corresponding ministries.

However, the general political state of affairs in the country and
the alignment of forces in the Politburo were apparently not conducive
to the triumph of a reactionary group of economists in the early 1970s.
Skipetrov's activity naturally provoked sharp protests on the part of
influential economists with other views. Skipetrov also apparently
frightened two proteges of Brezhnev, Iuri Arbatov and N. Inozemtsev,
the directors of the economics institutes of the Academy of Sciences
controlled by Skipetrov's subsection. In any event, a compromise
within the Politburo resulted in Skipetrov's removal from his position
and transfer to the leadership of another less significant subsection in
the same science section of the Central Committee of the CPSU.

As concerns Kapustin, his human qualities and experience as a
leader were sufficient to bring him to understand the limitations of
Skipetrov's policy. He did not cause a pogrom in the institute after his
arrival and was quite loyal in his attitude toward mathematical methods
in economic research, although he noticeably redirected the institute
to work on ideology.

THE ACADEM-GORODOK

At the end of the 1950s, a new branch of the Academy of Sciences
was established in Sibera, and a whole new town, Academ-Gorodok,
near the big industrial city of Novosbizsu, was built for this new branch.
N. Khrushchev patronized this town and even visited it once.

Mainly scholars from Moscow and Leningrad came to live in the
Academ-Gorodok. These scholars considered Academ-Gorodok--with
its possibilities of developing science in the new institutes, its relatively
better living conditions, and greater political liberalism--if not a para-
dise, then closer to the latter than some other places. Soon they realized that the Academ-Gorodok was nothing but a golden cage.

It is well known that in the Soviet Union there is an uneven distribution of income among different social groups. This social inequality
is greatly concealed in the big cities; for example, in Moscow many
apartment houses for the government officials are hidden in small side
streets, the location of the special food supply-stores for these officials
is known to few, etc. For the Academ-Gorodok, any social inequality
is readily apparent. The main living quarters, the research institutes,
and the university are situated in a very restricted area, all within
walking distance from one another. The living quarters are structured
in a following way. The villa of the President of the Siberian Branch
of the Academy of Sciences is in the forest, a considerable distance
from the other houses. Then there is a street with just cottages and
nothing else on it. One family cottage is given to academicians and

institute directors. The corresponding member of the Academy of
Sciences and deputy directors of the institutes, usually occupy only
half of the cottage. Doctors of Sciences, the head of divisions and
sections, live in apartment houses of a pretty high quality, i.e., high
ceilings, large kitchens, etc. The lower echelon of academics also
enjoy good living conditions, but of a lower quality than their senior
colleagues. The service and maintenance people live in big tenement
buildings, approximately two miles away from the main residential
area. Due to various shortcomings of food supply, different strata of
the population of Academ-Gorodok enjoy unequal access to deficit goods.
This conspicious inequality in distribution of housing and food leads to
a rather serious social problem: an extreme form of envy on the part
of one group of the population towards another.

The social ills of the Academ-Gorodok are further exacerbated by
the monopolistic character of research institutes in it. Since a scholar
can achieve promotion only within the framework of his own institute,
he must be very accommodating to his superiors. Should an employee
of the institute come into conflict with his boss, he would have to leave
not only the institute, but also Academ-Gorodok as well because of his
institute monopoly power. At the same time, leaving Academ-Gorodok
entails giving up your apartment since you cannot exchange it for another
apartment in a different city. The reader who is familiar with either
R. Kaiser's Russia, or H. Smith's The Russians, will be quick to
appreciate the difficulties that one encounters in apartment hunting in
the USSR. (17)

In view of the foregoing, it is easy to see how much more a con-
formist the scholars in Academ-Gorodok have to be vis-a-vis their
colleagues in Moscow and Leningrad. In spite of the above mentioned
difficulties, it is rather noteworthy that a number of dissidents emerged
in the Academ-Gorodok, and in some instances, the letter of protests
had been signed by up to fifty people. By hook, or by crook, practically
all of the dissidents were expelled from the city in the early 70s. The
majority of the scientists did not support one dissident, since they held
that the dissidents distracted them from their work and they feared the
government would cut their financial support.

Lastly, I want to point out a curious psychological trait in the lives
of the citizens of Academ-Gorodok. Since their community is quite
small, the frequency of scholars and their families meeting both on and
off the job is greatly increased. Under such conditions, appreciable
psychological strains make themselves felt. A suspicious glance of one
boss's wife cast at one of his subordinate's wife, may engender a long
and treacherous discussion concerning the husband's position in the
institute. The following real life episode illustrated the peculiar

mentality of the inhabitants of this small city. Once in Academ-Gorodok, academician L. Kantorovich, was taking a walk with a family of some friends of mine in a little forest which separated the university building from the apartment house area. My friend's wife was an extremely timid woman. She told Kantorovich that she was afraid of walking around alone to which Kantorovich replied, "Oh, come now, Luibochka! It is more dangerous when you are not alone..."

What has been said about the life of Academ-Gorodok has had and continues to have a great influence on the formation of a scientific community there. Gradually, there is a brain drain from Academ-Gorodok on the part of those scholars who come there from Moscow and Leningrad. To an ever increasing extent, the scientific community of the city is being formed by those scholars who come from the Volga region or the Urals and by graduates of the local university who come there from all sorts of provincial cities in the USSR.

Scholars in the Economic-Mathematical School

All this hold equally for the people involved in the economic-mathematical trend. The Siberian center for economic mathematical research was basically formed around two famous scholars: Leonid Kantorovich and Abel Aganbegian.

Kantorovich

Kantorovich came to Academ-Gorodok about 1960, having been elected a Corresponding Member of the Academy of Sciences in the Economics Department. Soon he became deputy director of the new Mathematics Institute, and he was able to attract a small group of mathematicians from Leningrad to his Institute. These mathematicians included G. Rubenstein, V. Bulavskii, A. Kaplan, and others. An economic-mathematical division was organized around them to work on linear programming and on the composition of programs for the solution of economic problems on computers. With the economists, these mathematicians tried to solve several concrete economic problems, notably the location of the optimal tractor fleet for an agricultural unit.

Makarov

Valeri Markarov came to this institute from Moscow. He had graduated from MGEI at the end of the 1950s, and even during his student years, Makarov had manifested an interest in mathematical problems. At the Mathematics Institute, Makarov first began to work on decompositional procedures and then on turnpike theorems. Makarov defended his doctoral dissertation in mathematical sciences. In the middle of the seventies Makarov became a member of the Communist Party. (18) After L. Kantorovich left Academ-Gorodok, he was appointed as the Deputy Director of the Institute of Mathematics. In 1978 Makarov was elected a Corresponding Member of the Academy of Sciences of the USSR.

In the Mathematics Institute the mathematician, A. Rubinov, worked on turnpike theorems with Makarov. In particular, they investigated turnpike theorems in which the technological possibilities are changed, but are treated as exogenous changes. However, the presence of anti-Semitism in the Mathematics Institute, supported by quite an influential group of workers, led to Rubinov's departure from Novosibirsk. New bright scholars were not invited to the Economic-Mathematical Division of the Mathematics Institute. To my best knowledge, in the last years the workers of this division did not develop new ideas.

Aganbegian

The basic groups of scientists working on economic-mathematical methods in the Siberian Branch were concentrated in the Institute of Economics and the Organization of Industrial Production (IEOPP). The present head of this Institute, academician Aganbegian, had graduated from MGEI in 1956, and after going to work for the State Committee on Labor and Wages, he quickly advanced and became deputy manager of the summary division. His first works in the sphere of mathematical economics included models of income distribution. In 1963, Aganbegian, a young Doctor of Economic Sciences, was elected a Corresponding Member of the Academy of Sciences of the USSR. He was then working in IEOPP as head of a division.

Prudenskii

At that time IEOPP was directed by German Prudenskii, an economist of the old school who worked on labor problems. Before the war, Prudenskii had published a book on methods which indicated that one worker could operate many machines. After the war, he entered the doctoral program of the Institute of Economics of the USSR Academy of Sciences and wrote his dissertation "with the help of friends."

Prudenskii was also active in administration. During the war he had been one of the secretaries of the Sverdlovsk Region Party Committee, and when the Committee of Labor and Wages was created in the mid 1950s, he became the deputy chairman of the Committee.

At the end of the 1950s, he received the title of Corresponding Member
of the Academy of Sciences of the USSR and moved to Novosibirsk for
the organization of IEOPP. Prudenskii was noted for his extreme
conservatism, but by using his experience in administrative work, he
was able to camouflage this conservatism. (19)

Aganbegian

Prudenskii happened to encounter Aganbegian,who had experience
in administrative battles from his days in the Committee on Labor and
Wages, where his superior in the department was Boris Sukharevskii,
a prominent specialist in administrative affairs. Having been the head
of the Plan-Coordinating Department of the Gosplan under Voznesenskii,
Sukharevskii was dismissed from work after Voznesenskii's arrest.
In the mid-1950s he was again promoted and finally became the deputy
to the chairman on the Committee of Labor and Wages.

Aganbegian was helped in his struggle with Prudenskii by a group
of young workers in his department, most of whom had come with him
from Moscow. (Some of them in the last years left Academ-Gorodok
for different reasons; among them was the well-known dissident I.
Khokhlushkin. It must be said that Aganbegian made a great effort to
enlist scholars for his division, and the people who came at his invitation supported him sincerely and helped him. Of course, the general
atmosphere in Academ-Gorodok also helped Aganbegian; basically the
town contained mathematicians, physicists, chemists, biologists, and
engineers. At that time the Siberian branch was headed by the well-
known mathematician and all-powerful academician, M. Lavrent'ev
As a result of the persistent struggle between Aganbegian and Prudenskii,
the latter was defeated, obliged to quit the battlefield, and move to
Moscow. Soon afterward, he died.

After Aganbegian became the director of the institute, Fedorenko
attempted to subordinate the IEOPP to himself to make it a subsidiary
of TSEMI, but counteracting forces did not allow Fedorenko to accom-
plish this. Fedorenko's trips to Lavrent'ev ended with nothing. Lavrentiev did not want to lose his own prestige; how could there be in his
jurisdiction an institute that was the subsidiary of TSEMI? Thus, the
IEOPP remained an independent force.

Aganbegian did not succeed in becoming an academician for a long
time. His candidacy, more than once approved by the Siberian Branch
of the Academy of Sciences, was more than once rejected at the Economics Department of the Academy of Sciences. Apparently, this was
the result of competition: to academician Fedorenko, Aganbegian was
enemy number one. Finally, at the end of 1974, Aganbegian was elected

as an academician. It is difficult for me to say what forces were working here, but it may be assumed that without the intercession of at least one of the influential Politburo members he would not have succeeded.

On the ideological plane, the IEOPP adopted a conservative position close to the views of Novozhilov and bizarre works on this trend have been written by Konstantin Valtukh and others. (20) The basic trend in the institute was toward optimizing the regional allocation of production, scheduling (e. g. , PERT), input-output tables, and so on.

The IEOPP

The IE and OPP occupied a leading place in the Soviet Union in works on the regional allocation of resources. Alexander Granberg, a doctor of economic sciences, did research in this area.

There were a number of people in the IEOPP who worked with PERT. In the early years of the institute this work was headed by Iuri Avdeev. However, due to differences of opinions with the head of the institute, Avdeev had to leave in the mid 1960s. Then something incredible happened in the history of Academ-Gorodok. The President of the Siberian Branch of the Academy of Sciences, M. Lavrent'ev, offered Avdeev a job in the Institute of Hydromechanics where he was head. This institute, of course, had nothing to do with Avdeev's main interests. I do not know why Lavrent'ev did what he did, but the fact remains that the monopoly of the IEOPP was disrupted in this way. For several years Avdeev worked in the Institute of Hydromechanics, but eventually he had to leave Academ-Gorodok. A couple of years ago he accepted another job in Odessa.

Practical developments in input-output tables have been made on the basis of the model elaborated by N. Shatilov. In this connection, the following incident is curious. In the mid-1960s, Aganbegian obtained access to N. Baibakov, the chairman of Gosplan. The latter ordered that Aganbegian be given all the information necessary to develop a usable input-output model. After several months of calculations on the model, a draft of an economic plan was produced which corresponded on the whole to the plan elaborated by Gosplan. The officials of Gosplan were victorious. It is also interesting to note that at the end of the 1960s space for a group of IEOPP laboratories was granted in the Gosplan building. Gosplan wanted workers from IEOPP located in Moscow to counterbalance TSEMI and NIEI and to work on the themes of Gosplan. The economist, Ozerov, headed this Moscow subsidiary of IEOPP, but no work came out of this subsidiary; Ozerov moved to Academ-Gorodok as deputy director of IEOPP.

The absence of innovative general theoretical ideas, the departure
of a number of leading scholars, and the lack of inflow of good scholars
from Moscow and Leningrad all combined to turn the IEOPP into rather
a mediocre institute with a narrow practical orientation.

THE INSTITUTE OF CONTROL (IPU)

The development of the Institute of Control (IPU), formerly the
Institute of Automation and Remote Control of the USSR Academy of
Sciences, operated in strict accord with one of Parkinson's laws, i.e.,
the construction of a new building is only completed for an organization
once the organization has lost its former glory. In its time, the IPU
was a leader in the development of the theory and practice of automated
control. A remarkable group of scholars, with academician Vadim
Trapenikov, as Director, worked at the Institute and attracted a large
number of talented young people. Gradually the early achievements of
the institute were all put into effect, but no new trends were developed.
Its older generation of scholars continued to develop what they had
begun and the middle generation and the young scholars searched more
intensely for new forms, particularly in economics.

Trapenikov

Academician Trapenikov displayed great interest in economics
despite his lack of education in the field. At times his work, especially
in modeling, was naive. With regard to the institutional area, his proposals connected with the intensification of decentralization and the
introduction of competition between the designing organizations were
of a progressive nature. In the middle 1960s Trapenikov, as first
deputy to the Chairman of the Committee on Science and Technology,
played a tremendous role in the preparation of economic reform in the
Soviet Union.

Braverman, Rozonoer, Malishevskii, and Razumikhin

Emmanuel Braverman and Lev Rozonoer were among the first
scholars at the IPU. Braverman is known for his works on the recognition of patterns. Using this theory, his group of workers conducted
interesting investigations on the branch structure of the Soviet economy
on the basis of published data on input-output. One of these works,
compiled by Vladimir Lumelskii, who recently emigrated to the United
States, was published in the early 1970s in the journal, Avtomatika i
Telemekhanika (Automation and Remote Control). (21) Braverman

later conducted original investigations in the sphere of revealing equilibrium in noncompetitive economics; the results of this study were published in the journal, Ekonomika i Matematicheski Metody (Economics
and Mathematical Methods) in the 1970s. (22) He died in 1977, but
until the last minute he continued his research. Not long before
Braverman's death I received his last book from him, Mathematical
Models in Planning and Control in Economic Systems. (23)
   The history of the development of Pontriagin's "maximum principle"
is quite complicated. But the engineers who apply these ideas to their
calculations know the name of Rozonoer, who did much to develop them
into practice. Rozonoer also contributed to mathematical economics,
attempting to generalize a number of results obtained independently in
thermodynamics and economics. A series of his articles on these
subjects was published in 1973 in Automation and Remote Control. (24)
In many respects, these works may help in understanding economic
mechanisms and the categories used in them.
   Andrei Malishevskii, a talented young scholar, also contributed to
the work on mathematical economics in connection with his interest in
the mathematical analysis of complex systems. (25) B. Razumikhin
used a mechanical analogy for investigating economic models, and he
did it in a very original way. A series of his articles on these subjects
was published in 1971-73 in Automation and Remote Control and finally,
in a book. (26)

Lerner, Aizerman, and Ivanov

   At the same time, the IPU developed and elaborated practical
schemes for the utilization of economic-mathematical methods and
computers. Initially these works were of an episodic nature. In the
mid-1960s, the group under the leadership of Alexander Lerner, known
in recent years as a pioneer in the movement for the emigration of the
Jews from the USSR, worked on organizing an engineering system for
the steel supply. A number of economic developments, particularly
ones involving the securement of spare machinery parts, were conducted by the workers in the Laboratory headed by Mark Aizerman.
   Later a division incorporating several sections was organized in the
IPU under the leadership of Iuri Ivanov. This division began to work
on the problem of planning the national economy. A large number of
highly qualified mathematicians who had experience in the application
of mathematics to engineering systems were enlisted in this work, but
there were no economists involved. The workers in this division,
however, were associated with economists and contributed to the move
toward teaching economics to their future colleagues from the Physics

Technological Institute, one of the best colleges in the country, with a
very powerful group of students. This college had a management faculty,
and students in the upper courses transferred to the base enterprises
and research organizations where they worked in the appropriate subdivisions and took courses at the same time. A number of the workers
at TSEMI gave a year's course on mathematical economics for these
students and their colleagues at IPU.

Relationships with Other Institutes

At this point I would like to touch upon a more general question
connected with the elaboration of economic problems in noneconomics
institutes. In the first place, this concerns the engineering institutes.
The workers at such institutes, for the most part, are incomparably
more educated and capable people on the whole than their colleagues,
the economists. Just this one fact creates the feeling in the workers
at these institutes that they themselves can develop economic problems.
But the knowledge and experience which the economists have also represent a sufficient value.

While IPU established contact with the economists, its counterpart,
the Cybernetics Institute of the Ukraine Academy of Sciences, shut off
interaction with economists. The Director of the Cybernetics Institute,
Glushkov, concentrated on competition with specialized economics institutes rather than communication with them. There is no doubt that
the presence of many institutes working on similar themes inevitably
engenders mutual competition. The competitive aspects and the desire
to distinguish oneself may sometimes work to the detriment of science.

IPU Seminars

The IPU understood the importance of solid relations among institutes. Concretely, this was embodied in the organization of a joint
weekly seminar for the workers of the IPU and TSEMI under my super-
vision. The workers of other economics institutes were also invited
to these meetings. Three groups of questions were examined at the
seminar, and among them was the consideration of Western economics.
The basic thrust of this lecture series lay in demonstrating both the
complexity of the modern Western economic system, in which vertical
and horizontal mechanisms are combined--in contradiction to the simplified representation of the West as a system whose economy resembles
a bazaar, with all its attractive aspects of a pure, uncomplicated and
unlimited market--and the tremendous role of a country's culture in
the process of developing its economic system, and hence the diversity

of economic mechanisms in contrast to simplified technocratic aspirations of creating the ultimate economic mechanism applicable to all countries.

Due to the tremendous assistance of Revold Entov, a large number of scholars from the Institute of World Economy and International Affairs (IMEMO) were enlisted. Ramses gave several lectures on Japan, demonstrating precisely how the peculiarities of the Japanese culture and way of life influence the development of the economic mechanism. In the lectures on the United States, Vladimir Shamberg showed new trends in the American economy. Iuri Chizhov, a worker in the section headed by Stanislav Menshikov, told of the work of this group on econometric models of the development of the American economy. Stanislav Menshikov, the former deputy director of the Institute of World Economy and International Affairs, did much for the development of the econometric trend in the institute and took an active part in this work himself. Later, for various reasons of a personal nature, Menshikov went to work in IEOPP, where he continued to conduct the research he began on econometric models of the American economy. Later, Menshikov went to work for the United Nations.

Victor Kuznetsov presented an interesting series of lectures on the mechanism of the French economy and the use of economic-mathematical models of planning in these mechanisms. He demonstrated how the correlations of social forces are taken into account in the models of the French economic system. R. Entov, a great connoisseur of Western theories and mathematical models regarding the circulation of money, acquainted the audience with these areas. From TSEMI, Boris Isaev brought up the system of national accounting used in the French economic system, and Vladimir Shliapentokh from the Institute of Concrete Social Research gave a brilliant survey lecture.

The second group of questions at the seminar involved the problems of macroeconomic modeling. The audience was acquainted with theoretical macroeconomic models and tests of their practical application. Lectures also were provided by the workers of TSEMI: Alexander Anchishkin, Valeri Grebennikov, Grigori Pirogov, and Erik Presman, among others.

The third group of questions examined at the seminars concerned general theoretical problems of the performance of a planned economy. This series of lectures sought to reveal the various competing views in this sphere. Ovsienko, Faerman, and I presented the subject of the modeling of the socialist economy on the basis of a unified model of the national economy. The audience also was able to become acquainted with the opposing viewpoint, represented in the lectures of Victor Volkonskii and Boris Mikhalevskii, which accented the economy as a

form of a complex of models. The reader can clarify some differences
between these approaches by consulting pages 114-15; 121-22.

In the mid-1970s contacts between economists and engineers from
IPU lessened. It seems to me that the main reason for this failure of
cooperation was due to the fact that old cadres retained their leading
positions in the institute and were quite incapable of participating in
the new fields of research. Fearing for their hegemony, they try
under one guise or another to block the development of new ideas.

This brings up a more general point, namely, of the type of organization in which it is possible to develop new ideas. If we admit that
new ideas can for a considerable time be developed within the framework of existing institutions, the latter eventually has to be changed
If the organization is relatively young, this reorganization is sometimes possible, e. g., the history of IEOPP. But as a rule such transformations are impossible; the old cadres will prevent it. (27)

4 Centers of the Economic-Mathematical School: Higher Education Institutes

THE G. B. PLEKHANOV MOSCOW INSTITUTE
OF THE NATIONAL ECONOMY (MINKH)

The MINKH became one of the new centers when the trend to develop economic mathematics started in the institutes of higher education. This institute grew out of a merger between the old MINKH, a pure trade economic institute subordinate to the Ministry of Trade, and the Moscow State Economics Institute (MGEI), subordinate to the Ministry of Higher and Secondary Specialized Education. This merger resulted from a series of events beginning at the end of the 1950s when the president of MGEI decided to expand and absorb MINKH, which was located next door and had comparatively good facilities for students. This proposal was put forth at a meeting of the Presidium of the Council of Ministers. Several minutes were allowed for discussion during which Anastas Mikoian, a member of the Politburo and a patron of trade, apparently said that in his opinion the two institutes should be merged, but MGEI should be put into MINKH because MINKH had a very important medal of the Red Labor Banner. The merger was ordered, and Afanasi Fefilov, President of MINKH, was names its president.

Fefilov

Fefilov was a decent, intelligent, progressive man of the older generation who had experienced the adversities of Stalinist power. Fortunately, in his case they were limited to his removal from quite a high position, head of the planning division of the Ministry of Trade. Due largely to Fefilov's personal abilities, work conditions in the amalgamated MGEI and MINKH were good and capable teachers were

91

enlisted, independent of their nationality. In this amalgamated institute
there were quite a large number of well-known Soviet economists of the
older generation, working primarily on applied problems. But as these
applied problems were national-economic in character, they were inter-
woven with fundamental theoretical problems. The majority of these
economists, many of whom were Jews by nationality, were noted for
their modern views. In contrast, the basic teaching staff of the institute
was noted for extremely reactionary views and anti-Semitism.

At the end of the 1940s, especially in the MGEI, which later gave
its basic group of economists to MINKH, a purge campaign had been
organized. Quite a large number of teachers were dismissed, with
those of Jewish origin foremost among them. Several of them were
rehired in the period of post-Stalin liberalism. Only in the 1960s,
when Fefilov was made the president of the institute, were the institutional passions quieted somewhat, or more precisely, repressed by
the president.

Mochalov

Unfortunately, after Fefilov retired on pension in the late 1960s,
the situation at MINKH changed again. A comparatively unknown,
middle-aged economist, Boris Mochalov, was appointed president.
Previously, Mochalov had been the secretary of the Party organization
of MGU, which was a very impressive position. As a result of a complicated struggle, he was removed from this post (secretaries are not
formally removed; they are simply not reelected). Mochalov represented the political views of the extremely reactionary part of the
Soviet Party apparatus. Immediately after his arrival at the institute,
Mochalov began a massive purge of the personnel. Using the traditional
biases of many at the institute, he unleashed an anti-Semitic campaign.
A large number of Jews were fired, and several leading professors of
Jewish origin died, easing Mochalov's problem. (1)

Mochalov's outrages provoked embarrassment among liberal-
minded people both within and outside the institute. Although not men-
tioning the firing of the Jews, an article against Mochalov appeared in
Literaturnaia Gazeta. Friends stood up for Mochalov; he remained
president. At a Party meeting at the institute there was a discussion
of the article, and no one could be found to support it. As usual after
a critical article was published in the Literaturnaia Gazeta, this newspaper would inform the readers of the punishment of the person who
was criticized. But in this case a different situation resulted. The
worker on the editorial board who had prepared the article about
Mochalov for publication was punished, and the pages of Literaturnaia

Gazeta were given to Mochalov in compensation for moral damage.
He soon produced an article seemingly without precedent in the major
press. In accordance with the demands of the reactionary forces,
Mochalov wrote about the necessity for the admission of students into
the universities in proportions corresponding to the social, geographical, and national composition of the population. As far as I know, the
question of national regulation of the student body had never before been
so obviously posed in the central press, although the press devoted
much attention to the structure of the student environment.

Against the background of such agitation of human passions in the
MINKH, scientific work went on. There were some scholars such as
Alexander Birman, the chairman of the Department of Finances, who
took a very active part in economic reform. Birman worked on such
critical problems as increasing the responsibility of the employers and
employees of the enterprises, the sources of financial security for the
enterprises, and similar problems in institutional economics. He
wrote some books and many articles about this in the journal Novy Mir
and Literaturnaia Gazeta, and they attracted much public attention. (2)
The immediate cause for Birman's resignation from the institute in
1972 was Mochalov's crude attempt to dismiss one of the leading members of the finance department by breaking all the rules for creating
vacancies. In protest to Mochalov's actions Birman transferred to
work in one of the research institutes.

Turetskii

The bulk of the reform minded scholars in MINKH did not use
economic-mathematical methods in their work. Such an economist was
Professor Shamai Turetskii. He had occupied prominent positions in
the Gosplan and even, it seems, remained a non-Party member; however, even Trofim Lysenko was not a member of the Party. Turetskii
was the author of a great number of books and articles, and he headed
the department of special problems in national economic planning.

Turetskii was notable among the traditional economists for a certain creativity. In 1963 at the MINKH, I took part in the discussion
after a speech in which he had noted that in pricing it is necessary to
account for the utility of a commodity. This was a reasonable demand,
since in practice the establishment of price in the USSR for capital
goods never considered the effects on the consumer. Of course, this
demand for the price, in the language of Western economic science,
looks trivial. However, there is an art to expressing this demand in
the USSR; one must break through the jungle of Marxist language and
also express price demands in a way that will be practically influential.

Turetskii was defeated during this discussion by his colleagues, the
political economists. I remember the speech by Grigorian, the head
of the political economy department. The essence of his criticism can
be reduced to the following: "According to Turetskii," said Grigorian,
"the result is that Marx did not explain everything, did not give exhaustive answers to all questions, but in Marx everything is said."
And with this, everything was said.

Turetskii's resilience as a scholar was matched by a resilience of
character. Although seriously ill, Turetskii lectured around the country
in order to discover the real socioeconomic processes in the Soviet
Union. He was a living history of the development of Soviet economics,
was able to discuss it, and loved to relate incidents which surely will
not be published for a long time. (3) Although creative, Turetskii was
on the whole an orthodox Marxist in economic theory, and a man
wounded many times--in the mid-1940s there was an abusive review of
one of his books in the journal, Bolshevik. On the other hand, he
wounded others in accordance with the rules of the game in his time,
and at times he wounded very painfully. High moral qualities were not
characteristic of him, either in Stalin's time or after it. Turetskii
died in his bed at the beginning of the 1970s, and the face of the president of MINKH did not reflect grief for the deceased when he stood in
the honor guard at Turetskii's coffin in the hall of the institute.

Itin

Another older economist who belongs to the group of reformers is
Lev Itin, the head of the economics department of industry at MINKH.
Itin was a man with a lively mind, who wished people well.

Itin did not work on economic-mathematical methods himself, but
he was respectful of them, tried to understand their essence, and expressed in some conversations a certain understanding of the new ways.
As chairman of the Faculty Academic Council, he often assisted in the
defense of dissertations on economic-mathematical themes. Itin had
to live through a lot at the end of the 1940s, when the purge of the
Jewish teachers began in the MGEI. By using his abilities for adaption,
he succeeded in keeping his job. In the mid-1950s, when Itin's doctoral
dissertation was being approved, he was viciously attacked. In his
dissertation about the economics of light industry, he included several
dutiful phrases, which corresponded to the then-current Party line,
about the necessity for advantageous rates of development in light industry. However, by the time the dissertation was up for approval the
Party line had changed and the well-known criticism of the woeful
economists had begun. The members of VAK had happily uncovered

another woeful economist, Itin. The case for the approval of the dissertation dragged on for a couple of years, but ultimately it was approved. Konstantin Klimenko, who was then the deputy to the chairman of the corresponding expert commission of the VAK, helped Itin tremendously. (4)

Breev

There also was in the MINKH a very noticeable group of people working on economic-mathematical methods. The basis for the application of these methods in the institute at the end of the 1950s was provided by the Department of National Economic Planning, which organized active work chiefly on the study of input-output tables. The work done by the leading teachers of the department, who were over fifty and had no previous knowledge of mathematics. The late Michail Breev, the head of the department, played a decisive role in the development of this trend. His personal traits are worthy of the highest esteem and he did much to preserve the membership of a department in which nationality was a thorny issue. Breev was a remarkably patient person who respected the views of others. In 1966 he invited me to give a series of lectures for the workers in the department. He wanted to further his own knowledge and to acquaint his workers with the new trends in economic science. In his introduction to my lectures and in his conclusion, Breev expressed disagreement with my views, but at the same time he emphasized his respect for my different perspective.

Feld and Smekhov

Professor Semen Feld was also an economist of the older generation. A very decent, gifted man who knew history, literature, and especially poetry well, he found it terribly difficult to live under Stalin. Perhaps because at that time he thought much and wrote little, he succeeded in preserving a freshness of perception and accomplished a great deal in the following years. In the mid-1950s, around fifty years of age, he began to work on mathematical models and Feld wrote a long book about the fuel-energy balance in the Soviet Union, in which he employed the corresponding mathematical methods. (5)

Boris Smekhov, of the same generation of economists, worked in the department. He also pursued economic-mathematical research and sought to find new approaches. There also were some young teachers working on mathematical methods in the department.

Although I held the workers in the Department of National-Economic Planning in high esteem, I must point out that some of their views on

mathematical modeling were quite conservative. They reduced the role
of mathematical methods to that of obtaining balanced and even optimal
plans, but they did not want to admit that the dual variables of an optimal plan (so-called shadow prices) were also prices and that a non-
Marxist view of the principles of pricing was needed. Apparently they
advocated the Marxist labor theory of value for too long to admit its
limitations.

Department of Economic Cybernetics

Another department working on mathematical methods in economics
appeared in the MINKH during the 1960s—the Department of Economic
Cybernetics. Only young workers ever staffed this department, and
they worked on problems connected with the optimal allocation of resources in industry and agriculture. This department is headed by
Ivan Popov, a middle-aged man, one of the pioneer in the application
of optimal planning methods to agriculture. In 1960 at a conference on
the application of mathematical methods to economics, he spoke on
these issues. Popov for a long time supported the best traditions of
the MINKH, as they were laid down by Fefilov. This was expressed
for example, in the following instance.

In TSEMI during the early 1970s, the Academic Council on the
awarding of doctoral degrees was already functioning, but it was heavily
overloaded. Therefore, a number of the workers in TSEMI defended
their dissertations in other institutions, especially at the special council
of the MINKH. Michail Zavelskii, one of the leading workers at TSEMI,
presented a dissertation there on problems of optimal planning. (I will
describe his work in connection with the evolution of the conception of
TSEMI.) Zavelskii was supported by the department at MINKH, which
Popov headed; by the TSEMI; by Fedorenko who went to the Academic
Council in person; and by others. For various personal reasons, bad
feelings existed between Zavelskii and Vladimir Kossov, one of the
workers at the Gosplan. Kossov drafted a letter that was signed by
three deputy heads of the Gosplan's departments and sent it to the
Academic Council of MINKH. The letter reviled Zavelskii's dissertation in every possible way. Zavelskii's main rival in the TSEMI,
Vsevolod Pugachev, came to a meeting of the Academic Council of
MINKH and delivered a crushing speech. (6) Nevertheless, in spite of
this unprecedented pressure on the members of the Academic Council--
usually the defense of dissertations takes place peacefully--all the members of the Academic Council of the MINKH present voted to award
Zavelskii the academic degree of Doctor of Economic Science.

Summary

In concluding the description of the MINKH, it should be pointed
out that the new president of this institute, Mochalov, actively supported
the development of the economic-mathematical trend. Mochalov employed the faculty of economic cybernetics and made Ivan Popov, the
head of them, his deputy. Vladimir Kossov, a specialist in input-output
tables, was appointed chairman of the Department of National-Economic
Planning after the death of Breev. It should not be thought that all this
contradicts what was said earlier about Mochalov. Political reaction-
ism gets along magnificently with reformism in economics, as is apparent in the Mochalov example. I think that Mochalov is supported on
the highest levels of the hierarchy by the same circles which support
TSEMI. We will have still another opportunity to mention these politically reactionary circles in the forthcoming discussion about the supporters of the economic-mathematical trend.

THE ECONOMICS FACULTY OF MOSCOW STATE UNIVERSITY

The graduates of the economic faculty of MSU are teachers, researchers, and party officials and a main source of personnel for the
leading ideological institutions throughout the USSR. This great responsibility fosters conservatism among the staff of instructors of the
economics faculty. But even in such a basically reactionary group,
there are some professors with either reform tendencies or sympathies.

The Department of Mathematical Methods for the Analysis of Economics, the only department in the branch of economic cybernetics,
stands out sharply in this reactionary setting. The department was
organized by Vasili Nemchinov at the beginning of the 1960s. It combined mathematicians who taught mathematics for the entire economics
faculty, and economists, who taught economic-mathematical methods.
It is also true that in addition some individual courses on economic-
mathematical methods were given by teachers from the Department of
National-Economic Planning.

Berri

Lev Berri, an economist of the older generation, headed this department. As of the end of the 1950s, around the age of fifty, Berri
began to work actively on economic-mathematical methods, having
previously paid them scant attention. Earlier he had worked on problems of technological progress, specialization, and cooperation in
industry. For the work on input-output tables, which Berri directed

in the Scientific Research Economics Institute of the Gosplan, he was awarded the title of State Prize Laureate. Berri was a benevolent, witty person, with a great interest in everything new. In spite of the fact that he was cautious, he helped establish new trends in economics, both by his friendly conversations with young scholars and with his appearances as a reader for dissertations devoted to new economic problems.

Lurie

The Department of Mathematical Methods for the Analysis of Economics was composed basically of workers who had come into the laboratory created by Nemchinov. Nemchinov had also invited Alexander Lurie and David Iudin to work in the department, and they became the leading professors there. Nemchinov needed full professors who were economists, but there were almost none among the specialists in mathematical economics. According to established practice, it was necessary to have a degree of Doctor of Sciences to receive the title of full professor. In terms of his scientific prestige, Lurie had the greatest chance to receive a doctoral degree, but Lurie had only a degree of Candidate of Sciences, which was close to a Ph.D. Therefore, Nemchinov asked Lurie before his appointment to speed up the writing of his doctoral dissertation and promised to help organize its defense. At that time, the defense would have been a problem because the councils for awarding the academic degree of Doctor of Economic Sciences were in the hands of traditional economists. Only toward the end of the 1960s were specialized councils for the defense of doctoral dissertations in the sphere of economic-mathematical methods created in TSEMI, MGU, MINKH, and IE and OPP.

It seems that Nemchinov succeeded in obtaining an exception so that Lurie was allowed a defense of his doctoral dissertation at a specialized academic council of the economic faculty of Moscow State University, which had previously only been able to award the degree of Candidate of Economic Sciences for people who specialized in economic-mathematical methods. Lurie put together a dissertation quite quickly after collecting and systematizing his separate publications on mathematical methods in the investigation of economics. The successful defense of the dissertation at Moscow State University was furthered by the fact that one of the dissertation readers was the famous mathematician, academician A. Kolmogorov.

Iudin

Iudin, Nemchinov's other important choice, was a mathematician
by education. Having studied the applications of mathematics to engineering he was one of the first Doctors of Mathematical Sciences to
work on the economic-mathematical trend. With his widely known
works on the mathematical methods used in economics, Iudin had done
much for the preparation of trained specialists and mathematicians,
and has stimulated them to master the new trends. In one of the institutes, he directed work for a long time on the application of mathematical methods for the solution of problems, several of which apparently also had natural economic applications. He succeeded in enlisting
good mathematicians to work in this institute and in motivating them
toward the use of mathematical methods in economics. Among these
mathematicians were Victor Volkonskii, Iuri Gavrilets, and Evgeni
Golstein, who later transferred to the laboratory headed by Nemchinov
and then to TSEMI.

At the Department of Mathematical Methods for the Analysis of
Economics, Iudin also succeeded in stimulating students and graduates
to investigate new economic-mathematical problems. Through the
lectures he gave on the operations research and with the seniors and
graduate students for whom he was responsible, Iudin developed methods
for stochastic programming in the resolution of economic goals, a
trend comparatively little developed in the Soviet Union. In fact, Iudin's
activity in the developing of the economic-mathematical trend was so
intense that he succeeded in involving his daughter and son in it. After
graduation from the mechanical-mathematics faculty of MGU his
daughter went to work in TSEMI; his son studied in the branch of economic cybernetics and after graduating from the university, also went
to work in TSEMI. Nemchinov tried very hard to help Iudin become a
Corresponding Member of the Academy of Sciences, but at the elections,
it seems, Iudin lacked one or two votes.

Most of the economists in the Department of Mathematical Methods
for the Analysis of Economics, by holding more than one office, were
also workers in TSEMI. This system gave students the opportunity to
obtain knowledge of the various aspects of the development of the
economic-mathematical trend from their original proponents.

Mathematical Economics: Personal Reflections

At Moscow State University, I gave a year's course on "The Theory
of Optimal Functioning in Socialist Economics." (7) This course reflected a series of problems which were the subject of my scientific
research on mathematical economics.

In my lectures, I tried to impart to the students a significant interest in the economic problems connected with mathematics. At the same time I attempted to show them the limitations of the application of mathematics, indicating the vital connection of economics with the culture of a people, their traditions, and so on. I wanted the students to obtain the best representation of the general processes of the functioning of diverse economic systems through mathematical methods, and I tried to show the students the importance of the differences in specific mechanisms of economic functioning in different countries through knowledge of the humanities. I liked the student environment in economic cybernetics. (8) It satisfied my desire to assist in the education of a new generation of people in Russia. An evolutionist by conviction, I thought that the improvement of the economic mechanism must take place gradually, as the necessary conditions were created, and first and foremost among these conditions was an educated person able to use modern knowledge. I never discussed current political themes with the students since I understood the danger for them as well as for myself. Only in conversations with students after the lectures did I touch on moral and ethical problems. I recognized the importance of these problems for the following reasons.

In the post-Stalin period, a number of new scientific trends were advanced, and with the removal of the taboos on cybernetics, genetics, and mathematical methods in economics, etc., students had increasing opportunities to master modern scientific methods. The level of student social thought was raised significantly; students evinced a tremendous understanding of the role of the social system. The fact that Khrushchev dragged Stalin off the pedestal and the new leadership in its turn reduced Khrushchev's status, negated the deification of the ruler from the consciousness of many people. However, only a relatively small group of people understood the role of moral and ethical norms. The moral and ethical theme usurped by official organs had become an indecent topic for conversation among decent people. There was not yet sufficient understanding of the fact that the tragedies of the twentieth century were the result of a loss of absolute values, i.e., of the rejection of independence, of the glorification of the means in and of themselves, and of attempts to define the value of the means from the viewpoint of the sublimity of the ends. (9)

Many mathematicians were working with the economists in the department. They taught not only general mathematical disciplines, but also special courses connected with the mathematical analysis of corresponding economic models (models of equilibrium, turnpike theorems, etc.). General courses in mathematics were given in the branch of economic cybernetics and in other branches in the economics faculty by such qualified teachers as Pavel Medvedev, Igor Nit, and Tatiana Faleks. In the branches of political economy and international economics, the students also were given an elementary knowledge of higher mathematics. A number of mathematics teachers tried to connect mathematical analysis with economic problems, especially price-formation (the idea of duality). However, the students in these branches basically received a traditional education.

The presence of two types of education for economists--with the application of mathematics and without it--is a phenomenon characteristic of economics education in the Soviet Union. It would not be justified from the point of view of the specialization of the students because all of them have to know economic-mathematical methods. There is now a sufficient number of specialists in the country to warrant courses in mathematical economics at all the economics faculties. The two types of education in the USSR are now mainly a result of the fact that the old economists do not want to give up their positions to economists who use mathematics.

The traditional methods for the education of economists affected the branch of economic cybernetics also. Giving lectures to the highest classes (the fourth and fifth), I was able to sense the overall deficiencies in the general preparation of specialists in economic-mathematical methods. In the beginning, the students studied mathematical disciplines and social sciences in which there were no mathematics. Moreover, these social sciences were based on traditional obsolete dogmatic concepts.

The almost complete isolation of mathematics from its applications in the first courses affected the students' approach to the later courses; here, though they studied special disciplines in which mathematical knowledge might have proved useful, they already forgot much of their math, and they had also already assumed a scornful attitude toward the knowledge of social science that lay at the basis of the special disciplines. I was especially aware of this attitude in the capable students. They emphasized study of the mathematical aspects of a problem over the social aspects. It is true that this was also influenced by the fact that many of them, unable to study with the mathematics faculty of the university, were tempted by the abundance of mathematics in the branch of economic cybernetics.

Economic-Mathematical Methods: Other Developments

In order to achieve a better understanding of the connection between mathematics and economics, from the start of economics education it is necessary to give lectures on the economic disciplines which organically absorb new economic concepts together with mathematics, just as is done, for example, in the physics faculties.

The department was not limited to teaching. Under the leadership of Nit, the deputy to the chairman of the department, scientific research work was organized as well. Through contracts with the enterprises and other institutions, practical goals were posed and resolved in the sphere of capital goods supplies. These contracts helped to attract the teachers and graduate students in the department for the solution of everyday problems. Famous young mathematicians from the department of probability theory at Moscow State University, Valerie Tutu-balin and Iuri Tiurin, for example, took part in this work. Supplementary payment, the opportunity for business trips (on small means and divided among the faculty), and other benefits which the "self-support theme" provided secured the continuance of the faculty's interest in undertaking the work.

The Department of Mathematical Methods for the Analysis of Economics plays a large role in the general form of the scientific atmosphere in the economics faculty. The existence of students studying mathematics within the faculty obliged the department of political economy to have on its staff a number of teachers who had a least some idea of mathematical economics. More than that, the recognition in Party documents (the resolutions of the 24th Congress of the CPSU on mathematical methods in economics) obliged the leaders of the economics faculty to be more flexible. Under the current conditions, it had already become uncomfortable to argue with economist-mathematicians unless one had at least a knowledge of the mathematical language used in economic problems.

In 1970 a resolution was adopted to train the economics faculty members in economic-mathematical methods. This resolution was quite in earnest, and it was more than a token gesture. Every semester a group of five or six members, as a rule over thirty years old, were chosen and freed from their usual tasks. In the group there were also Ph.D.s and in most cases at least one full professor, even if he was from the department of political economy. Daily courses in economic analysis were conducted by teachers from the Department of Mathematical Methods for the Analysis of Economics. Courses were given on mathematical economics and on mathematics alone. I gave a thirty-six hour course to such groups, presenting ideas of the optimal functioning of the socialist economy.

It must be said that the students really wanted to understand the conception of optimal planning; at the same time, it was very difficult for them. My former students will forgive me for such a stupid comparison, but I would compare the difficulties in explaining the theory of optimal planning to them with trying to explain to primitive people the idea that the earth is round. After all, for the ordinary consciousness engaged in daily business in a limited area, the idea that the earth is flat is entirely natural. The idea that the earth is round suggests the seemingly apparent impossibility of people walking around upside down. The students had three types of difficulties characteristic, in general, of traditional economists. The fundamental problem was that the students absolutely could not get used to the fact that all the analyzed corollaries were correct relative to the premises accepted. Beginning with their ordinary knowledge, they tried to refute the corollaries. The teachers of these groups had a hard time teaching the students that if there was no agreement with the corollary, it was necessary to examine the premises from which it flowed. When the question of the premises arose, the fundamental difficulties also appeared. An obvious axiom such as "an economic system has constraints on resources" was not always understood. Such arguments as the following were usually offered against it: there is, after all, technological progress, and expansion of production is taking place constantly. The most difficult axiom for the traditional economists to accept concerned the individual's preference for a type of good because of its utility. The individual's demand for various goods was examined by traditional economists from a position of prices and expenses; internal values in the invididual were ignored. The following question, for example, was not often posed by traditional economists:

Two bachelors go into a store where there is a great selection of wares. They receive the same wages and the prices in the store are identical; i.e., the influence of prices and income is eliminated. These buyers will surely choose different goods, but what forces them to do this?

Traditional economists were not, as a rule, predisposed to credit the role of psychophysiological factors in the behavior of Homo Economicus. Traditional economists were ill-accustomed to the ideas of Olds, Delgado, and other prominent neurophysiologists who spent the last twenty-five years investigating centers of emotions in animals and man, and whose works suggested the profound forces which individualize a person's value perception.

Finally, there are difficulties connected with the fact that the students did not quickly assimilate the language of mathematics. The demand for the mathematical notation in economics obliges one to introduce precisely the corresponding known and unknown parameters and the connections between them. Furthermore, the economist must be able to translate from mathematical to economic language the algorithmal solution to economic problems in order to construct modern mechanisms for the functioning of an economic system.

I am deliberately emphasizing the role of mathematics as a
language necessary for economic investigations. In the understanding
of this trivial idea may lie the key to understanding the basic difficulties
of economists and other scholars in the social sciences who attempted
to use mathematics. The greatest difficulties arose during the transition from the formulation of the task in economics language to its
mathematical formulation. The discipline of thought which is demanded
here is achieved at a very high cost. It is not by chance that among the
textbooks on mathematical logic it is noted that in order to read the book
no preliminary specialized knowledge is required, other than the culture
of mathematical thought. In teaching mathematical economics to people
who have not had special preparation, the above-mentioned considerations are often ignored. These considerations are very important for
many countries which are beginning to join the culture of the world.
The majority of those who teach mathematics to economists have often
cursorily cited the mathematical formulation of the economic task and
rushed on at once to the exposition of linear algebra or another corresponding area of mathematics. A squall of involved mathematical con-
structions bursts upon the student uninstructed in strict methods of
reasoning, a squall in which his desire to enter mathematical economics
can easily drown. Such, briefly, is the pedagogical and scientific life
of the department. Human relations in the department are no less
remarkable.

The Staff

On the whole, the staff in the Department of Mathematical Methods
for the Analysis of Economics was very good. Its workers labored to
protect the department from "Black Hundreds" (as was called an extremely reactionary force in tsarist Russia) who somehow occasionally
managed to penetrate the department.

Gerasimov

At the beginning of the 1970s, for example, such hooligan types as
Gerasimov were forced to leave the department. A mathematician by
profession, Gerasimov came to the department after receiving his
Ph.D. under the mathematical faculty of Moscow State University.
His advisor, Landis, was a famous mathematician and a very decent
person. After a short time, Gerasimov showed his true colors and
succeeded in becoming a very necessary person for the reactionary
forces on the faculty. His administration of mathematics examinations
was a case in point. Mathematics was listed among the entrance

examinations for the economics faculty of Moscow State University.
Approval for the program of examinations was given by the special
commission chosen from the staff of the mathematical faculty at Moscow
State University. This commission had to coordinate the entrance examinations in mathematics for all the faculties of MGU and also had to
direct a group of teachers from the mathematical faculty who controlled
the examinations in mathematics for the entire university. Gerasimov,
the senior examiner in mathematics for the economics faculty, barri-
caded the doors and did not admit to the examination certain teachers
of the mathematical faculty, and among them such respected scholars
as Professor Nikolai Efimov, a Lenin Prize Laureate, and Professor
Sergei Fomin. Gerasimov's hooliganism was, of course, sanctioned
by people who were interested in securing admission to the economics
faculty for the necessary students. In spite of the scandalous nature
of the preceding, Gerasimov received thanks from the university,
signed by one of the vice presidents, for the successful examinations.

Petrovskii

Concerning the activity of the Department of Mathematical Methods for
the Analysis of Economics, one might ask the question: how could such
a staff survive surrounded by reactionary forces ? It must be remembered that this department was created in the early 1960s, when economic-mathematical methods were not yet advocated by the central
Party press. Academician Ivan Petrovskii, president of the university,
played a decisive role in its acceptance. Because the leadership of the
university was very conservative, Petrovskii was unable to influence
everything in a progressive way. But his support undoubtedly led to
the creation of new departments and the selection of a staff of leading
teachers connected with the development of the long-term trends in
science. It was Petrovskii who quickly responded to Nemchinov's proposal to organize a department for the application of mathematical
methods to the analysis of economics.

   After Nemchinov's death, the department was threatened by the
dark forces in the economics faculty. Vladislav Dadaian had the duties
of an acting chairman of the department for a brief period of time. One
of the young economists who came to Nemchinov's laboratory, Dadaian
was quite a brilliant man; he wrote fiction, was interested in UFO's,
and had one of the best libraries in the USSR on this subject. As an
economist, he devoted much attention to general theoretical questions
of the application of mathematical methods to planning, and he later
wrote several books on these problems, combining traditional economic
views with an examination of various ideas on the problems of economic-

mathematical research, for example, the problem of the criterion of optimality. Dadaian also did experimental calculations for the development plans of the union republic and the country.

Of course it was difficult for Dadaian to defend the department from the many monsters on the economics faculty of Moscow State University. I was told that Petrovskii went specially to a Party meeting of the economics faculty which took place soon after Nemchinov's death. At this meeting, the fate of the department was to be decided. Petrovskii was not a member of the Party, but his position permitted active participation at the Party meeting. Petrovskii demonstrated in every way his respect for the trend developing in the department and for the people participating in it. During the break, he strolled along the corridors with two leading workers in the department, taking them by the arm. It is precisely due to Petrovskii that academician, Nikolai Fedorenko, was appointed after Nemchinov to the position of chairman of the Department of Mathematical Methods for the Analysis of Economics. Fedorenko also did much for its preservation and development. But in 1970, for nominal reasons--the recurrent criticism of the Academy that the leading scholars occupied too many positions--Fedorenko left the chairmanship of the department. Petrovskii approved Stanislav Shatalin, who as new chairman of the department, retained for himself the important job of deputy to the director of TSEMI.

I witnessed Petrovskii's influence on the selection of the leading teachers at the university directly. In order to strengthen the development of the trend of optimal planning, it was decided in 1970 to invite three new workers to the department of mathematical methods for the analysis of economics; Victor Volkonskii, Nikolai Petrakov, and me. We all continued to work in TSEMI and were registered in the department as part-time workers. At the same time great cutbacks were taking place for part-timers in the system of higher education. I don't know the real goals that motivated the commission of the Central Committee of the Communist Party under Arvid Pelshe, the member of the Politburo who recommended such cutbacks, but this ruling did curtail the preparation of specialists. Even under these circumstances, however, Petrovskii, after becoming acquainted with the recommended candidates, selected the three part-timers for the department. After Petrovskii's death, the department situation was unstable, but the department survived, and its leader, Shatalin, tried to continue its best traditions.

5 The Main Center for Economic-Mathematical Research: The Central Economic-Mathematical Institute of the USSR Academy of Sciences (TSEMI)

GENERAL COMMENTS

The development of the theory of economic-mathematical modeling in the 1960s and 1970s was largely spearheaded by the activity of TSEMI. (1) The evolution of ideas regarding mechanisms for the functioning of the Soviet economy developed in TSEMI can be demonstrated by refraction through the system of this institute's management. TSEMI was characterized by a remarkably developed diversity in the use of mathematical methods. This diversity gave the institute many opportunities for survival; the institute could switch hats at a moment's notice.

Fedorenko

It is particularly important to note that N. Fedorenko, the director of TSEMI, played a part in making possible the development of new trends, although he rarely encouraged them actively at first. (The workers who conducted new trends did not receive in the beginning prizes or other limited advantages.)

Fedorenko must be given his due. He consciously implemented the policy of diversity at the institute. One parable he often cited was derived from the time when he served in Germany after the war as an officer working on dismantling German equipment. One day, noticing three unfinished buildings standing next to each other, Fedorenko asked what they were. It turned out that these were three different uncompleted factories for the production of synthetic benzine. Because it was difficult to give a preference in the planning to any one type of factory and since each factory's output had special importance, it had been decided to build three different types of factory at once.

Using the idea of diversity which he had applied at the institute, Fedorenko at the same time served various groups in the Politburo, making "a simultaneous play of several billiard balls in the pockets," as they say in the Soviet Union. For a long time, Fedorenko had no strong support in any one group; i.e., he was nobody's man. He wanted to create a reliable system from unreliable elements, and he succeeded at it for quite a while. Fedorenko tried to take part in Kosygin's group on the development of reform. At the end of the 1960s during one of Kosygin's reform meetings, Fedorenko made a well-received speech. Kosygin suggested that he be included in a group of four to five leading workers on the reform. Many people were already congratulating Fedorenko on his success, but after several days, when the order of the Council of Ministers came out, Khachaturov, then the Academician-Secretary of the Economics Department of the Academy of Science, had been appointed to the group instead of Fedorenko. Someone had convinced Kosygin that Fedorenko should not be given power. I don't know whether Fedorenko later got into one of the groups; however, in later years one of the groups actively supported him.

Diachenko and Tikhomirov

On the subject of affairs within a diverse institute, I should point out that the variety of viewpoints in TSEMI was immense. In TSEMI one could even see zealous supporters of traditional economic theory; especially prominent among these were Iuri Tikhomirov and Vitali Diachenko (the son of the deceased economist Vasili Diachenko). They saw their goal as giving a truly Marxist meaning, i.e., the Marxist formula as seen by the majority of Soviet economists, to mathematical methods in economics.

Diachenko was a man of little ability, a lover of life, a scribbler, with a traditional economics education, and he did not know mathematics. Therefore, there was usually no harm in his activity. However, when changes occurred in the ideological climate of the positions Diachenko represented, he would cease to be peaceful and would become a very dangerous conservative force.

A more colorful figure was Tikhomirov, an industrious and active man, who by profession was an engineer, or maybe an agronomist. He was known for his invention of herring bones (equipment for milking cows) which brought him a medal during Khrushchev's rule. I don't know why he abandoned agriculture, but in the early 1960s, around forty years of age, Tikhomirov went to work in the Laboratory of Economic-Mathematical Methods. In this Laboratory, he worked on the creation of a Marxist economic theory of price formation.

In 1963 Tikhomirov prepared the manuscript of a book which the
reviewers approved, apparently without reading it. By chance I was
given this manuscript to read. I cannot say that I went through the
manuscript with a fine-toothed comb, but I read the whole book, and
I found pages worthy of mention. The author attempted to show that
the use of shadow prices, as prices in an optimal plan contradicts the
demands of Marxist economics because these prices are marginal,
while the prices must be the average of socially necessary labor expenses. A statement of this sort in and of itself is ordinary, but the
author's following feat was not ordinary. In order to prove the correct-
ness of his statement, he took the average estimates and rebuilt the
production plan according to them. Of course, this plan produced
better results than the plan obtained from the solution to the initial problem of linear programming or the plan equivalent to it in accordance
with the shadow prices of the optimal plan. Tikhomirov was victorious;
the estimates of the optimal plan were disgraced. The plan using the
prices based on average expenses was still more optimal. Later Tikhomirov prepared a thick tome on price theory, which assimilated a
huge collection of quotations from the classics of Marxism. He spoke
more than once at meetings of the Academic Council of TSEMI. Fortunately, he was not taken seriously at the institute. His job was ad-
ministrative--academic secretary of the Scientific Council on Optimal
Planning--and when he left TSEMI, his departure went unnoticed.

GEAM

In the presence of the diversity in TSEMI, there is always one
trend which is considered the main movement. One main trend, after
being used, is exchanged for another, through the process of human
relations which I have called "GEAM" (in Russian these letters spell
out PUPU, a word which has a universal meaning!). This name reflects the fact that in TSEMI the advance of any new main trend and its
rotation on the plan of human relations suggests the attitude of a king
toward his favorites. At first, the favorite receives gifts from the
king; then comes a period of equalization; then abuse; and ultimately,
his murder. Of course, not all the favorites go through all the stages.
It must be noted that the first phase of favoritism is very insidious.
The proposals which are made to the favorite create the illusion that
he is not merely the favorite, but is a member of the coalition which
wants to achieve the realization of the stated goal through joint effort
under a certain division of labor (each does what he can). The gifts
to the favorite and the favors from membership in the coalition are
very similar. It is necessary to be a good diagnostician to determine

which is the case even in the beginning of a particular disease when there are symptoms common to other diseases. A good doctor can define the actual disease and take measures for its cure.

The second phase for the favorite, equalization, appears initially in petty jabs from the king. The favorite perceives them as some sort of misunderstandings, the intrigues of his enemies, who are the viziers of the king. It is well known that the goal of the king's viziers consists not only of coping with current affairs, but also of seeking a man with kingly ideas; the kings themselves often do not have such ideas. They usually find people with such ideas, and favorites are made of them. But when the favorite becomes close to the king--the king often gets advice from him, gives him everyone's favorite leg of pheasant from the table, etc.--then the viziers begin to feel that they are being forced out. A certain conflict is created between the formal power of the viziers and the informal power of the favorite. The favorite is usually occupied with the development of ideas; he has not been through the "school of feudal intrigue" (the Strugatskii brothers' expression). The viziers, on the other hand, are only concerned with staff affairs, and they have experience here.

They begin to open the king's eyes to the favorite, and if there is a chance, even threaten the king with deposition, if he does not quickly remove the hated favorite. The king leans toward their opinion because he has already elicited much input from the favorite and fresh brains are needed. Therefore, the conflict between the formal and informal power is usually resolved by the removal of the favorite. Depending upon the circumstances, the favorite moves with varying speed into the next stage--abuse. In this stage the favorite keeps an unimportant position. After all, the favorite could reach the last stage--death.

Fedorenko must be given his due. He did not reach the stage of killing his favorites. Furthermore, after a favorite passed the stage of abuse, he remained at the institute and had the opportunity to continue his research. His second chance was the result of the outstanding administrative abilities of the director, who was capable of ignoring personal dislike for a former favorite in the name of the development of the institute. Of course, the development of the institute helped the director's career, but it is important to keep in mind that in this case the director's career in many respects coincided with the development of science.

OPTIMAL PLANNING

During the period in which the institute was created, optimal planning of multistaged systems was chosen as the basic trend. In the beginning of the development of the theory of optimal planning, the model of the national economy was examined in the form of an optimal problem without emphasis on the number of variables and limitations. In the work of Kantorovich, Lurie, and Novozhilov, the national economy was examined as a simple structure. Such a representation yielded many valuable ideas such as approaching the national economy from the position of optimality, understanding the role of prices as instruments for the composition, and implementation of the plan. However, it was not enough to be limited to such a representation of the national economy because when the national economy is described through concrete technological methods and products, the problem dimensions are unworkably large. By breaking the problem into parts, however, one could solve the local problems and coordinate the solutions with the general demand of the system.

Pugachev

At around this time, Dantzig-Wolf's algorithm, which is based on a decompositional procedure, had already appeared in the West and was known in the Soviet Union. Since the late 1960s, a group of mathematicians in the Laboratory of Economic-Mathematical Methods (Victor Volkonskii, Iu. Gavrilets, and V. Pugachev) and my group in the Institute of Economics had begun to work out analysis methods for an economic system in hierarchical system form. The group of mathematicians in the Laboratory of Economic-Mathematical Methods primarily sought good computing methods to solve problems concerning large systems, but they also saw in this scheme the prototype of a system of national-economic planning. The ideas of this group were most consistently realized in Pugachev's work. Pugachev had come to the laboratory, which was under Nemchinov, soon after it was opened. Pugachev was then a young engineer with a mathematics education, after graduating from one of the air force academies, having taught there, and he had received the degree of Ph.D. in Engineering. Noted for his receptivity to economic problems, Pugachev brought to their examination the practical principles of an engineer. At the same time, he had a striking desire for power and a wish to obtain higher positions, which he justified by saying that qualified people were needed to develop the new trends.

When TSEMI was organized, the projects developed by Pugachev concerning the optimal planning of hierarchical systems were strongly advocated, and Pugachev began to play the role of the favorite. Fedorenko gave him gifts such as prizes, missions abroad, and so on, but Fedorenko did not want to give him the power of deputy director.

Pugachev was an active young Russian, longing for power--a dangerous figure to have close to the throne: a Party member with a knowledge of mathematics and an understanding of economics. After passing through the first phase of favoritism (gifts) and having failed to be transformed from a favorite into a grand vizier, in 1964 Pugachev decided to transfer to the Gosplan in the new division on the Application of Mathematical Methods and Computers in Economic Activities, which was headed by Iakov Oblomskii. Oblomskii had a Ph.D. in economics, but had no previous connection with mathematical methods in economics. He manifested a moderate progressivism, apparently the result of Tevosian's school, where he had worked for a long time as deputy to the secretariat. (Tevosian was the Deputy Chairman of the Council of Ministers in the 1940s-1950s.)

Several young, newly-appointed Jews were working in the section, an unusual phenomenon for the Gosplan of the 1960s. Oblomskii's deputy was Natan Kobrinskii, a man who had worked for many years in mathematics. For various reasons, primarily ones connected with his Jewish origin, Kobrinskii was obliged in the late 1940s and early 1950s to stay out of Moscow. During these years, Kobrinskii taught in Penza and began work on cybernetics. He was asked to Moscow as deputy to the head of the Chief Computer Center of the Gosplan. From there he went to work with Oblomskii as his first deputy. After working for several years in the Gosplan, Kobrinskii went back to teaching. He settled down in the Moscow Economics Statistical Institute as the head of the Department of Economic Cybernetics and put out a useful book on economic cybernetics. (2) A cautious man, he tried to reconcile economic-mathematical methods with Marxism.

The division on the Application of Mathematical Methods and the Computers in Economic Activities had a miserable existence in the Gosplan and was alien to its workers. Apart from the fact that this section had ideals unacceptable to the apparatus of the Gosplan, it was also seen as a meaningless structure because it was not responsible for anything. It was not by chance that after Oblomskii's death in the late 1960s the section was absorbed; it was made part of the section of summary planning. Vladimir Kossov, a former worker at TSEMI, occupied the position of deputy to the chief of this section with responsibilities for applications of mathematical methods in economic activities.

But let us come back to 1964 when Pugachev was invited to work at Gosplan as the second deputy to Oblomskii. While he worked in this section, Pugachev did a number of useful things. Under his control, an order was prepared for the Gosplan concerning the development of optimal plans in all branches. This order strengthened the groups on optimal planning in the branch research institutes. While he was working in Gosplan, Pugachev came up against tremendous difficulties, conditioned in many respects by the fact that the people above him were not professionally competent in mathematical economics. Pugachev longed for independent work which would at least give him room to turn around. I don't know what would have happened if Pugachev had been given such an opportunity. With his longing for power and lack of fastidiousness as to means, as well as his impatience, he could, as they say, "have cut a lot of wood." But although it once seemed as if Pugachev might have a chance to obtain independent work by replacing Nikolai Kovalev as director of the Chief Computer Center of the Gosplan, this opportunity was not given to him. His flirtation with this power came about as follows.

Pugachev's Decline

Prior to his appointment to the Computer Center of the Gosplan, Kovalev had had no connection with economic-mathematical methods; he was typical of the new type of leader. Because he occupied the position of the leader of a semi-research institution, he needed an academic degree based on his own scientific works, but he had little time for science sinee he was always occupied with practical activity, so the workers subordinate to him wrote him a book which he published under his own name. (3) At this time, however, a group of sharp-tongued economist-mathematicians, among them, Albert Vainshtein, academician A. Kolmogorov, and Corresponding Member B. Gnedenko, decided to do battle with ignorant writings on economic-mathematical models, and a critical review of Kovalev's book appeared in the news-paper, Izvestia. Kovalev had chosen his writers badly, and the mistakes in the book and the bad review made it seem that he would be removed from his position. Moreover, a commission created in the Gosplan for the verification of the Chief Computer Center's work was yielding uncomplimentary results. Nothing, however, came of these criticisms; in fact, the review in Izvestia actually helped Kovalev be-cause the honor of the Gosplan was at stake. Kovalev kept his position until he died several years later.

Pugachev, therefore, was not given the position as head of the Computer Center. His impatience predetermined his rapid departure from the Gosplan, approximately a year and a half after he came, and his return to TSEMI. In 1965, when Pugachev returned to TSEMI, which accepted him out of a certain degree of kindness since he had been dis-missed from the Gosplan with a reprimand, the place of favorite was already occupied. Thus Pugachev remained in TSEMI in a secondary role, consumed with ambition, and ready for any provocations in the name of obtaining power. He did not advance in his work after getting involved on the computing aspects of the multi-staged system of optimization. He was deprived of a scientific environment; no self-respecting, creative scholar wanted to have anything to do with him. (4) Such was the price of amorality; yet he was a very capable man!

Volkonskii

After Pugachev left TSEMI for the Gosplan, Victor Volkonskii became the favorite, and many people in the institute called him prince because of his aristocratic Russian last name. He was a young mathematician, Kolmogorov's graduate student, and he had successfully defended his Ph.D. dissertation on the probability theory. He was thrown out of MGU, where he was then a graduate student, for his abnormal interest in social problems. Next he worked in the Institute of Weights and Measures, and then in the institute where David Iudin was working. From there he went to the Laboratory of Economic Mathematical Methods.

While continuing the ideas of hierarchical planning, Volkonskii's conception differed from Pugachev's. While Pugachev focused attention on the fact that one indivisible model was needed for the analysis of the Soviet economy, Volkonskii concentrated on the necessity for elaborating the model's structure. This structure involved two model groups. In the first group were bloc models, i.e., macro-models of the national economy and models of individual branches of industry, factories, etc. These models called attention to the peculiarities of each level of the managerial hierarchy, for example, the essential role of the integer variables in models of the development of the branches, where much significance was attached to the building of new enterprises. Algorithms were developed for the analysis of each kind of bloc model.

Parallel to the bloc models were functional models: models of price-formation, capital investment, financing, and so on. These models stood by themselves to a certain extent. It cannot be said that Volkonskii did not understand that the prices flowed from the plan. At the same time, however, he focused too much attention on the independence of these models; he separated them from bloc models which already included these problems. Furthermore, both the bloc and the functional models were insufficiently coordinated by Volkonskii into a unified theoretical scheme; their synthesis was not thoroughly established.

Analysis of Economic Problems: Personal Interpretation

Such an approach to the analysis of an economic system recalled traditional economic thought. It cannot be said that all the phenomena listed above do not exist in economic reality. The problem lies in how to study them. For traditional economic theory and practice, it seems natural to divide these problems and to make the study and the implementation of each of them independent.

The traditional economic theory does not know how to integrate these problems, (5) but without a proper economic theory it is impossible to coordinate the many bloc and functional models. The value of a consolidated mathematical model of the national economy is apparent. With all its limitations, it allows one to see the process of coordinating actions of blocs at various levels and to perceive how different functional parameters (prices, capital investments, etc.) are formed in the course of the very process of functioning.

Volkonskii's conception of the combination of bloc and functional models did not satisfy the director because of the limitations described above, and he rapidly passed through the second and third phases of favoritism but saved his position as head of the section. His passage was accelerated by the arrival of E. Faerman, Iu. Ovsienko and me with our conception of a planning economic system. Our work had the following features.

First, we were trying to develop the problem of the global criterion of optimality. Strictly speaking this problem still belongs to the stage of development of the ideas of optimality as applied to the representation of the national economy as a simple structure. Various types of palliative criteria, given in a general form, are characteristic of this stage. The next stage is characterized by more detailed elaboration of different aspects of criteria based on the idea of utility. The criteria we developed were unique in that they were based on constructing norms of consumption, on which people could be completely satisfied, and measuring deviations from these norms (levels of dissatisfaction) by their influence on the average life-span; it seemed to us that average life-span is the major indicator of the development of mankind. The criterion was formulated as the minimum of integral dissatisfaction on the entire path to the achievement of norms. Such a criterion permitted the elimination of the difficulty of formulating additional time constraints for cases where the planning period is limited. The time for the achievement of the established norms and the share of GNP on consumption and accumulation were sought in the course of solving the problem. Second, we were trying to describe the unit in the systems of production, which then was seen in the production operation.

Furthermore, we were not simply trying to postulate the hierarchical structure of the economy. We analyzed various sorts of technological hierarchies which could be utilized in the construction of
different mechanisms for the operation of the economic system. The
main idea of our research was to enable us to determine the following
characteristics of a unitary process: the optimal input-output and the
optimal managerial structure. Finally, we were trying to give a more
extensive economic interpretation of the decompositional procedures to
call attention to the fact that mathematical methods of problem-solving
can be translated into economic language and can give economists
methods for the organization of planning processes under conditions of
decentralization.

On the basis of such ideas, Faerman, Ovsienko and I later demonstrated the essence of price-money relations under socialism. We
demonstrated that these relations flow from the nature of complex
systems, i.e., systems in which every unit had freedom to make choices
of allocating its own resources but at the same time did not have information about internal resources of all other units. Prices were global
parameters, condensed information concerning the whole system.
That was why they could be guidelines which allowed every unit to choose
the best input-output, i.e. to maximize profit and simultaneously to
move toward equilibrium along the system as a whole. Such an idea
allowed one to look in a new way at the arguments in the Soviet Union
about what gave birth to the price-money mechanism. These ideas
meant that propaganda need not make excuses for the introduction of
profit as a criterion for the activity of the enterprises as if profit were
a capitalist category. Profit, in our representation, was a category of
complex systems.

The hierarchical idea of economics allowed us, further to demonstrate that from the point of view of the use of prices all the levels of
the hierarchy were, in principle, equal. The existing theory negated
the use of the price mechanism on a level higher than the factories and
considered prices within the factory as some sort of calculation quan-
tities without an economic nature. As a result, the State Committee
on Prices set the prices on the level of the factories, but the system of
planning inputs-outputs was different--the Gosplan gave the plans to the
ministries; the ministries had to pass the plans to the Chief Departments; they in turn had to pass them to the factories, and the factories
transferred them to the workshops, etc. The hierarchical development of prices together with the plan would relieve the central organs
of much calculation of prices for the factories. By way of illustration,
in the Ministry of the Chemical Industry's system about a third of all
the types of produce were consumed only within the given ministry.

In the book Optimality and Price-Money Relations (Moscow, USSR, Nauka: 1969), written with Josef Lakhman and Iuri Ovsienko, we gave a more complete account of the examined group of economic problems.

A few words about Lakhman. He is a capable person, with a sense for what is new. For a long time after he graduated from MINKH, he had to work as an editor, first in a publishing house and then with the journal, Voprosy Ekonomiki. Lakhman was the editor of Kantorovich's first article in this journal and assisted in its publication. Then Lakhman worked for many years on trade economics, examined mathematical methods in this sphere, and was involved in the creation of automated systems for the management of GUM (the largest store in the Soviet Union). Upon coming to work at TSEMI in 1964, he soon began to work on problems in the theory of optimal planning. The basic result of this work was the book mentioned previously and a number of articles in leading economic journals.

1966

In 1966 our group was transformed to a section, and in 1967 in a division numbering about thiety people, mainly highly skilled mathematicians who for various reasons, but chiefly because of their Jewish origin, had not been able to find professional employment elsewhere. The division's major task was to develop a general theory of complex systems. By way of applications we were expected to elaborate new approaches to the formation of a socialist economic system on the basis of integrating various economic mechanisms. The division consisted of two sections and two groups. B. Mitiagin was the head of the section of functional analysis. Such brilliant mathematicians as A. Dynin, A. Katok, G. Khenkin, and V. Levin worked with him. The work of this section was primarily concerned with the functions of the system in the situations of certainty. A number of highly original results produced by this unit was published in parts in the collection Mathematical Economics and Functional Analysis (Moscow, USSR, Nauka: 1974). I would especially like to call the reader's attention to the article by Katok concerning the role of money in a model of economic equilibrium.

The group headed by Vladimir Lefebvre dealt with the problems of conflicting structures. Partly the results of their work have been incorporated in Lefebvre's book to which A. Rapoport wrote a marvelous introduction. (6)

Another group headed by Vadim Arkin worked on the problems of risk and uncertainty in complex systems. The original results produced by such members of this group as E. Presman, V. Rotar, and I. Sonin were published in part in the collection Problems of Probability in Management (Moscow, USSR, Nauka: 1977).

Finally the section which I headed--I simultaneously occupied the
position of a head of the division and the section in keeping with the
customs of TSEMI--was concerned with general problems of complex
systems and their applications to economics. I personally worked with
such remarkable algebraists as B. Moishezon, V. Danilov, V. Iskovskikh,
and G. Tuirina. I would especially like to emphasize the contributions
made by philosopher-engineer-mathematician, Victor Polterovich in
the fields of mathematical analysis of formation of complex networks
and different kinds of mechanisms. A number of his publications have
been translated into English. I myself, published several articles
which dealt with methodological problems of complex systems from the
standpoint of value theory. In cooperation with Solomon Movshovich
and Iu. Ovsienko, I published the book Growth and Economic Optimum
(Moscow, USSR, Nauka: 1972) which reflected some of the work that
was being done in the section concerning economics. Some comments
on Movshovich, who shrewdly combined the understanding of the content
aspect of economic goals with the mathematical apparatus for their
analysis, need to be made. A very capable man, Movshovich was able
in the mid-1940s, to study in one of the privileged institutes concerned
with physical and technological problems. He studied there for only a
year, however, and then due to circumstances beyond his control, transferred to the Moscow Machine-Tool Instrument Institute. After his
graduation, he worked as an engineer at a factory for electric meters
near Moscow. "Without a break in production," Movshovich graduated
from the mathematical faculty of Moscow University and went to work
at the institute where David Iudin was. There he became very interested
in the mathematical themes close to economics, and he later went to
work in TSEMI. Movshovich successfully defended his dissertation for
the academic degree of Doctor of Economic Sciences in TSEMI and
waited about five years for its acceptance by VAK.

The 1970s

My division was established near the time of my transition from the
first stage of favoritism to the second. I had an opportunity to stay in
the second stage for about three years. In 1970, I entered the third
stage, favoritism. This was accompanied by different types of attacks,
at first minor, and then later, more severe accusations that my division did not offer ideas which had practical applications. Because our
scientific work was highly appreciated, this division continues to exist.

In April 1972 B. Moishezon, one of the leading scholars who worked
in the division, decided to emigrate. At this time, since emigration
from the USSR was rare, Moishezon's decision generated a lot of

unofficial discussion. An open discussion concerning Moishezon's decision was officially avoided. Instead, Fedorenko announced a meeting, which included division members and the top executives of the institute, with the following agenda: the current research program of the division. As usual, I opened the meeting with a speech, and a number of people asked questions, but suddenly Fedorenko asked, "What is the attitude of the members of the division to the Moishezon's decision to emigrate from the USSR?" I was prepared for this bitter question, because I knew that I was in the third stage of favoritism and at any moment could be moved to the fourth. I decided I had to assume complete responsibility for Fedorenko's question and answer it, because I had previously assured several anxious members of my division that there was very little likelihood of this issue being raised at this meeting. My response to Fedorenko was that the division is not prepared to discuss this question, and I was to blame; because the only member of the division who was a member of the Communist Party was on a business trip, there was no one present who was obligated to publicly accuse Moishezon. Then after the meeting, Fedorenko decided to dismiss the division, but the sections and the groups were saved and were subordinated to the deputy director, N. Petrakov.

In June 1973, I resigned because I had decided to emigrate. Immediately, the section which I headed was dismissed and its members dispersed among different sections. In 1974 V. Lefebvre emigrated, and the members of his group moved to other research institutes. Two years later, during the reorganization of TSEMI (further discussion of that reorganization is included at the end of the chapter), the section headed by B. Mitiagin was dismissed and its members moved to other sections. Some of them, Dynin, Katok, and Mitiagin himself emigrated.

On the ruins of the division, new sections were built. In 1977 Iuri Ovsienko was appointed as a head of a section; earlier he had joined the Communist Party. The purpose of this section was to write a textbook on Soviet economics. Fedorenko had this idea for a long time. He had asked me to write this book as early as 1968 and had repeated the request over the years, but because I had had bitter experience being a favorite, I had no interest courting his favoritism again. In 1978 V. Arkin was appointed the head of a section which dealt with probabilistic economic processes.

Danilov-Danilian

It is time to come back to 1967, when I passed the first phase of favoritism and was replaced by a new favorite, Victor Danilov-Danilian. At first, Danilov-Danilian worked in my section, but soon, as the

favorite, he was given an independent section. A mathematician by
profession, Danilov-Danilian graduated from MGU in the 1950s. He
was a competent and accurate mathematical economist who also had a
tremendous knowledge of music and a unique collection of records. He
was somewhat lacking in creative activity in the socioeconomic sphere,
which is important for a favorite. Therefore, he was unable to formulate a new platform for the institute, and the hopes pinned on him were
not justified. He soon entered the third phase of favoritism: abuse.
At that time, Danilov-Danilian, together with Faerman, who began to
work separately from Ovsienko and me, did a lot of work on the preparation of a book which systematizes the basic results obtained by
TSEMI on the theory of optimal functioning in a socialist economy. (7)

In 1971 a collective group of favorites, including Baranov, V.
Danilov-Danilian (now as one-third of the triumvirate), and M. Zavelskii,
was organized. Baranov, who had experience in work on input-output
tables, as one of those who received the State Prize for the elaboration
of input-output tables in 1968, and organizational skills, headed the
division. Danilov-Danilian and Zavelskii worked with him as heads of
sections. Zavelskii, who had a sharp awareness of social problems,
worked with the others on elaborating models in which the emphasis
was on the representation of the economy as a model of equilibrium.
Regions were selected as initial objects; this revealed the problem of
the interrelations between the central power and the republics in the
area on the use of the securities created by them.

In the previous research, with the global criterion of optimality
clearly posited, the present problem was not manifest; it silently moved
about as an unclear assumption about the equal weights of all the participants in the criterion. In the meantime, this problem was acute because
many republics have rich natural resources and think that their federal
governments are robbing them, which is one of the reasons for the
growing nationalism in the republics. After posing the problem and
understanding its difficulties, the authors tried to conceal it.

In the elaborated model dealing with the introduction of regions,
the question of the connection of regional and branch management was
formulated clearly. In previous works on optimal planning, only one
type of unit, which in essence was understood as the branch aspect of
management, was examined. The authors of the new program in
TSEMI produced drafts on the coordination of branch and regional aspects of management. Finally, attention was focused on questions of
the social mobility of the population and on incentives for attracting
workers to certain regions. These problems also had not figured
earlier in models of the optimal functioning of the national economy.
Great attention was called to the practicality of this model's implemen-

tation. The work's attraction lay precisely in the creation of an experimental model suitable for the goals of practical national-economic
planning. It is possible that in the maximum program, it was even
proposed that the work conducted be capable of becoming a competitive
variant of the national economic plan. In any event, the plan attracted
several political leaders who were antagonistic to the Gosplan.

Baranov

Baranov's program for the work of the division was announced as
the battle plan of TSEMI. Work plans in all other divisions of the institute were to be subordinated to and coordinated with the new program.
The staff of Baranov's section approximated 150 people. The diversity
of trends cultivated in the institute included not only various applications of mathematical methods in economics, but also various paths to
the same goal. To put it more simply, Fedorenko encouraged competition at the institute among different groups following different paths
to the same direction. Following the proverb, "the pike is in the river
so that the carp won't fall asleep," Fedorenko created a paralleled division which was headed by the "pike," Pugachev. It is true that Pugachev's
program differed in some respects from the program of his rivals. In
it, the accent was on the computing aspect of the already posed traditional hierarchical system of optimal planning. Pughachev contacted the
Chief Computer Center of the Gosplan and succeeded in enlisting Victor
Cherniavskii, a Doctor of Economic Sciences, to help with the work. A
man of the older generation, an economist close to the traditional form
of thought in economic ideology, Cherniavskii joined quite actively in
working on the application of mathematical methods to economics, particularly in the sphere of branch planning. Before his transfer to
TSEMI, he had worked for several years in the division on the Application of Mathematical Methods and Computers for Economic Activities
in the Gosplan.

On the whole, Pugachev's division, in fact smaller in number than
Baranov's section, played a secondary role in the atomic project, as
by analogy the project with the experimental model of optimal planning
was called.

NONOPTIMAL PLANNING

The third division, long-range planning, created for competition
with Baranov's division, was headed by the "half-favorite," Boris
Mikhalevskii. (8) Mikhalevskii's basic interest was concentrated
around the elaboration of statistically verified models of medium-range

planning. In the ideology of planning, he was basically oriented toward
the production function and its disaggregation and aggregation. The
very attempt to connect macro-economic models with branch models of
the national economy is attractive. It stands out against the background
of the above-mentioned conceptions of planning, in which significance is
not attached to macro-economic specificity.

Mikhalevskii

Mikhalevskii graduated from the history faculty of Moscow State
University in the beginning of the 1950s. Even at the university, he
manifested great interest in social and political questions. After obtaining access to the German archives brought to the Soviet Union after
the war, he did a comparative analysis of the laws adopted during the
1930s in Fascist Germany with those in the USSR. It turned out that
many of these laws were very much alike and sometimes as little as
two weeks separated the adoption of a law in Germany and the adoption
of a similar law in the Soviet Union. (9)
    At the university, Mikhalevskii, to some degree, sided with
Krasnopevtsev's group, who after Stalin's death tried to write a new
book on the history of the Communist Party in the Soviet Union and to
send it to Poland for publication. In the mid-1950s the members of
this group were arrested and sent to concentration camps. Mikhalevskii's
participation in the group was not proven, and he was not arrested, but
his known closeness to these infidels was a strike against him. For a
long time he could not get work in his field, and at one time he was even
obliged to work as a stevedore. Finally he was hired as an editor for
the journal, Voprosy Ekonomiki, from which he went to the Scientific
Research Institute of Labor. I don't know when Mikhalevskii began to
get interested in economics and particularly in mathematical economics,
but I do know that he had defended his Ph.D. thesis in economics and
had studied mathematics in the mid-1950s. Therefore, when Nemchinov
created his laboratory, Mikhalevskii's invitation to it seemed entirely
natural.
    For a long time he was the only Ph.D. in Economics at the labora-
tory. The workers called him KEN (kandidat ekonomicheskikh nauk)--
Ph.D. in Economics. Mickalevskii was a person of democratic convictions. Apparently the idea of optimization as the embodiment of
centralized planning was basically foreign to him. In the fall of 1965
at a small TSEMI meeting, our collective work was being discussed.
Mikhalevskii, who took part in the discussion, suddenly began to reproach us, saying that our work contradicted the decisions of the
September 1965 Plenum of the Central Committee of the CPSU, which

was aimed at developing initiative and decentralization. The reproach
was not completely fair, as the basic idea of our work was decentralization (mathematically corresponding to the decompositional procedures).
We also spoke, though to a lesser extent, about market, but of course
all questions of decentralization considered in our work were devoid of
social thematics (forms of property, etc.). More precisely, all our
suggestions were directed at improving the technology of planning
within the framework of that same social system.

What was unusual in Mikhalevskii's remarks was the political evaluation of our work. Although it was 1965 and the chairman took Mikhalevskii to task for unfair criticism, it was still unpleasant to have your
work contrasted with the decisions of central Party organs. However,
never before had I heard any political reproaches from Mikhalevskii.
While this particular incident was not in keeping with Mikhalevskii's
usual behavior, I have focused attention on it to emphasize that in a
struggle of passions, progressively-minded scholars who are, on the
whole, decent, sometimes resort to political indictments when dealing
with opponents.

Mikhalevskii's "scientific" criticism of the idea of optimality was
also somewhat unusual; it was not really criticism in essence. Mikhalevskii was an ironical sort of person, and when there was talk of optimal models among a group of people, he maligned them and scoffed
at them in every way. If one of those present was in the mood for a
serious conversation, it was difficult for him to change Mikhalevskii's
tone. I remember at the end of 1963 when the director proposed that
Iu. Gavrilets, B. Mikhalevskii, V. Pugachev and I prepare a speech
together on the development of theoretical research in the institute.
The discussion quickly reached a deadlock because of the noted peculiarities of Mikhalevskii's criticism. I proposed that we split up into
pairs and try to prepare the speech in tandem, and it fell to me to work
with Mikhalevskii. I was prepared for a serious discussion with him
about the theoretical problems of optimality I had put forward, but
Mikhalevskii suddenly began to agree with me on all points. As a
scholar, Mikhalevskii preferred applied research; he was not inclined
toward theoretical research.

Mikhalevskii must be given his due: he had an excellent knowledge
of Soviet statistics. At the end of the 1960s, for example, he wrote a
report with Fedorenko and Shatalin to the Central Committee of the
CPSU about Gosplan's work. In it, inapplicable methods of planning
not dealt with in the press were revealed; it appeared that the country
was heading for a severe financial crisis. The group of questions examined in the classified report testifies to its political acuity. Passions
raged about this report for quite a while; it had advocates and opponents

on the level of the Central Committe of the CPSU, Gosplan, and the
Presidium of the Academy of Sciences. This variety of reactions
demonstrates that there was no solidarity among the leadership of the
country. The matter ended with a compromise between the warring
sides. The scapegoat turned out to be Mikhalevskii who was removed
from his position as head of the division but allowed to remain as head
of the section, so that he did not suffer materially.

Knowledge of Soviet statistics had further repercussions for
Mikhalevskii. Apparently he was thinking about emigrating, but his
access to classified material prevented this. Shortly before his death--
he perished tragically on a canoe trip in May of 1973--he refused to
work on the area of economics which involved classified material, and
said he intended to return to research on the German economy, the
subject of his work as a young man.

Mikhalevskii's Articles

Mikhalevskii advocated economic-mathematical methods, since he
had been the deputy to the editor-in-chief of the journal Ekonomika i
Matematicheskie Metody, for a long time. It seems to me that on the
whole, he headed the journal well. He allowed various points of view,
secured orders for articles from the leading Western economists, and
permitted their publication. It is also important to note that there were
almost no abusive articles "unmasking bourgeois economists" printed
in the journal, and that the leadership of the journal was more than
once reproached by the workers in the science section of the Central
Committee of the CPSU.

Mikhalevskii published many works on mathematical economics,
which were basically devoted to Western economic models and conceptions, but I do not know a man in the Soviet Union who can say that he
read these works and understood them. For a long time, my friends
and I were curious why we could not understand Mikhalevskii's works.
Finally, one of my friends decided to organize a group of sufficiently
objective and qualified people with whom to discuss an excerpted article
of Mikhalevskii's. This friend did not like Mikhalevskii, and the feeling
was mutual; thus, do human passions further the development of science.
He chose the article, "A Single-Sector Dynamic Model with Structural
Disequilibria," published in the journal, Ekonomika i Matematicheskie
Metody (vol. 6, no. 4, 1970). A young mathematician from the Institute
of Economics of the Academy of Sciences who was working on macroeconomic models was invited to speak on the article.

The bulk of the article was an exposition of an article by a Western
economist, M. Bruno, "The Estimation of Factor Contribution to Growth

Under Structural Disequilibrium" (International Economics Review, vol. 9, no. 1, 1968), to which Mikhalevskii conscientiously gave the corresponding reference. Mikhalevskii was trying to generalize the results of the Western scholar to a case with three production factors, including in the model natural resources as well as labor and capital, with a more general group of production functions. However, these generalizations proved to be incorrect; the elementary mathematical errors were disgraceful. The appearance of such an article was possible because no one reviewed Mikhalevskii's work before it was published, since he was one of the leaders of the journal. The members of the editorial board who were able to understand the text did not want to spend time reading articles which were remote from their own interests. After our discussion of the article, we appointed the main speaker to go to Mikhalevskii and tell him about the mistakes we found. Mikhalevskii listened silently and indifferently to these remarks, although in essence they discredited the article.

Another article by Mikhalevskii, "A Qualitative Definition of a Developing System," published in Ekonomika i Matematicheski Metody (vol. 8, no. 1, 1972) occupies a special place. I do not want to cite separate excerpts from the article because they might seem humiliating. On the whole, the tone of the article is striking in its boundless pseudoscience. It is written in a language, which I think is impossible for any Soviet economist-mathematician to comprehend. In an article of twenty-one pages, there are quotations from 158 publications of Western authors. Because Mikhalevskii was known for his negative attitude toward abstract theoretical problems, this article is even more amazing with its especially abstract character on the channel of systems theory. The article was like a burst of wounded pride, an attempt to show that its author, too, was capable of the highest level of theoretical analysis.

Baranov

At the beginning of the 1970s, it became clear that Baranov's work program was threatened. The difficulties in the realization of the program elaborated in Baranov's division were first and foremost engendered by the necessity to find statistical data for the experimental model. It was also difficult to work out computer programs for the equipment available.

As always, personal relations interfered. These difficulties arose under quite objective conditions. In an oligarchical system of management, it is necessary to assign one person to establish external connections. This person was Baranov, the most appropriate person for the given role. However, he became distracted by diplomatic work, and he spent less time on the scientific development of the program. As a result, Danilov-Danilian and Zavelskii decided that the work program prepared as a monograph could be published without Baranov, although Baranov had taken part in the elaboration of the programs and the participants had agreed to a three-way union. It is possible that under normal circumstances, when scientific works are signed only by those who really contributed to the scientific elaboration of the problem, such a division of functions seems justified. Under established conditions, however, of leaders signing scientific work in which they did not participate directly, the conflict between Baranov and his colleagues became more acute.

The previously mentioned difficulties, which were revealed in the implementation of the project for the experimental model of optimal planning and the new opportunities for Fedorenko to distinguish himself, led in 1972 to a replacement of the favorites. The old favorites continued to work on their model; everything had not yet been squeezed out of them. But they were deprived of their former prestige and the corresponding blessings, first and foremost the hiring of new workers. Thus Baranov, Danilov-Danilian and Zavelskii passed through the first phase of favoritism and entered the second.

The 1975-90 Plan

The new opportunities for TSEMI were connected with the elaboration of a long-range plan for the development of the USSR during 1975-90, proclaimed at the 24th Congress of the Party. This plan was described in a document to which great significance was attached. It was to replace the old Party program in which Khrushchev, in response to the Chinese pretensions of arriving at Communism, outlined a no less adventuristic program of great leaps, the building of Communism in 1980. After Khrushchev's removal, this program has been mentioned as little as possible.

According to the established tradition, no one bore responsibility for the quality of the perspective plan for 1975-90. It is not by chance that the joke about Khodzha Nasreddin is recalled in this connection. Somehow, passers-by noticed Nasreddin standing near a tea-shop with his donkey, before which was lying a copy of the Koran. They asked him what was the meaning of this. To this, Nasreddin replied that he had made an agreement with the emir to try to teach the donkey to read the Koran in ten years. The agreement, added Nasreddin, was safe; in ten years, the emir would die, or the donkey would die, or Nasreddin would die himself.

True, in the work on the composition of the new perspective plan there were difficulties in principle for TSEMI and its director--the opposition of the competing organization, the Gosplan, and the forces standing behind them.

In any event, in 1972 Fedorenko began to develop the problems of perspective planning energetically as the primary work. After tremendous effort in overcoming the opposition of several workers in the Gosplan and the Central Committee of the CPSU, Fedorenko succeeded in enlisting in TSEMI a group of leading specialists from the Scientific Research Economics Institute of Gosplan (NIEI) who were working on perspective planning. Among them were such scholars as Alexander Anchishkin, Emil Ershov, Nikolai Soloviev, and Iuri Iaromenko. These scholars were anxious to move to TSEMI because it was difficult for them to work in a bureaucratic institute with a director who had comparatively little influence and was trying to exploit them mercilessly.

Anchishkin

Alexander Anchishkin, a Doctor of Economic Sciences, headed the newly-created division at TSEMI; in fact, he was its complete ruler. He was an economist of the new generation. His father, Ivan Anchishkin, was quite a famous economist. Ivan Anchishkin was known not for his scientific works--he was an extremely conservative economist--but for his honesty. In 1948, while secretary of the Party organization of the Institute of Economics of the Academy of Sciences, at the meeting for the discussion of the cosmopolitans, he very actively restrained the passions of such black-hundred types as Lazutkin and those like him. (10)

Alexander Anchishkin was a decent, cultured man with diplomatic abilities, who worked on scientific problems. After graduating in the mid-1950s from the Economics Faculty of MGU, he worked for many years in NIEI, where he obtained much knowledge and experience in the sphere of perspective planning. By inclination, as Anchishkin said, he is a practicioner. He is one of the best econometricians in the Soviet Union, and recently, he was elected as a Corresponding Member of the Academy of Sciences.

Basically, Anchishkin was concerned with the direct preparation of the proposals of the Academy of Sciences for the perspective plan. For a while he stayed at the Uzkoe Rest Home of the Academy of Sciences outside of the city with Fedorenko and Shatalin where he succeeded in gradually enlisting new qualified workers and in expanding the research. Thus, Iuri Levada, Doctor of Science in Philosophy and one of the leading sociologists in the Soviet Union, was enlisted.

The theoretical foundation for the investigations conducted on

perspective planning in the section was the production function, as well
as the growth theory. This trend in mathematical-economic research
had been very little developed in the USSR because optimal planning and
input-output tables had for a long time obstructed other significant
trends for the composition of perspective plans. In the Soviet Union,
there still is not much work to be done on the assimilation of Western
achievements in growth theory; these theories are primarily an object
for criticism as anti-Marxist offspring.

Anchishkin was soon declared the favorite of TSEMI. In 1972-73
he was in the first phase of favoritism; at meetings the director pro-
nounced his name with an emotional tremor, adding many epithets to
it. All sorts of blessings flooded Anchishkin's division.

Leibkind and Maiminas

Parallel with the creation of the new-favorite-set-of-problems (the
question of perspective planning in TSEMI) another set of problems also
began to be developed. These problems were postulated by Iuri Leibkind and Efrem Maiminas, Doctors of Economic Sciences. This set of
problems also concerned the questions of perspective planning, and
was connected with the formation of a tree of goals and the elaboration
of programs.

Such a trend has great interest on a theoretical plane. It is common
knowledge that in the army, on a line with the fronts (the analogue of the
territorial administrations), with subdivisions specializing in the form
of adopted equipment (the analogue of the functionalist aspects of management), such a structure as an operation is still used. In economics,
elaborations of programs for the implementation of individual complex
jobs (operations) also have meaning. Such is the experience of the
United States, the Soviet Union, and other countries. The difficulties
lie in joining the general development, including both its functional and
regional aspects, with the elaboration and implementation of many such
programs. (11)

A section was also created for the favorites, concerned with these
problems, and Leibkind was made the head. He was one of the first
young people who came to the Laboratory of Economic-Mathematical
Methods. In the mid-1960s, he went to work in the Division on the
Application of Mathematical Methods and the Computers in Economic
Activities in the Gosplan. There he worked for many years, particularly on introducing computers to the mechanization of the existing
technology of planning. Leibkind was among the new type of managers
in science who combined an ability to work with people, with the knowledge of the system functioning in reality, and the understanding of the
contemporary scientific methods of investigation.

Maiminas was the leader of this trend. He was invited by Nemchinov to work at Moscow State University in the Department of Mathematical Methods for the Analysis of Economics. Maiminas' basic work
in this department had been his teaching duties. However, he received
half of his salary as head of a section in TSEMI. Usually the situation
is the reverse; a worker in the Academy of Science receives half his
salary from the educational institution. An active person, Maiminas
had a gift for precise thought and many characteristics of a fighter.
However, his caution prevented him from achieving a higher position,
but perhaps it enabled him to maintain what he had achieved. Maiminas
prefered to work on new problems unconnected with ideology. His book
on economic cybernetics was devoted to the technology of obtaining and
processing economic information. (12)

Leibkind and Maiminas also passed through the first phase of
favoritism in 1972-73.

The development of the two last trends at the institute provoked
certain contradictions in its ideological platform. Although Fedorenko
continued to say that all these trends enter into the system of optimal
functioning in a socialist economy, it was apparently necessary to alter
this platform and to put the work into a more general program in which
optimal functioning would occupy the proper place.

"A new invention," wrote Victor Shklovskii, "does not destroy the
old, but only narrows the sphere of its application. After all, prose
was developed in art later than poetry, but poetry has remained." (13)

SUMMARY

In conclusion I would like to say a few words about the foreign
policy of TSEMI. Right from the beginning Fedorenko was interested
in enlarging the institute and making it an empire. He was quite suc-
cesful in achieving this in the 1960s. Thus colonies, branches of
TSEMI, were established in Leningrad and Tallin. These branches
were founded on the basis of previously existing organizations which
had mathematicians on their staff and computers and did not really
know where to direct their efforts.

The Leningrad branch of TSEMI (LOTSEMI) grew into quite a large
organization. V. Novozhilov, the famous Soviet economist, worked in
LOTSEMI until the last day of his life. Another economist, F. Diderikhs,
in spite of his political confusion and devotion to Marxism and all this
after he spent about twenty years during Stalin's time in the labor camps,
did a lot of good for the economic-mathematical trend. He did his best
in trying to cultivate an interest for economics among those mathematicians who were in the majority at LOTSEMI.

Among the mathematicians who were engaged in economic research
at LOTSEMI, one first of all has to point to Boris Pittel. His work in
the field of probabilistic economic models on the basis of maximizing
the level of entropy was of a genuinely pioneering nature in the Soviet
Union. Pittel energetically tried to use these models for improving the
work of municipal transportation systems in Leningrad. In 1975 Pittel
emigrated from the Soviet Union and has recently been tenured by the
State University of Ohio. The other interesting mathematicians at
LOTSEMI were Vladimir Lifshits, who introduced a number of good
ideas from mathematical logic into linear programming and emigrated
from the Soviet Union in 1976, and V. Varshavskii, who worked on the
games of automatons. Concurrently with the expansion of the empire,
Fedorenko was greatly concerned with strengthening his division by
attracting whole groups of scholars interested in mathematical economics
from other institutes. Such was a group from the Institute of Labor,
which included N. Rimashevskaia, V. Kuznetsov, and N. Rabkina, etc.,
who were working on the problems of the standard of living. As I have
already indicated, Fedorenko was able to bring one group of scholars
from NIEI who were working with the econometric models of long-run
planning.

The Decline of TSEMI

In recent years, however, the "imperial might" of TSEMI has been
under decline. For various reasons TSEMI not only lost its branches
in Leningrad and Tallin and the power to involve work groups from
other institutes, but also has started to lose its own scholars as well.

In 1976 TSEMI received a "strong blow" from the right. An authoritative commission was organized by the Moscow Party Committee to
conduct an investigation of TSEMI's activities. An unusually high percentage of people from TSEMI who emigrated to the West served as an
immediate pretext for the attack from the right. As a main instrument
for improving the personnel situation in TSEMI, the commission proposed that two deputy directors, Iu. Oleinik and S. Shatalin, be fired;
eighteen sections, most of which had either Jews or nonparty members
for their heads, be disbanded; and certain scholars be expelled for one
reason or another. The disbandment of the sections which were headed
by the Jews was an offering to the anti-Semitic policy of the government.
The rational from this decision ran as follows. The percentage of Jews
in TSEMI was pretty high, although there were no Jews at the top level
and the lowest level; e.g., there were no Jewish janitors. The pre-
dominant number of Jews were concentrated at the middle level, i.e.
heads of sections. The presentation of such a huge percentage was

believed to be dangerous for the stability of the institute; the emigration of the head of a section could paralyze its activities. So here we have a vicious circle: Jews were fired because they might emigrate, and they they emigrated because they were fired.

However, TSEMI came under attack not only from the right but from the left as well. In 1976 there emerged a powerful competitor of TSEMI, the All Union Institute of Systems. D. Gvishiani, the deputy of the Chairman of the Committee for Science and Technology, also known for his liberal views, became the head of this institute. One of the main lines of work of this institute was the system research in the field of economics on the basis of mathematical models. The leading role in this work was held by a couple of dozen scholars who came there from TSEMI. At first the work in mathematical economics was headed by ex-deputy director of TSEMI, S. Shatalin, who was then replaced by the ex-head of the section of TSEMI, V. Davilov-Davilian. L. Kantorovich with a group of his colleagues also came to work at VNIISI.

At this point it is hard to say what contribution this new organization can make to the development of economics. However, potentially this organization has a lot of momentum and can replace TSEMI as the main center for economic-mathematical research.

6 Four Circles of Hell

SUBSTANCE OF THE ECONOMIC DISPUTES

Soviet scholars and politicians can be divided into three groups depending upon their relation to the existing political system. The reactionaries stand for a return to the old Stalinist system in which rigid administrative methods dominate. It should be noted that these people reflect the views of a large number of practical workers, who also dream of a return to the blessed Stalinist times, when there was iron discipline in the country, no difficulties, for example, with manpower supplied by rigid labor assignments and camps with millions of prisoners who provided factories and construction sites with cheap labor. The conservatives are those who are prepared to defend the existing political system in any way possible. The overwhelming majority of economists and politicans belongs to this group. It is then also possible to divide both the reactionaries and the conservatives into at least two groups, the flexible and the inflexible ones, from the standpoint of their ability to change some of their views within their limited political framework. Finally, the modernizers are those economists and politicians who wish to change the existing political system in a liberal way. Every scholar or politican who is involved in economics has developed his own views about the Soviet political system. If this view is not expressed directly or indirectly, we shall consider this economist a conservative, insofar as he silently supports the official view.

Modernizers

I should like to pay more attention here to the modernizers. All the modernizers are united in speaking out against the existing order and thus threatening the interests of people who represent and guard it. We can go even further and divide the modernizers into three groups distinguished by their attitudes towards the limitation on political power.

The radical modernizers seek to organize a modern market economy within the boundaries of a democratic system. Generally such radical demands are put forth by the Soviet dissidents. Some of them fight for the construction of "socialism with a human face," as it was developed by the Czechoslovakian economists in the mid-1960s.

A second group of modernizers, the reformers, express views regarding the improvement of the functioning of a socialist economy. While not directed towards the liquidation of the existing political system, such an improvement nevertheless demands a limiting of political power, either through experimentation or through wide-ranging reform.

Some economists have tried to modernize the economy inductively, i.e., through local experiments which demonstrate that new types of organization are possible and promise considerable economic effectiveness. But when the workers' collectives are given new forms of organization, they may become independent in many ways, and considerably fewer functions will be left for the party apparatus. Let us note, however, that this opposition group has not touched on the existing economic theory. The experiments conducted by this group have been limited by a framework of relatively small units, in which the new type of organizations do not require an extensive application of economic theory. Moreover, these reformers have not understood that the reforms they have introduced in their individual units are not applicable to the economy as a whole or that the overall economic mechanism would have to be changed in order to make these individual reforms effective in a general case.

Some economists attempted to bring about a reform deductively, i.e., applying it to the entire economy. This modernization took place with the well-known economic reform proclaimed by Kosygin in 1965. Most specialists on the Soviet economy would agree that Kosygin's movement came to a halt in large measure because it required extensive limiting of the role of the Communist Party. The economic conception of the reform was insufficient; it was based on the dominant economic theory. This is not surprising when one looks at the research and commentary of the economists conceptualizing the reform, e.g., Evsei Liberman. As we noted earlier, this theory could not insure the implementation of a developed economic mechanism in the 1930s; for the same reasons, it would not have been able to insure the functioning of the Soviet economy in the 1960s.

The third group of modernizers I shall call cosmetologists. They

attempted to bring about changes in the existing political mechanism
by redistributing political power between politicians and scholars. A
lot of them have an inclination to be liberal people, but it is very easy
for them to convert to reactionary views if the reactionaries agree to
share the power with them. The cosmetologists also could be sub-
divided into several subgroups depending upon the extent to which their
ideas change the existing technology of planning.

Nikita Moiseev, a Corresponding Member of the Academy of
Sciences, in an article in the newspaper Izvestiia at the end of the 1960s
addressed himself directly to the necessity of creating at the top level
scientifically based decision-making mechanisms in which scholars
would be included. The evidence of this tendency toward scientific
method and the utilization of academics was linked to hypermodernist
views on the functioning of systems in conditions of uncertainty. The
works of Russel Ackoff and Herbert Simon were particularly interesting
in this respect. (1) Some Soviet mathematicians and engineers who
were applying mathematical methods in economics translated Ackoff's
books A Concept of Corporate Planning and On Purposeful Systems
(together with F. Emery) into Russian for their publication in the
Soviet Union. (2)

Another subgroup of the cosmetologists sought to change the technology of planning by proposing a new concept of optimal planning. Included in this group were such administrative figures as academician
A. Aganbegian, and N. Fedorenko. These economists exerted great
pressure on the development of mathematical modeling in economic
theory.

The third subgroup of cosmetologists was primarily concerned with
some changes in the existing technology of planning through the use of
some mathematical methods, such as input-output tables and the accompanying computer technology. This subgroup of economists was represented by V. Kossov, the deputy of the director of a department of
the Gosplan, and by academician, Anatoli Efimov, the former director
of the Scientific-Research Economics Institute of the Gosplan of the
USSR. The most extreme spokesman of this reformist school of thought
is one of the leaders of the economic-mathematical school, V. Glushkov,
academician and Vice-President of the Ukrainian Academy of Sciences
and Director of the Kiev Institute of Cybernetics. Glushkov played an
important role in advocating the use of the computer to help run the
economy. Glushkov knew no economics. Like any denier, he utilized
the most primitive economic notions as a result of his common sense.
Glushkov attempted to use computers to create a rigidly centralized
system in which salaries were paid and goods were purchased by
computer in order to curtail theft.

Economic Theory

To better understand the positions taken by the above mentioned groups of scholars and politicians, we need to classify Soviet economics. We shall primarily deal with economic theory here, not with applied economics. Economic theory can be divided into two areas: mathematical modeling and institutional theory.

Mathematical modeling involves a series of questions whose exact answers can be derived from mathematical models and experiments. Within the scope of modeling is the investigation of hierarchical systems, an inquiry which uses various kinds of economic parameters (prices, money, etc.). Institutional theory concerns problems such as the formation of financial sources of enterprise through credit, private resources, grants, or other means. Depending on the source studied, institutional economists consider different means of choosing the economic leadership (appointment, elections, self-appointment). Consequently, this part of economic theory defines different economic systems, such as socialism, communism, and capitalism. To a greater or lesser extent, each of the two areas of economic theory touches on Marxist ideology.

The previously discussed classifications, both of people involved in economics and economic theories, could be expressed in the following table.

With human nature such as it is, conflicts occur among these various groups of scholars involved in economics; both reactionaries and modernizers fight with conservatives; the reactionaries and modernizers fight each other. At the same time there are internal conflicts within each group. It is difficult, for example, to achieve unity among the subgroups of the modernizers because they have opposing methods of influencing the political system. The radicals want a fundamental change in the political structure, while the reformists and cosmetologists respectively want only its limitation or preservation. The radical ideas are too dangerous for the powers-that-be, thus causing those in power to consolidate against the radicals. The other two groups of modernizers try to divide the powers-that-be and in this way to enlist the support of politically powerful individuals for the introduction of their new ideas. However, there is a conflict between the cosmetologists and the reformists that, even given their similarities, does not allow them to unite. The reformists think, not with basis, that if the views of the cosmetologists are accepted, the rulers will get the ideas that the way for the "salvation of Russia" has been found and thus will reject reformist's views.

TABLE 6.1. The Conflicting Political Groups and Their Attitudes to Different Parts of Economics

Attitude to the Existing Political System / Part of Economics	Methods which Could Be Investigated by Mathematical Models But Are Not	Institutions	The Attitude to Marxist Ideology
I REACTIONARIES			
Inflexible	#	+	#
Flexible	-	+	E
II CONSERVATIVES			
Inflexible	+	+	E
Flexible	-	+	E
III MODERNIZERS			
Radicals	-	-	E
Reformers	-	-	-
Inductively	+	E	E
Deductively	+	E	E
Cosmetologists	-	+	E
Proposer of a new Optimal Planning Concept	-	+	E
Proposers of some Mathematical Methods	-	+	E

Notes:

Strong support of the existing situation

+ Support of the existing situation

- Negative attitude to the existing situation

E Positive attitude to some aspects of the existing situation and negative to other aspects

Attitudes to Economic-Mathematical Methods

Let us discuss now the struggle between different groups of scholars involved in economics from the standpoint of their attitude to economic-mathematical methods.

Mathematical Knowledge

First of all economic-mathematical methods are distinguished primarily by the fact that they are put forward in a new language which is incomprehensible to the majority of Soviet economists. After the destruction of the economic-mathematical trend during the 1930s, the teaching of mathematics in the economics institutes was severely reduced, and even the rudiments of higher mathematics which the students did encounter were not connected at all with economic themes. The majority of economists who received their education in the 1930s through the 1960s, and they are the majority, do not know mathematics, and it is difficult or impossible for them to assimilate it at this point.

Second, the consistent application of mathematical methods in economics in many respects undermines Marxist theory because Marx dealt with economics most completely; there is no such systematic investigation into humanities and social problems in Marxism. Many major problems touched upon in Das Kapital are being analyzed today with the help of mathematical models. As a result of this analysis, the limitations of Marxist views are being revealed. This is particularly apparent with the use of the methodology of optimal planning. It engenders qualitatively new economic phenomena, even if they are clothed in the usual ideological Marxist rhetoric. Optimal planning, in fact, subscribes to a methodological idea contradicting the labor theory of value, since it maintains that the mathematical parameters used have an economic meaning in expressing the estimates of scarce resources. When the question of the optimal plan estimates was discussed for a particular problem concerning the best use of resources in factories, the traditional economists said that the estimates were simply technical parameters used for the solution to the production problem. Such an answer is impossible at the level of the national-economic model; it belongs in pure economics. The mathematical models are thus perceived fearfully by the generation of economists educated on Marx's Das Kapital.

Third, mathematical methods in certain areas of economics carry with them modern knowledge, and permit Soviet economists to become acquainted with many achievements of Western economics as they learn modern methodology. At the same time, because of the lack of knowledge of Western economic conceptions for the past 100 years, it is difficult for the majority of Soviet economists to master this investigative methodology.

Economic-mathematical methods entail the improvement of the methodology of management. Knowledge of these methods enriches the economists' intuition, and allows them to think more subtly. Only in individual cases, when the model can be saturated with formalized information, can it be used directly for automating the management process. This is why economic-mathematical methods are, in principle, an element of the general knowledge base of any economist, no matter what revolutionary ideas he maintains.

While I have great respect for the courage of the radicals and reformers who are not older than forty and try to achieve socioeconomic transformations, I would like to point out that many of them, although very progressive in institutional economics, reject ideas about mathematical modeling. There are no specialists able to use modern mathematical methods of economic analysis among the radicals and reformers.

Labor Value

They defend Karl Marx's theory of labor value and, within its framework, they attempt to give recommendations for the improvement of the Soviet economic system. One of the active reformers, for example, gave lectures entitled, "K. Marx's Labor Theory of Value and the Improvement of the Mechanism of the Socialist Economy."

The paradox of the position lies in the fact that the Soviet attitude toward the law of labor value often acts as litmus paper to test one's affiliation to the advocates of decentralization and reinforced market relations. This is provoked by the fact that the law of labor value is recognized by many economists as a synonym for the market. For the majority of economists, the Marxist theory of value is true; they think that this theory correctly explains the market mechanism. That is why the economists who reject the effect of the law of labor value are in their own minds those who advocate centralization. It does not matter to them if this rejection is made on the basis of a conservative Marxist point of view--that under socialism the law of labor value will not function and everything will be rigidly planned--or of the Western theories of value and concomitant ideas for constructing a flexible mechanism for the functioning of the economy.

Market Economy

In this connection we run into important negative aspects of the radicals' actions. A prominent industrial society like the Soviet Union

cannot be governed on a primitive understanding of a
Seeing the successes of the Western countries and un
their economic mechanism, a significant portion of t
gentsia, including a number of economists, thinks th
would be to transfer to a system of private enterpris
of competitive forces. They imagine this mechanism very primitively,
as an auction or bazaar, i.e., as a system in which the results of production activities are manifested only after the fact. As a rule, there
is no recognition of the fact that the market represents a developed
mechanism of horizontal relations directed at anticipation, with a complex structure of institutions: banks, stock exchanges, etc. Further
more, under conditions of dynamic large-scale production, the market
mechanism must be connected with the vertical mechanisms of management. The history of Western economies testifies to this; the development of vertical mechanisms came from below, as multileveled hierarchical complex, and from above as a realization for the necessity of
strengthening the role of the state in the economic mechanism. The
whole point lies in the degree of strength in the connections between the
vertical and horizontal mechanisms.

Such considerations are also not always usual for radical Soviet
economists. While seeing the advantage of the market economy, they
have not sufficiently thought out the question of how the market is connected with the state. It seems to them that it is all very simple and a
matter of common sense. Moreover, a lack of understanding of the influence of a country's culture on the development of its economic mechanism leads to Soviet attempts at blind imitation of the experiences of
some Western countries. The lack of education of radical Soviet economists could prove threatening in a crisis situation if in place of the
centralizers, the marketeers seized power. With their primitive understanding of the market, they could produce economic anarchy in the
country, anarchy which could engender a centralization even more rigid
than that now in existence. Yet the radicals did not want to learn the
new economic ideas. It may be that they had no time, because they
were concerned with stormy, and sometimes very stormy, current
events.

I tried to make contact with one such radical. The first thing he
said to me was that my developed principles of the optimal functioning
of a socialist economy supported the present centralized system of
planning and therefore, were worthless. I agreed with him; the reasons
for my agreement can be understood from the previous exposition of the
role of the cosmetologists. At the same time, I told him that in the
problems I had elaborated there were also scientific results which
could help him understand the functioning principles of the system he

was proposing. Realizing how difficult it is to understand a new point of view from books, I suggested to him that we meet a few times so that I could explain to him the basic principles of the theory of optimal economic functioning. He did not accept the suggestion, although we maintained friendly relations. He knew of my sincere respect for his desire to democratize economic life, but also of my critical attitude toward his quite primitive theoretical knowledge.

Conflict between Social Progressiveness and Lack of Knowledge

The conflict between social progressiveness and lack of knowledge in the sphere of mathematical modeling of economic processes is typical of other groups beside the Soviet economists. In 1967 I happened to meet the well-known radical Czech economist, Otto Shik, when he visited TSEMI. The first thing that he said upon seeing me was that an optimal plan could be developed in 150 years, and I agreed with him. However, I noted that the main concern in the economic theory of optimization was not the composition of the optimal plan. The basic goals of this theory were to enrich the intuition of practical workers by helping them understand how to synthesize vertical and horizontal mechanisms. To illustrate this position, I asked Shik how, for example, the rate of interest would be established in the system he proposed. Since he assumed that the state would influence the formation of value parameters, this category was needed. Shik informed me that there would be no problem because in Marxist theory rate of interest was a category of men's relations to production, not of productive forces, and that it was necessary only for stimulation. His answers to questions about the role of taxes, the connections of taxes with prices, etc., were also incomprehensible.

The most bitter attacks on the economic-mathematical trend are coming from the economists of the older generation who spent their whole life defending Marxism, and it does not matter whether these economists are cosmetologists, reformers, conservatives, or reactionaries.

Strumilin

The most active and highly respected pogrom leader against optimal planning, a heavyweight fighter who was the patriarch of Soviet economics, was the recently deceased academician, Stanislav Strumilin. Quite a brilliant man, he had understood the necessity for conformism in the struggle for survival as early as the 1920s. In the 1930s, when the discussion about declining rates was taking place, Strumilin supposedly said, "It is better to stand for high rates than to sit in prison for low ones."

Strumilin's criticism of the optimalists in the 1950s-1960s was
virtually a prepared indictment of them. None of the other heavyweight
economists produced such open political accusations of the optimalists
in such a concentrated form. Strumilin accused the advocates of the
optimal planning theory of deviations from Marxism. As an example
of such deviation, he cited the optimalists' proposal to construct prices
on the basis of marginal instead of average costs. Strumilin also revealed the reasons for such apostasy: the influence of vulgar Western
political economy. Finally, Strumilin maintained that if the proposals
of the advocates of the optimal planning theory were accepted, the
workers' standard of living would deteriorate. Strumilin explained
this deterioration by the fact that the prices for consumer goods would
increase. It never occurred to Strumilin that according to the optimization theory an increase in the prices for consumer goods, generally
speaking, does not occur, because the prices in force are quite close
to the prices of equilibrium for many goods. An increase, however, in
the wholesale prices for the capital heads is offset by a decrease in
turnover tax. The budget does not suffer here because rent payments
and capital interest increase. If the articles written by Strumilin a-
gainst the optimalists in the 1930s and 1940s appeared these people
would be sent to Siberian camps, but in the 1960s this criticism could
not produce such results.

Kronrod

Iakov Kronrod, a Doctor in Economic Sciences, can be included
among the pogrom-leaders in the middleweight category. He was an
industrious, brilliant man, with an excellent knowledge of literature,
a philosophical turn of mind--and, it seems, a prewar philosophy
education--and a comparatively young wife. He read the New York
Times very often in the special repository of the Institute of Economics.
Kronrod supported the economic reform in the 1960s.
    As a rule, traditional economists have criticized the theory of
optimality without proposing answers to the new questions posed by this
theory, but several of the pogrom-leaders, lacking the corresponding
mathematical education, nonetheless tried to produce their own theories
of optimality. At the end of the 1960s, Kronrod prepared a paper in
which he attempted to put forward a theory of optimality. For example,
he proposed a criterion of optimality which had an integral character.
The time for the planned period was determined by the period of the life
expectancy of capital goods. The output of consumer goods, measured
in terms of labor cost, was maximized for the planned period. Kronrod
did not understand that such a criterion lacks logic, because the life

expectancy of capital goods is an unknown variable and must be found
in the solution of the optimization problem. Labor cost, as is well
known, is an average quantity and is the result of the proportions of
different technologies used for producing a given product. In the meantime, the intensities of the use of various technologies are also unknown parameters in the optimization problem. Kronrod's paper was
severely criticized during the discussion. After this, as far as I know,
he did not undertake any new elaboration of problems in the theory of
optimality. In the conflict with his opponents, Kronrod stopped at
nothing; he publicly announced more than once, in particular at a 1968
scientific session devoted to the 150th anniversary of the birth of Karl
Marx, that the advocates of the theory of optimality were burying
Marxism.

Kronrod was injured by his own colleagues many times and quite
painfully for his views, and he was injured with his own weapons. The
last time was in 1972-73 for his interference in the philosophical area
of political economy. The classics of Marxism-Leninism have taught
that the indicator of the development of a society is the level of labor
productivity achieved in it. In 1936, Stalin announced that socialism
in the Soviet Union was basically built. By the 1970s, it had been being
built for more than thirty-five years already; at the same time, the level
of Soviet labor productivity in the USSR was lower than that of the developed capitalist countries. Economists began to think of how to
remedy the situation. In this connection Kronrod proposed to develop
the Marxist theory of formations in approximately the following manner.
On the one hand, he introduced a broad concept of the era, using the
Communist era as an illustration, and on the other, a narrower concept
of the mode of production. After this, he proposed the concept of the
developed socialist mode of production which would enter into the
socialist formation of the Communist era. When this mode of production was created, a level of labor productivity, exceeding that of the
capitalists would have been achieved. However, Kronrod did not take
into account that such a proposal threatened political unpleasantness;
if there was not yet a developed socialist society in the Soviet Union,
then how could it set an example to the East European socialist countries,
several of which have also basically built socialism? To counter the ill
effect of Kronrod's postulations, it was announced that the Soviet Union
had a developed socialist society. Kronrod was subjected to powerful
criticism and even persecution for his theorizing. During the reorganization of the Institute of Economics, he was removed from the position
of head of the section of political economy and at one time was only a
provisionally appointed senior researcher.

During the months when Kronrod was being criticized for his

philosophical works, he and other reactionary economists prepared
and later published in the journal, Planovoe Khoziaistvo, articles
against optimal planning, the best tradition of name-calling criticism. (3)
Economist-mathematicians who had tried to help him when he was being
persecuted were insulted by this performance. In the middle of 1973,
while coming out with the recurrent pogrom against the optimalists at
a meeting organized by the journal Planovoe Khoziaistvo, Kronrod
cleverly tried to separate Fedorenko from the optimalists and to put
all the blame for the ideology of TSEMI on S. Shatalin and myself. He
knew that I already intended to emigrate, and if one remembers that
every emigrant is a renegade, the conclusion is clear. Before this,
Kronrod had not made any political accusations about me and had even
tried to demonstrate signs of his respect to me. I offered Kronrod and
several other gifted people similar to him but not involved in economics
one naive question: "Why do you resort to name-calling; why do you
sew the label of anti-Marxist onto your opponent instead of acting only
within the bounds of logic?"

For these scholars the unofficial argument of the inadmissibility
of the new trends was that it is necessary first to reestablish Marxism
in the Soviet Union, because the propagandists of science had made
Marxism banal and were even hiding a number of Marx's manuscripts.
After this, they continued, if it was discovered that it was impossible
to explain certain phenomena with the help of Marxism, they would then
determine the advisability of instituting new means.

This argument reminds me of the following allegory. Imagine that
one hundred years ago a catastrophe had taken place on earth. As a
result, the country in which the inventor of the steam engine was living
was cut off from the rest of the world--I don't want to get involved in
the argument about whether this country was Russia, since I had been
taught in the postwar Stalin period that the Cherepanov brothers in-
vented the steam engine--and the inventor fell into a coma and awoke
after one hundred years had passed. The first thing he asked was,
"What is the coefficient for the efficiency of the steam engine?" He was
told that it was 3%, but he knew that in his time the coefficient had been
equal to 5%, and it was theoretically possible for it to be even 8%. Then
this inventor exclaimed with youthful enthusiasm, "To work, comrades;
we must reestablish the previous coefficient for efficiency and then go
further." However, information from the outside world indicated that
there were already electric locomotives, rockets, etc. in other countries,
and his comrades suggested that instead of spending energy on building
steam engines, it would make more sense to turn to the development of
new types of transportation. To this the inventor answered, "Well,
first let us reestablish the lost capacity of the steam engine, squeeze
out of it all that we can, and then let us go further."

In personal conversations, as if by agreement, Kronrod and his fellows cited the same arguments, but they could not often come to an agreement because they were fighting among themselves. (4)

Levin

One example of older generation economists who was a lightweight attacker of the theory of optimal planning is Grigori Levin. Levin had a certain amount of knowledge in the sphere of the economics of construction. He was quite a capable orator and demagogue. Personally, Levin was well liked. For a long time he was not a Party member, but several years ago, about the age of sixty, he joined the party. He decisively rejected the prices of the optimal plan and was against including the capital interest in expenses. He debated this with approximately the following pseudo-scientific arguments: "Capital investment is not a condition of growth, but the result of growth."

At the end of the 1960s, Levin undertook the defense of his doctoral dissertation in the Institute of Economics. In this dissertation many economic-mathematical methods were criticized, but Levin's arguments were ignorant, and furthermore, he spurned his opponents as anti-Marxists. The defense of the dissertation attracted a huge audience of several hundred people, who came expecting a show. It was clear that if Levin could defend the dissertation, a certain precedent would be set. Among those sitting in the hall were two or three people who wanted to obtain quite high positions in science in the same way that Levin sought to advance, without knowing the new methods of economic analysis. Because Levin was up in arms against not only the economist-mathematicians, but also against other economists who supported the necessity for calculating the period of recoupment, the whole council voted against him.

It is interesting to note that class solidarity among the Soviet economists sometimes plays a more powerful role than national enmity. Thus, the defense of Levin's dissertation was supported by economists of Russian origin, none of whom could be accused of loving Jews, but who could fearlessly be included among the conservatives. It was basically Jewish economists, standing for a different class position than Levin's, who came out against this Jewish man. A tremendous fuss about Levin and all sorts of scenes followed his defense.

It would seem that in the face of the common enemy the economists who did not accept mathematical methods and economists using these methods would have to unite. However, they also have a conflict among themselves, and the basic reason is the attempt to replace one monopoly in science by another. (5)

Input-Output Tables Advocates Versus Optimalists

The combat between the advocates of input-output tables and the optimalists was quite cruel. In 1958 at a meeting of the Moscow Mathematical Society at Moscow State University, L. Kantorovich gave a report on optimal planning. A group of workers at the Laboratory for Electronic Control Machines, who were working on input-output tables tried to obstruct Kantorovich, almost accusing him of plagiarizing the ideas of J. Von Neumann. I also remember combative debates as early as 1960. At that time, Alexander Kronrod and V. Belkin had already written equations for calculations of prices on the basis of input-output tables. Kronrod abused the ideas of linear programming in every way. He thought that they were an unworthy object of study for a prominent mathematician, because any mathematician acquainted with linear algebra could invent these methods. I replied that we would allow his point, that the methods of linear programming were quite easy to invent, but the value of these methods for economists was not measured by the labor expended to create them. They were interesting because they assisted in the development of a new economic ideology, new principles for planning in which, as Kantorovich noted, the prices came out as an implement for the composition of the plan and its realization.

There were also more than a few arguments among the proponents of various trends on the theory of optimal planning, but the character of the arguments depended on the type of personality involved. (Fortunately, in this case the number of pogrom-leaders of Pugachev's type was small.) One of these arguments concerned the methods of describing an economy. The disparity centered around two methods of description: one utilized models of vector optimization, known in the literature as models of equilibrium; and the other depended upon models with the global criterion of optimality.

A discussion about these two methods of description took place in 1968 at the All-Union Conference of Sociologists in Sukhumi between V. Shliapentokh, who defended the equilibrium models as a method for description of the economic system, and me, representing the position which described systems with the help of the global criterion of optimality. The conference proceedings, including our speeches were published, (6) but the essence of our disagreements came to the following. Shliapentokh thought that a system did not have criteria of optimality and that, therefore, it was necessary to describe an economy with the help of models of equilibrium. (It must be noted that at this time, Western models of equilibrium were relatively unknown to Soviet economists working on mathematical economics, but optimal models were prevalent, and only a limited number of mathematicians, first among them, Pittel, had then become interested in these models.) My position was that a system had a criterion of optimality, and it could be determined from without, from the suprasystem. Pointing out that the human race was transient, that it occupied a definite place in the evolution of the world, organic and nonorganic, my position was expressed in the fact that I proposed that the criterion of the development of the human race was its creation of a new and more perfect form than itself. The peculiarity of this form, as distinguished from certain biological forms, lay in the fact that it was created outside of its creator; usually the forms were changed by using the previous form as their substrate. I thought that the available knowledge and resources should be accepted as constraints for the system. Already acquainted with Olds' works on emotional mechanisms, I thought that the emotional structures of individuals also had an objective basis and were therefore constraints.

Ideologically, in the eyes of the leading progressive sociologists who had come to the conference, Shliapentokh's position was remarkably attractive. Every mention of my criterion engendered in these sociologists indignation, since it suggested to them a utopia in which the dictator knows what the people need. It was natural that Shliapentokh's position provoked indignation from the reactionary sociologists who were also at the conference. On the other hand, although my ideological scheme was closer to the reactionary sociologists in that it retained the criterion of optimality, on the whole it was foreign to them, if only because it used mathematical methods with which they had little familiarity. Only later did I understand that out entire discussion about the presence or absence of the criterion of optimality was merely the result of our lack of understanding of the fact that mutually transforming methods for the description of systems exist. The introduction of the criterion of optimality is nothing other than a method for expression in the models of equilibrium of the principle of distribution of income; this principle as the criterion of optimality is also based on considerations outside of the model. The presence of the managing organ is not connected with these methods of describing the system.

Summary

Even thought I now acknowledge the idea of mutually transforming methods for the description of a system, I by no means believe that the boundaries among various methods for the description of a system should be erased. Each method has definite images which stimulate our understanding. Furthermore, as follows from the experience of the historical development of the variation principle of mechanics, the

methods for describing a system also play an important i\
The Church used the variation principle in order to prove\
of God, since in this principle lies the aspiration of nature\
fection, the attainment of the maximum-minimum. Therefc   ..um-
ber of scientific materialists even rebelled against the variation principle and its proponents because they thought that it would strengthen
the Church they hated.

Finally, I want to mention that it is extremely characteristic of
the present state of affairs in Soviet economics that it is often impossible
to answer the question of whether a certain economist or economic institute as a whole is progressive or regressive. As a rule, if an economist is progressive in one direction, he is regressive in another.
The terms progressive and regressive can be used only relative to the
established conditions. Concerning the absolute evaluation of the trends
themselves, the answer to this question is that all trends are necessary.
The only exceptions are the trends whose examinations on the whole are
subject to the action of the law of the excluded middle and this relates
primarily to the mathematical modeling.

On the question of the possible preservation of the diversity of
opinions in economics, depending on the interrelations among the economists, the following may be assumed. The sharpest criticism of
pluralism in economics is from the economists of the older generation,
who have inherited the Stalinist style of scientific life. Among the
young and middle-aged economists, who were basically educated in the
post-Stalin period, one encounters such critics quite rarely. But if
leaders should ask to destroy the plurality in economics, then it must
be assumed that a sufficient number of critics also will be found among
the new generation of economists, if only because the majority of them
do not have and are not now obtaining the corresponding knowledge of
new trends in economics.

CONFLICTS BETWEEN SCHOLARS AND PLANNERS

During the last twenty years, experience has been gained in introducing economic-mathematical methods at various levels of they Soviet
managerial hierarchy. Presently, under pressure from the country's
leaders, the automated management systems (ASU) are being introduced
into factories. These systems, based on primitive mathematical models,
are part of the present planning technology. The immediate effect of
the ASU is not great, and sometimes it is even negative because of the
increased expenses for servicing the computers. Apparently, the effect
of computers was basically indirect. I was able to observe this in an
assembly shop for cameras at the Leningrad Optical Factory. The

introduction of a primitive computer, for example, required the creation of a warehouse to allow the present inventory of components to
appear rapidly; thus, the introduction furthered a rise in the number of
production sites, with all the concomitant results. After the production
was regularized, the computer could be removed; in fact, in this case,
it stopped working.

The introduction of automated management systems at the higher
levels of management comes up against great difficulties. Various
trends in the development of Soviet economics cannot but touch upon
the interests of managers on different hierarchical levels. Thus, economic mathematical methods require a great deal of additional knowledge, which the manager often cannot master. The introduction of
these methods also might lead to a partial reduction of the managerial
personnel, a problem that authorities face in overcoming resistance.
For example, the workers at the former section on the Application of
Mathematical Methods and Computers in Economic Activities unsuccessfully tried to automate the existing planning technology. One of
the decisive reasons for this failure was the fear that with less need
for manual workers, subdivisions would be consolidated. In more
complicated situations when the introduction of mathematical methods
entails a transformation of the existing planning technology, to relate
the difficulties simply to the conservatism of the planning apparatus
would be an oversimplification; the immediate reason is the incapacity
of the existing economic system to assimilate it. Let us start at the
higher level of the hierarchy.

The Introduction of Input-Output Tables

In order to accelerate the introduction of input-output tables a
special laboratory was created several years ago in the Scientific Research Economics Institute of the Gosplan. F. Klotsvog headed this
laboratory, and it was given special premises in the Gosplan building.
However, no serious shifts took place with the introduction of input-
output tables in Gosplan's procedures. The workers' negative attitudes
toward input-output tables were partly a reason for it. These attitudes
were expressed by the chairman of the Gosplan, N. Baibakov:

Unfortunately in recent years, theoretical and methodological
work on the balance of the national economy has grown weaker.
One of the reasons for this was apparently the exaggeration
of the role of input-output tables and the opposition by several
scholars of the latter to the balance of the national economy.
While not at all minimizing the significance of input-output

tables, it must be emphasized that it is a component part of
the balance of the national economy which proposes the use
of the entire complex of balances--material, cost, labor.
Therefore its future development and improvement, including, naturally, its mathematization as well, is a
matter of the utmost importance. (7)

It seems to me that the main reasons for the difficulties in introducing input-output tables are rooted elsewhere. While I was studying
problems on the introduction of new technologies, I noticed that attempts
to introduce the new production technologies were remarkably difficult
because they interfered with the production force and distracted people
from their tasks. If the technologies were really new and embraced
many parts of the enterprise, it was necessary either to stop the enterprise, at times right next to the old one, using its infrastructure, experienced workers, etc. After the new enterprise has assimilated the
production output, the old one was closed. The idea, popularized in the
Soviet Union, of introducing new technologies without stopping production can be successfully realized only with relatively small changes in
technologies.
Input-output tables can be related to new management technologies
of management; they affect quite seriously the entire technology of
planning. If one takes into account that the work of the Gosplan cannot
be stopped for any amount of time because the management mechanism
could thus be paralyzed, there remains the route of the creation of a
parallel to Gosplan. This Gosplan would master the new planning
technology, and various types of situations would be rehearsed, simu-
lating the interaction of the Gosplan with the workers in the bureaucra-
cies, but under new conditions. After the new planning technology was
mastered to a sufficient degree, it would be possible to curtail the work
of the old Gosplan. Sufficiently powerful divisions working on planning
questions with the use of new methods in the chief Computer Center of
the Gosplan and the branch research institutes could play an essential
role in the formation of a more perfect system of planning which would
parallel the Gosplan. I understand that the concept of two Gosplans
would raise very acute political problems, but it seems to me that the
established political situation in the country and the presence of various
groups in the Politburo would allow the idea of a second Gosplan to be
realized, even from a political point of view. I expressed the idea of
two Gosplans several times at TSEMI and even in print, in the form of
incidental remarks. I did not hear arguments against my idea, but at
the same time, the singularity and political ramifications of this proposals did not provoke sympathy for it.

Mathematical Methods on the Factory Level

One of the main reasons for the weakness of the introduction of
developed mathematical methods on the level of the factories is that the
economic mechanism decisively resists these methods in many cases.
Only in a small number of cases have the results of solutions to these
problems not come into conflict with the demands of the planning system
currently in force. At the end of the 1930s, for example, Kantorovich
solved the problem of the "Veneer Trust." Because the goal in the
problem was an increase in the output of production without decreasing
the value of other indicators, the method was successfully introduced.
Analogous cases were encounterd subsequently. The majority of problems are characterized by improvement of some indicators with decline
in the value of others. There are other problems whose solution contradicts the accepted system of stimulation. In the latter case, these
goals are not introduced in practice, although a temporary show is
made of their introduction.

After the war, Kantorovich and a group of Leningrad mathematicians
introduced methods for linear programming in the cutting of metal at the
Egorov Train Car Factory in Leningrad. Breakage of metal was significantly reduced, but then Kantorovich ran into trouble. The problem
was that the Egorov Factory was an important supplier for the "Vtorchermet," an organization which collects scrap. The reduction in breakage led to a decrease in the factory's deliveries to "Vtorchermet." The
latter did not fulfill its plan and was threated with a work stoppage.
Kantorovich was called to the Leningrad committee of the Party and
was threatened with a lot of trouble. Fortunately, the results were not
disastrous.

In the connection, I would like to point out that the situation of the
planning of breakages is the usual state of affairs in Soviet industry.
One of the ceramics factories had succeeded in lengthening the firing
time of the ovens and cutting down breakage of the articles. Because
of this, however, they did not fulfill the plan for the delivery of fire
clay (broken ceramic articles used in the production of new bricks).
It was fortunate that another ceramic factory had a large waste of production, and the leaders of this factory rescued the factory in difficulty
by giving it the necessary amount of fire clay.

I understand that steel mills, as a result of technological demands,
have to foresee the delivery of a certain amount of scrap. However,
if the suppliers of scrap, improved the use of metal and lowerd the
need for it, then it would be rational for these enterprises to overlook
the plan and not to punish them for working well.

It is well known that Soviet planning is conducted "from what has

been achieved" (the Ratchet Principle); i.e., annually a certain growth
is achieved, depending upon the current demand level. In the Egorov
Factory, which successfully introduced methods of linear programming,
a very high percentage of output of finished goods (approximately 94%)
was achieved. However, the ministry to which this factory was subordinate, following the principle of planning "from what has been
achieved," automatically decreased the level of allowable waste for the
factory by another 7 percent. The Leningrad branch of the Steklov
Mathematics Institute of the Academy of Sciences, where Kantorovich
was then working, wrote a letter to the ministry. In this letter, the
institute, with its lofty scholarly authority in the sphere of mathematics,
maintained that there was no such thing as 101 percent output of finished
goods.

Localized Optimization Problems

In 1961 I also happened to run into difficulties in the introduction
of localized optimization problems. While working on the introduction
of mathematical methods at the Moscow Factory for Small Cars (MZMA),
I decided to organize work on the basis of principles of optimization in
the factory's pressing shop for the primary material processings. Kantorovich agreed to participate, and a group of mathematicians who had
experience in this area came from Leningrad. Rubinstein headed the
current task force. It must be said that Rubinstein was more than a
brilliant specialist in linear programming. He was well acquainted
with the technology of press production since he had worked on mathematical methods for the efficient cutting of metal. In Leningrad he was
sometimes even asked to consult on corresponding technological questions. L. Grinman offered considerable assistance on the automation
of management processes. The head of the technological department
of the factory, a very progressive person, willingly provided the materials needed for the work.

After some time, the work was finished and a chart for the efficient
cutting of metal was composed, but efficient cutting required that a
certain set of parts be obtained from one certain type of sheet. As a
result of this, the daily structure of production of components did not
correspond to the proportions of components needed for assembly. Of
course, over a week's time, the balance of supply and demand of components was attained, but during the course of the week it was necessary
to maintain reversible surpluses. Supplementary warehouse premises
and several workers for the transport of these surpluses to and from
the warehouse were needed in order to do this. However, it was only
possible to build additional warehouse facilities in Moscow by resolution

of the USSR Council of Ministers. It was also difficult to increase the
number of transport workers because the wage fund, which was strictly
limited, would have to increase. Unfortunately, we were caught in the
midst of a routine campaign to decrease the percentage of maintenance
workers, and the transport workers were included among the latter.
As a result of these constraints, we did not succeed in introducing the
new measure, which had promised the factory a yearly saving of hundreds of thousands of rubles and required only small capital investments that would have been quickly recouped.

Transportation

In explaining how the existing Soviet system of stimulation opposes
the introduction of mathematical methods for allocation of resources,
the example of transportation is cited. A well-known means of making
transportation more efficient is the reduction of the volume of transportation. The leaders of the transport organizations receive a bonus
for an increase in the volume of transportation, and the drivers are
paid depending on the volume of work they carry in ton/kilometers.
Thus, the introduction of optimization methods in certain parts of the
economy runs into difficulties, which are connected with the imperfec-
tion of the whole economic mechanism. At times, against the interests
of the managers the Party organs oblige them to introduce optimal
methods of planning, but the effects of these are short-lived, for example, as with the introduction of optimal transports of sand in Moscow,
which at one time was decisively supported by the Moscow City Committee of the Party. The reconstruction of the whole economic mechanism, however, demands tremendous work and must begin from the
top. Moreover, to think that the change in the planning technology will
greatly improve the economic mechanism in the existing political system
is unrealistic; social and political factors affecting the effectiveness of
this mechanism are still too great.

THE ATTITUDE OF THE POWERS-THAT-BE TOWARD
THE ECONOMIC-MATHEMATICAL TREND

Several features I have demonstrated in the diversity of trends in
Soviet economics are evidence that we are witnessing a renaissance.
However, this observation raises an important question: What are the
political premises for the stability of this diversity?

It is obvious that the established political regime in the Soviet Union
has a tendency toward unification. This tendency lies deep in the nature
of bureaucracy since it is incapable of managing a whole variety of

conditions. At the same time, by virtue of dire necessity, bureaucracy is compelled for different reasons to deal with the existing diversity of conditions and to make many concessions.

Administrative Competition

During Stalin's time, diversity of opinion and competition were allowed in some branches of industry. Great significance was attached to this. In the aviation industry, for example, parallel design offices, headed by Tupolev and Miasishchev, were created for the planning of heavy bombers. Separate plans for fighters were developed in the two design offices headed by Iakovlev and Mikoian-Gurevich. This competition, implanted and controlled, was capable of being destroyed from above at any moment. In fact, Miasishchev was dismissed from work several times and then reinstated.

In the Khrushchev period, competition was allowed among missle design organizations. The head of one organization, Chalomei, sometimes beat his competitors not because of the quality of production, but rather because Khrushchev's son was working for him. He and Khrushchev's son went with applications to the Central Committee of the CPSU, but after Khrushchev's retirement, his son quickly was transferred into the Institute for Electronic Control Machines.

During the Khrushchev period, the revival of economics began, accompanied by the creation of new economics institutes (laboratories) and new views on the development of economics. However, Khrushchev operated in the old tradition of claiming that a good idea was his idea.

In 1958 Khrushchev decided to seek advice from specialists before the reorganization of the Machine and Tractor Stations (MTS) and the sale of their equipment to the kolkhozes (collective farms). He invited agrarian economists, workers at the Ministry of Agriculture, the chairmen of the kolkhozes, and others to a conference. Among those present was a famous Soviet economist, a Doctor of Economic Sciences, Vladimir Venzher. In Stalin's work, Economic Problems of Socialism in the USSR, he had sharply criticized Venzher and his wife Sanina for their proposal to reorganize the MTS and to sell equipment to the kolkhozes. (8) Khrushchev had known Venzher since the 1920s. Venzher had been a member of the Red Guards from the Khamovnicheskii region in Moscow during the Revolution and after this was connected with Party work, where he met Khrushchev. Before the conference, Khrushchev reportedly told Venzher something like, "Don't think that this is your proposal; your proposal was different and incorrect." Such an attitude toward an economist's proposals was conditioned by the fact that the leader of the state, because of his functional role as the government's head, was trying to show the people that he was the creator of new ideas.

It may be that the case of Evsei Liberman was a natural exception
to what had been said about the attitude toward economists' opinions
during the Khrushchev period. Publicity by the central Party press
was given to Liberman's proposals for improvement of the economic
mechanism through the intensification of the profit role. (9)   After the
removal of Khrushchev, when economic reform began, Liberman was
forgotten. It is true that none of the Party leaders was officially named
the author of the reform. Thus, although various views were permitted
in economics, the same spirit of facelessness of the economists remained when they entered into governmental decisions.

The spirit of modernizing was prevalent during the time of Khrushchev, and it was possible that Khrushchev was ready to support even
the reformists since he was sometimes inclined toward limiting the
Party power.

The Post-Khrushchev Period

The post-Khrushchev period has been a period of searching for
equilibrium among the reactionaries, conservatives, and modernizers.
Apparently, the overwhelming majority of the representatives of the
Politburo's various groups was especially opposed to the radicals, and
most of them were arrested or exiled from the country.

The left wing is always the most dangerous for authoritarian systems
because it calls for the creation of a society with a division of powers
and limitation of and compulsory replacement of the leaders in accordance with the law. The radical reactionary wing is also unacceptable
for many of the leaders, but their attitude toward it is more tolerant,
because in principle the right does not fight against the foundations of
the social and economic systems in force; rather, it demands only that
they be made more rigid.

It can be assumed that the modernizers in the Politburo are represented primarily as reformers who could produce in a comprehensible
form an alternate program of development or so-called economic reform. The reactionaries, apparently, adhere to their opinions about
the necessity for a return to Stalinist methods, but do not combine this
with any serious proposals for improvements.

For a long time, until the end of the 1960s, Brezhnev's role possibly
lay in balancing these two opposing groups within the Politburo. The
reformers could not triumph, because the Party functionaries, defending the stability of Party privileges, possessed enough power to deter
reformist victory. In spite of a number of opposition maneuvers, never-
the less they were obliged to discontinue the economic reform and even
in some respects to return to the past; the role of the physical indicators

of the plan for the enterprises was again strengthened and the role of
the value parameters have been diminished. The scholars who proposed the improvement of the economy from above were criticized.
The members of the Politburo supporting the improvement of the economy from below, also were apparently obliged to stop their activity.

This support can be documented by the speeches of the Politburo's
former member, Gennadi Voronov. These speeches defended the complex links in agriculture which were to embody the suggested new production procedures. A number of Politburo members were against
these links. It was clear that through the direct connivance of several
Politburo members, the initially successful experiment with complex
links within the limits of the state farm, Akchi, in Kazakhastan fell
apart in 1971. The organizer of the experiment, Ivan Khudenko, was
sent to prison on trifling accusations and died there in 1974.

The Politburo

Apparently the Politburo's reactionary factions prefer a rigid
economic mechanism. However, some of them hold rather romantic
views on the nature of this mechanism, fastening their hopes on a spon-
taneous outburst of energy, which is characteristic of the Russian
people in a crisis. The economic program of these extreme forces is
the program of Russian nationalism as reflected in Ivan Shevtsov's
book. (10) There are persistent rumors that Dmitrii Polianskii, a
former member of the Politburo, supported the publication of Shevtsov's
book.

Many Stalinists want a return to the former times, with a certain
amount of modernization added. The reactionaries also want growth
in military power and are ready to use new means to acquire this, if
the means do not lessen their political power. The reactionaries do
not oppose the introduction of new means if they strengthen the regime.
However, the introduction of such new means is connected with the
demand to forego ideological principles to a certain extent, or rather
to relax their interpretation, which tens of thousands of their adherents
want to preserve. Experience has shown that these reactionaries are
ready to give ideological concessions to strengthen the regime. It is
natural that such reactionaries must unite with modernizers, such as
the cosmetologists. The reactionary group of the Politburo also could
not completely succeed because enough Politburo members fear the revival of Stalinism. Thus, it is possible that there are several powerful
groups in the Politburo, though none are completely unified. Each of
these groups in the Politburo needs proposals to oppose groups competing with them.

In the post-Khrushchev period, both old and new economics institutes, created around new trends in economics during Khrushchev's
period, were firmly established and developed. The diversity of viewpoints on the development of economics as of the mid-1960s came to be
represented not only by individual economists--this was typical of the
workers, for example, at the Institute of Economics--but also by organizations. Now the government often examines the proposals of the
leaders of the large collectives, for example TSEMI, not of the individual collaborators.

The diversity of trends in economics has developed a firm political
basis. The competition among these institutes is no longer organized
by just one person; it is based on oligarchical or so-called collective
leadership. Each Politburo group supports the institutes which develop
proposals for it, and the balance of power between powerful opposing
groups in the Politburo guarantees the existence of these organizations.

The Soviet Media

I will try to demonstrate the last statement with the following example. In 1972 three issues of Planovoe Khoziaistvo, under one very
pretentious title, "Belated Acknowledgements and Fruitless Borrowing,"
three articles by Adolf Kats, Doctor of Economic Sciences, were published. (11) They criticized the bourgeois essence of Western econometric research and were directed against the Soviet scholars, who on
the basis of the production function, were conducting economic-mathematical and econometric research on the development of the Soviet
economy. The very fact of the appearance of three articles by the same
author in one journal in the same year is an unusual phenomenon for the
Soviet press. Usually they print one and extremely rarely, two articles.
The length of each article was also unusual; the first article was eighteen pages; the second twenty-one pages, and the third nineteen pages.
Usually an article devoted to an important theoretical problem occupies
no more than fourteen pages in a journal. Above and beyond these
factors, a large part of the text was set in brevier (large type). After
considering the pretentious style of the articles, it became obvious,
knowing the procedures in Soviet journals, that permission to print
these articles might have been given on a very high level, the secretary
of the Central Committee of the CPSU or a member of the Politburo.

Then Iuri Belik's article directed against mathematical methods
applied to predict economic development appeared in Planovoe Khoziaistvo.
Ia. Kronrod's article directed against the ideas of the optimal functioning of the socialist economy developed in TSEMI appeared in the same
issue. (12) All three authors fulminated against the new trends in

economics and used the lofty positions of Marxism-Leninism and the
resolutions of the Communist Party as rationales.

In early June of 1973, a review unexpectedly appeared in Pravda
by I. Soloviev and criticized the authors of these articles. (13) The
authors were accused of directing their remarks against the resolutions
of the 24th Congress of the Party, which stipulated the development of
the economic-mathematical trend. This criticism also was written in
the very best tones of the Party press. When I discussed this review
with friends, they were extremely embittered by the tone of the criticism, because the means employed for the defense of progress were
reactionary. (14)

There was also a humorous side to this affair. The surnames of
two of the authors, Kats and Kronrod, were Jewish, and the third
resembled a Jewish surname, Belik. In fact Belik is a true Russian;
he works in the Central Committee of the CPSU, which already precluded his being Jewish. Many of my acquaintances who were not in
economics called me in those days with the question, "Does another
anti-Semitic campaign begin?" The Jewish surnames of the authors
and the common stereotype that only progressive people could be criticized by the Soviet Press for any revision of the Party resolutions
gave rise to the opinion that progressive Jews were being abused. Of
course, only a member of the Politburo could sanction the publication
of such an article in Pravda.

At the end of June 1973, Planovoe Khoziaistvo organized a discussion of the article in Pravda, or more precisely a condemnation of
it. Pravda is viewed in the USSR as a "holy" newspaper and that is why
it could not be criticized by the public. Therefore, in a quite verbose
account of this discussion published in Planovoe Khoziaistvo (15) the
article in Pravda was not mentioned and it was said that this was only
a meeting of the editorial board of Planovoe Khoziaistvo with the participation of scholars, practical workers in planning, and representatives of the press that had been organized to "continue the discussion
of problems of theory and practice in national-economic planning."

Around 200 workers from various scientific and nonscientific institutions of Moscow, including the Academy of Social Sciences under
the Central Committee of the CPSU, were present at this very impressive assembly. Forty people gave speeches and thirty eight of them,
including all the authors of the articles in Planovoe Khoziaistvo, condemned the article in Pravda. It must not be forgotten here that Belik
works in the apparatus of the Central Committee; he is a consultant,
which is somewhat higher than an instructor, and he came out against
the central organ of the Central Committee of the CPSU. Several of
those speaking mockingly demanded that the author of the article in

Pravda come to the conference, understanding that Soloviev is a pseudonym for an official opinion. Only two people, the director of the
Institute of Economics, Evgeni Kapustin, and the deputy to the head of
the Gosplan's summary section, V. Kossov, came out with mild support
for the article in Pravda. (16)

The Gosplan's board also discussed the article in Pravda. Although
the resolution about the "anti-Marxist character of many branches of the
economic-mathematical trend" was already prepared, and the speakers
opposed TSEMI, the first meeting of the board ended unsuccessfully for
its organizers. Academician Nikolai Nekrasov, the chairman of an organization subordinate to the Gosplan, came forward and announced his
disagreement with the criticism of TSEMI. To his announcement he
added the following words, "Science can get by without the Gosplan, but
the Gosplan without science--no." Nekrasov was supported by several
other people.

The chairman of the Gosplan, N. Baibakov, who was conducting
the board meeting and saw the situation taking shape, interrupted the
meeting and said that it would be necessary to return to this problem
again. Indeed, in September 1973, the board adopted the earlier prepared resolution, which condemned the economic-mathematical trend
for its anti-Marxist character.

In October 1973, a conference of economists organized by the
science section of the Central Committee of the CPSU took place. All
the major speeches were made by scholars developing the new trends.
Among the speakers, the majority were people working on the new trends
or supporting them.

The Battle Continued

The leading people in the field of ideology continued the argument
about unification and diversity in economics. The chief of the science
section, S. Trapenikov, in an article decisively had called for a battle
against diversity and the introduction of conformity of ideas. (17) In
listing the needs for the future development of the economics of socialism, Trapenikov wrote:

. . . Our university community and most of all the teachers
of economics have become sharply aware of the need for the
theoretical elaboration of the economics of socialism. This
is more noticeable because the universities and engineering
colleges do not yet have a stable textbook on the economics
of socialism. . .

And finally, economics itself has begun to sense the need
for a profound analytical elaboration of the economic theory
of socialism, as never before. After all, it is not a secret
that among the economists themselves various interpreta-
tions are frequently appearing on a whole number of important problems in economic theory. Take, for example, the
problems of value, price-money mechanism, and accounting under the conditions of developed socialism, or the
problem of the application of mathematical methods in economics. All this speaks of the fact that it is necessary to
survey again and again in the most attentive manner all the
aspects of the development of our economics and develop a
unified authoritative opinion on all problems of economic
theory. And first and foremost, this must be done by the
scholars and economists themselves, summoned to give a
scientifically based answer to the burning questions put
forth by economic development by the needs of today and
the inquiries of tomorrow.

Thus life itself dictates to us the necessity for self-
critically approaching the analysis of the development of
our economics. The entire complex of theoretical and
scientifically applied problems must be examined; a fundamental shift toward the study of the modern economic
basis, of really existing, mature, developed socialism
must be made. At present, as never before, the problem
arises of the elaboration of a large scale state plan for the
development of economics, along with how to unite and
concentrate the efforts of scholars in the solution of urgent
problems posed by our Party (p. 5).

However, the following was also written in the same issue of the
journal by academician Petr Fedoseev, vice-president of the Academy
of Science responsible for the humanities and social sciences, and
the director of the Marx-Engels-Lenin Institute under the Central Committee of the CPSU:

It must be noted that the indicated reconstruction of the
work of the scientific economics institutes is accompanied
by a number of difficulties. For example, there still remains a certain group of economic scholars which cannot
cope with new conditions, and cannot direct its energies to
the solution of the most important problems standing before

the national economy. They devote their basic attention to
conducting abstract discussions on questions about the object of economic theory, about the essence of commodity
production, about the nature of a commodity, etc. There
is no doubt that these questions by themselves have great
significance and at all costs must be investigated, but the
discussions which we have in mind are conducted by these
economists as a rule at one and the same level, without
apparent progress. Of course such fruitless arguments
can only be considered as marking time, with certain of
these "theoreticians" often dogmatically approaching the
work which research economists are developing on various
trends in our economic theory and practice. After hearing
the word "goal," they are ready to shout: 'This is teleology';
the term 'needs' they inevitably connect with vulgar political economy, and the one who mentions 'utility' is immediately accused of 'resurrecting the theories of Bohm-Bawerk,
the theory of marginal utility,' etc. Such an approach, to
our mind, is not constructive and interferes with the development of economics, although we must always keep our
powder dry and fight an unremitting battle against bourgeois ideology, against the spreading of its influence.

. . . Attention must be focused on the insufficient harmony
in the work of our economic scholars, which is particularly
expressed in the opposition of their approaches to others,
leading to a certain 'self-isolationism.' And we must also
reckon with this. Some theoreticians (sometimes) demand
that certain approaches to the solution of scientific and
practical economic problems be condemned and even forbidden, and, on the other hand, that their own be made
law. Here, in our view, a certain matter of principles
must be revealed in the sense of not allowing a monopoly
of one approach, not hastily closing off new developments
which at first glance can seem somewhat pretentious. It
is better to criticize the precocious, very hurried conclusions in a comradely way, and not to drive them from
the threshold.

The most important thing is necessarily to verify any
conception put forth with the theory and practice of Marxism-
Leninism, to verify it strictly and objectively. (pp. 60-61)
(Emphasis added) (18)

THE FUTURE OF THE ECONOMIC-MATHEMATICAL TREND
IN THE SOVIET UNION

The outcome of the battle between the advocates of unification and diversity in economics is difficult to determine. It depends on many things and first of all on the political situation in the future. Let me examine this situation briefly.

Brezhnev's era started in the early 1970s after victory was impossible for one group of the Politburo. Brezhnev proposed a policy of preservation. His politics sought to implement the solution to the problems of the country's development through external forces, i.e., by improving relations with the West. It was calculated that this would strengthen the Far Eastern position in the battle with China, particularly because it would lead to the withdrawal of part of the Soviet army from Eastern Europe and relocation to the Soviet-Chinese border. Loans then could be obtained from the West for the expansion of industrial production, especially in the East, and the West could supply new military technology, and so on. Brezhnev's policy of preservation, however, has not lead to stability. It is difficult to expect a prolonged improvement in Soviet relations with the West because of the incompatibility of the democratic and autocratic systems and the absence of guarantees from the Soviet Union's autocratic political regime to fulfill long-term agreements. The West had proceeded very cautiously with the allocation of credit and such assistance.

Chinese Implications

However, in my opinion, the main factor contributing to the worsening of relations between the USSR and the West lies in the new orientation of the present Chinese leadership. It is important to remember that Mao after breaking away from the Soviet Union practically stopped the process of industrialization. The Cultural Revolution had reinforced this course. Under these conditions, in spite of a bitter ideological struggle and Chinese irredentists' claims, China was not a serious military threat to the Soviet Union. However, the present Chinese leadership has proclaimed a return to the course of industrialization. The Western powers and Japan have made clear their desire to help in the modernization of China because now it is less dangerous to them than the Soviet Union.

With this state of affairs, the Soviet leaders are reexamining their attitude toward the internal situation in the country and their views on detente. It may be assumed that there is an attitude in the Politburo favoring the course of liberalization for the country. This will provide

an opportunity both for a serious improvement of the economic mechanism and better relationships with the West, particularly to counter-
blanance China. Apparently the liberal opinion encounters a strong
opposition from some members of the Politburo since it might lead to
a considerable loss of their power. It may be also assumed there is a
view that it is necessary to rigidify the internal political structure and
get ready for a preventive war against China, while at the same time
trying to neutralize the Western powers.

Evidently, some members of the Politburo would be glad to see
good neighbor relations restored between the USSR and China. In this
case it would be possible to rigidify the political system in the USSR,
much to China's delight, and simultaneously eliminate the threat of a
war. China, however, would have to agree to restore such relations
only if the USSR accepted China's leading role in the Communist movement and in the Third World and agreed to share with China the sparsely
populated regions of the Far East and Siberia. This could be carried
out either under the guise of brotherly help of all the Communists or
under the guise of returning to China lands that had once been conquered
by Russian Tsars. However, giving back the conquered
territory would be going against the whole history of Russia. The known
exceptions have been of a temporary nature. Poland and the Baltic
Union Republics may have seceded from Russia under Lenin but they
were reannexed by Stalin; moreover, the latter also enlarged Russian
territories.

Other Politburo Opinions

In addition to the views expressed here, some other opinions might
also be current in the Politburo. But in any case, the position of the
reactionary group, which insists upon a strong political regime that
will enable them to preserve their power and at the same time be sufficiently strong for a possible war with China, is apparently gaining
momentum. On the basis of what has been written I will put forward
a paradoxical statement. The economic-mathematical trend, although
it has some anti-Marxist flavor, is first of all supported by the flexible
reactionaries and conservatives. The Politburo's liberally oriented
members, although willing to support a variety of opinions in economics,
still treat the economic-mathematical methods negatively because they
see in them a tool for strengthening a rigid political and economic
system.

Cooperation with the cosmetologists who advocate economic-mathematical methods would require considerable concessions on the part
of authorities. Of course, the economic-mathematical trend has a

certain unpleasant aftertaste for the authorities because it is connected
with the direct rationalization of their work. If an engineer uses mathematics, then as they say, "Forget about him." But when a planner
uses mathematics, because the authorities are directly included in the
planning mechanism, the new methods cause them discomfort.

Those cosmetologists who demand the inclusion of scientists in the
decision making mechanism are especially unpleasant to the political
leaders. For example, the Politburo did not enlist the aid of N. Moiseev,
a corresponding member of the Academy of Sciences, when formulating
the policy on the computerization of the Soviet economic system. In the e
beginning of the 1970s, he was not even invited to the All-Union Conference, "Application of Mathematical Methods and the Computers in
the National Economy," a conference which was very impressive and
was attended by several members of the Politburo. Sorrowfully,
Moiseev departed at the time of the conference for a winter economic-
mathematical school in Drogobych.

Semen Zukhovitskii, a mathematician of the older generation who
recently emigrated to Israel and was a great enthusiast about economic-
mathematical methods, ran this school at which hundreds of young
mathematicians and economists regularly gathered. Moiseev's anti-
Semitism was well known. He prefered not to admit Jews into the
schools he had organized on mathematical economics and the theory of
control. One can imagine the degree of his despair if he decided to go
to a school organized by the Jewish Zukhovitskii and to take part in the
discussion of several speeches there, and to give a speech himself.
Moiseev had tried to earn the praise of those in power and had put
forth proposals for improving work at the computer centers. Moiseev
was also trying very hard to prove that prices must correspond to labor
expenses in accordance with the Marxist labor theory of value.

Essentially closer to the authorities is the group which supports
the automation of the existing technology of planning. However, the
leader of this trend, academician V. Glushkov, is somewhat feared in
the Politburo, because he wants to automate absolutely everything.
This, combined with his tremendous thirst for power, makes Glushkov
somewhat dangerous, but he is needed for action. It must be assumed,
judging from the fact that Khrushchev was able to smear Marshall G.
Zhukov, that the autocrats can remove a technocrat who has gone too
far, if need be.

Among the cosmetologists' several ideas, apparently the closest
of all to the conservative forces in the Politburo is Nikolai Fedorenko's
trend of optimal planning of the nation's economy. While Glushkov and
Moiseev hold real doctorates in mathematics--they were awarded academic titles not for great scientific results--academician, Fedorenko,

is by comparison not a scholar at all. At the same time, he is a gifted
person in his own right, well aware of the techniques for achieving
power. All this increases the opportunities for him to communicate
with those in power. Among all the leading cosmetologists, he is one
of a few who are culturally compatible with the ruling clique.

In spite of the reluctance on the part of the leaders to cooperate
with the cosmetologists who could change their position if they thought
it would strengthen their regime, it must be noted that direct enlistment of scholars in the mechanism of decision making is by no means
a new phenomenon. Experience shows that the enlistment of prominent
economics scholars in the administration of the country has produced
varying results. Such prominent economists as A. Turgot and J.
Schumpeter proved to be nonproductive as ministers. At the same time,
E. Bohm-Bawerk, F. Wieser, and J. Keynes, upon being enlisted in
state activity, positively influenced the economic development of their
countries.

I do not know of cases in which the enlistment of prominent mathematicians in the government of a country has produced good results.
It is well known that Napoleon, himself quite an educated person, tried
to utilize a large group of scholars in the state government. At one
time, the famous mathematician, Pierre Simon de Laplace, was appointed Minister of the Interior. However it was very quickly revealed
that Laplace could not cope with his duties; he overlooked an important
conspiracy. Napoleon was said to have removed Laplace from the
position of minister because he applied "infinitesmal ideas to vastly
important state affairs."

Reflections

If democratization of the country does not take place, there is little
hope that the performance of the Soviet economy will be appreciably
improved, no matter how favorable the conditions might be for further
development of the economic-mathematical methods. Democratization
of the Soviet society and adequate development of an economic mechanism based upon the concept of mixed economy hold out the greatest
promise for an increased efficiency of the Soviet economy. The mathematical methods could occupy a prominent place in the creation of
such a mechanism. The necessity of democratizing the country becomes
all the more evident if it is remembered that the Soviet leaders are not
so much interested in the improvement of the economic mechanism on
the basis of the new methods of planning, as in using these methods to
cover up their ambitions to have a rigid political regime and create an
illusion that these methods might increase the efficiency of the economic

system. It was not by accident that the concept of <u>economic optimum</u>
was once branded by a Soviet economist as the <u>optimum for the people.</u>
   Generally speaking, leaders all over the world are eager to use
any means at hand to increase their power. The difference among
societies lies in how subject are the innovative proposals to preliminary
control, selection, limitation, and replacement if it becomes clear they
are not effective. In the Soviet system, the mechanism for selection of
new proposals for the improvement of the national economy takes place
under secret conditions; good conditions for analysis and discussion of
the proposals do not exist. The decision to introduce such proposals
is made by the highest Party and government circles according to their
own considerations. Criticism of the decisions made by these circles
is forbidden.
   The rise of T. Lysenko, in fact, became possible as a result of
such a decision-making mechanism. If Lysenko were to be removed
from his position, this would not mean that "Lysenkoism" as a social
phenomenon would be eliminated. The conditions giving rise to
"Lysenkoism" would remain about the same as they were during the
period of Lysenko's prosperity.

Amalgamations

   It is well known that the process of creating industrial amalgamations
in place of the chief departments of the ministries, now taking place in
a slowed policy has, first and foremost, a political character. If one
keeps in mind that almost two-thirds of the entire apparatus of the
ministries is concentrated in the chief departments, the replacement
of these departments by amalgamations would decline the staff in the
ministries. Then the number of ministries would decline as well, and
new consolidated ministries would be organized. The heads of these
new ministries would be appointed by the Party leaders who succeeded
in reducing the power of the Council of the Ministers.
   At the present time, with the application of mathematical methods,
proof is already appearing of the need for amalgamations. Beyond all
these mathematical exercises are primitive economic considerations
about the need for amalgamations. One such work contends, with the
help of mathematical models, that in the metallurgical industry amalgamations are needed according to the object principle because, as
mathematical analysis demonstrates, there are strong connections
between the factories by delivery of commodities.
   In the meantime, such works are not so harmless; after all, the
amalgamations according to the object indicator will lead to the destruction of the Ministry of the Ferrous Metallurgy, the chief departments

of which are organized according to the technological principle. For
example, there is a chief department of refractory bricks in the Ministry
of the Ferrous Metallurgy. This department is organized according to
technological principles because all factories which are consolidated in
the department use similar technologies. It is possible to abolish this
department and to involve its factories in different steel mills which
demand refractory bricks. In this case the steel mills will be organized through the use of the object principle. Both the technological, as
well as the object, principle have strong and weak points. It would be
very naive to say that one principle was better because it alone has
advantages, but this kind of naivete has been demonstrated by the proponents of the amalgamations.

Since Brezhnev does not possess enough power "to wring the necks"
of the managerial class, the idea of amalgamations has not yet succeeded.
But if tomorrow a new political leader succeeds who has greater power
than Brezhnev, or at least equal to that of Khrushchev's, there will be
again a new series of experimentations which would have as their main
goal the strengthening of the personal power of the leader. There is
danger that a new leader might see in the mathematical methods and
computers the same panacea against all illnesses as Khrushchev saw
in "corn for the agriculture."

Thus, in my opinion, the future of the economic-mathematical
methods in the Soviet Union is a rather promising one, for regardless
of the political orientation of new leadership, reactionaries or liberals,
the economic mathematical methods can be used as a tool for improving
the economic mechanism. The effect that might ensue from using these
methods under different political conditions is a subject for further
research.

Notes

CHAPTER 1

1. M. Bongard, <u>Pattern Recognition</u> (Moscow: "Nauka," 1967), p. 255.

2. In this connection Lvov's article in the journal <u>Novy Mir</u>, which
was devoted to the medieval French philsopher, Petrus Ramus, represents a significant interest. The questions raised in the article about
Ramus' attitude toward Aristotle are surprisingly similar to today's
problems in the USSR concerning the attitudes of scholars toward Marx.
The relations of the innovator Ramus with his enemies, the zealous
defenders of Aristotle, are also interesting from the point of view of
tolerance. I share the approach of the Western scholars to Marx, who
acknowledge his great role as a scholar, but in addition recognize his
limitations. I became acquainted with these views in the Soviet Union
from the manuscript of the Russian translation of B. Seligman's book,
<u>Main Currents in Modern Economics</u> (translated by A. Anikin, L.
Afanas'ev, Iu. Kochergin, R. Entov, Moscow: Progress Publisher,
1968). In this manuscript, the above-mentioned opinions about Marx
were cited. I also will note that in the Russian translation, the entire
section devoted to non-Marxist socialism was omitted.

3. I myself succeeded quite easily in publishing criticism of Engels
in 1959 in my book <u>The Economic Effectiveness of Complex Mechanization and Automation in Machine Construction</u> (Moscow: Gosplanizdat,
1960). Below, I quote quite a large excerpt from this book, demonstrating how concrete this criticism was:
     . . . in our literature, in order to characterize the change
     in the structure of expenses taking place in the growth of

167

labor productivity, the following position is quoted from
Capital: 'An increase in labor productivity lies precisely
in the fact that the portion of present labor decreases and
the portion of past labor increases in such a way that the
total sum of labor contained in a good decreases; thus it
follows that the quantity of present labor decreases more
than the quantity of past labor increases.' (K. Marx, Kapital,
vol. III, Politizdat, 1955, p. 271)

This quotation is taken from Part Four of Chapter 15 in
the third volume of Capital, which was redone or supple-
mented in several points by Engels. It explains the increase
in the expenses of materialized labor by the fact that expenses
for the wear of the main part of constant capital are increased, i.e., the expenses for depreciation increase:
'. . . Most typical of the increase in the productive force
of labor is the fact that the basic portion of the basic capital
experiences a very powerful increase, and in addition the
portion of its value which is transferred to the goods as a
result of wear also increases.' (Ibid.)

From the analysis of the first volume of Capital, carefully edited by Karl Marx, flows another characteristic of
the increase in labor productivity. In the first volume of
Capital, Marx indicated that with the appearance of powerful machine industry the expenses of materialized labor in
the value of a good absolutely decrease in connection with
the wear on the basic capital, although the value of the
machines is higher than the implements of labor used in
manufacturing:
'The comparative analysis of the prices of handmade or
manufactured goods and the same goods produced by machine
produces in general the result that in the machine product
a portion of the value, transferred from the means of labor,
increases relatively, but decreases absolutely. That is, its
absolute quantity decreases, but its quantity in relation to
the entire value of the product, for example, a pound of yarn,
increases.' (K. Marx, Kapital, vol. I, Politizdat, 1955, p. 396)

Karl Marx explains the decrease in the sum of expenses
for depreciation of the basic means by an increase in the
durability of the machines with the growth of their productivity, the more economical use of production investments,
etc.

4. A. Katsenelinboigen, "Domestic Factors Shaping Soviet Foreign Policy: Economic Conditions and Cultural Forces: Perceptions: Relations between the United States and the Soviet Union. United States Senate Committee on Foreign Relations, 1978, pp. 59-64.

5. In the 1960s A. Fraenkel's and Y. Bar-Hillel's book, Foundations of Set Theory (Amsterdam: North Holland Pub. Co., 1958), was translated in the Soviet Union. In this book, the authors demonstrated the diversity of schools in the sphere of mathematics and explained the necessity for this. It is well known that pluralism is the basic enemy of monism, and theoretical substantiation of the impossibility of a simple proof of the truth or falsity of various views agrees poorly with official Soviet ideology; the latter recognizes the presence of only one truth and the ruling cadre possesses it.

Another example was in 1969, at the eve of the 100th anniversary of the birth of Lenin, when academician, Andrei Kolmogorov, made a speech on the development of probability theory. Dialectical materialism suggests that everything in the world is connected. However, the axioms of probability, in whose development Kolmogorov played a leading role, postulate the independence of events. In his speech, Kolmogorov dialectically extricated himself from this contradiction.

6. For a long time Konius' works were not published in the Soviet Union. There was something tragic in Konius' meeting in Moscow in 1972 with Leonid Hurwicz, a famous American scholar in the sphere of economic-mathematical methods. Hurwicz brought Konius a book recently printed in the United States. In this book were references to Konius, and his name had been credited to a certain type of demand function proposed by him in the 1920s.

Konius is presently working in the Scientific Research Economics Institute of the Gosplan of the USSR, conducting investigations in the sphere of consumer demand. He gave a speech concerning the results of his investigations in 1973 at one of the seminars at the Central Economic Mathematical Institute. It is true that like many economists of the older generation, Konius is trying even now to unite the theory of marginal utility with Marxism.

7. With Kubanin, the authorities arrested a worker at The Central Statistical Administration, Solomon Kheinman, who had somehow participated in the elaboration of the data used by Kubanin. Kheinman was in exile until 1956, then returned to Moscow, and is now successfully working in the Institute of Economics of the USSR Academy of Sciences. He has done much to acquaint Soviet economists with

Western economics. He has been favorable to the new trends in economics; in particular, he offered his services more than once as a member on dissertation committees in mathematical economics.

8.   Boris Markus, Labor in a Socialist Society (Moscow: Gospolitizdat, 1939).

9.   Only later did I find out certain details of how my affair at the factory had begun. I heard about them in 1957 from the well-known economist, Victor Belkin. As a result of established living conditions, Belkin had been obliged to continue his study at the evening division of the Moscow State Economics Institute in 1953. During preparation for examinations, he met Valeri Belkin whom I mentioned, and who for some reason was also combining work with study. During these studies, Valeri Belkin taught Victor Belkin how one must live in the real world. One of the principles was the following: usually there are people who are necessary to you and people to whom you are necessary. For success in life, it is necessary to be able to "sell" the people to whom you are necessary to the people whom you need. By way of example, Valeri Belkin cited the incident with me: how he sold me to the people he needed.

Valeri Belkin had a great career in the early 1950s: he had become the secretary of the Proletarian Regional Committee of the Komsomol, then the assistant of Politburo member Lazar Kaganovich, who was at that time the chairman of the Committee on Labor and Wages. Kaganovich's falling star apparently struck his assistant as well. Belkin was transferred to work as the head of the section of personnel in the Scientific Research Institute of Labor and Wages, and then he began to work on questions of the professional preparation of personnel. I happened to meet him at this Institute, and he even asked me to transfer to work with him later. After Valeri Belkin became the head of a Laboratory on the Professional Preparation of Personnel under the Committee of Professional and Technical Education, he tried to defend a doctoral dissertation, but I don't know the results.

10.   Shamai Turetskii, who worked for many years in Gosplan, told me that Voznesenskii's political ideal, as the latter assured him in private conversation, was Catherine the Great. Voznesenskii thought that Russia must be a rigidly centralized state with an enlightened monarch. Planning must embrace all the links of the national economy; everything must be planned to the last bolt.

11. In the evening at a banquet--and there were banquets almost every day and sometimes even twice a day--Ostrovitianov, in a quite ironical tone, proposed a toast to the economic-mathematical trend and to me as its representative. Ostrovitianov must be given his due; he could speak well and sometimes told jokes quite successfully. In my answering toast, I proposed to drink to Ostrovitianov, who had gone further than the everyday application of mathematics to economics and had begun to introduce it in social life. As an example I cited the famous formula ascribed to Ostrovitianov, of how to determine the age of the wife of an academician. According to this formula, the age of the academician's wife is equal to 100 minus the age of the academician. It is true that Ostrovitianov himself did not follow this formula, but several academicians did.

12. Totalitarian regimes accept the principle of uniformity in all spheres of social life. In this respect the following remark, reputedly made by Stalin in the postwar period, is very interesting. Once Stalin asked the Minister of Cinematography how many movies were being produced in the Soviet Union and how many of them were very good. The minister replied that out of approximately fifty movies produced annually only seven or eight of them were very good; Stalin said, "Well, then go and produce seven or eight movies."

13. J.M. Keynes, The General Theory of Employment, Interest and Money (Moscow: Inostrannaia Literatura Publisher, 1948).

14. See Alexander Gerschenkron, "Samuelson in Soviet Russia: A Report," The Journal of Economic Literature 16 (1978): pp. 560-73.

15. Kommunist, no. 15, 1971. I happened to meet Iovchuk in the mid-1950s. At this time I had been invited to take part in the collective work of the Philosophy Institute of the Academy of Sciences and the Sverdlovsk State University on the study of the cultural and professional level of the working class in the Soviet Union, based on the example of the Urals. The basis for the invitation was my publications on questions of the technological progress and organization of labor.

Iovchuk headed this collective work because he was a worker at the Philosophy Institute of the Academy of Sciences and knew the Urals. In the early 1950s, he had been one of the secretaries of the Sverdlovsk province committee of the Party after having been removed from the post of secretary of the Central Committee of the Communist Party of Belorussia. I happened to speak with him several times and he gave me the impression of a man inclined, in spite of his position as a leading member of the Party, to be responsive to new and challenging ideas.

16. See Kommunist, no. 15, 1971, for the articles or speeches of
Michail Suslov, Petr Demichev, and other marshals on the ideological
front.

17. Ibid., p. 101.

18. Ibid., p. 103.

CHAPTER 2

1. I once told my friends in jest that it was possible that alcoholics
were the only people in the USSR who really use the methods of linear
programming. It is they, the folk experts withdrawn into obscurity,
who created the methods of linear programming long before Kantorovich and Dantsig. Not realizing their genius, nor understanding the
significance of what they created, they have used these methods in their
daily humdrum lives.

What problem does an alcoholic solve? The criterion of optimality
for an alcoholic is the maximum alcohol content he can obtain in the
purchased alcoholic beverages. Let us designate the unknown quantity
of a certain kind of wine that he had bought as x_i; $i=1, 2, \ldots, n$. The
alcohol content in each unit of wine we will designate α_i. Then the
criterion of optimality is expressed in the form $\sum_i \alpha_i x_i \to$ max.

As constraints, the alcoholic has money "resources" which will be
denoted as d, and the prices for a bottle of wine, p_i. The integer constraint on the variables reflects the nature of the bottling process.

On the whole, the problem he solves has the following form:

$$\sum_{i=1}^{n} \alpha_i x_i \to \text{max.}$$

$$\sum_{i=1}^{n} p_i x_i \leqslant d$$

$$x_i = 0, 1, 2 \ldots$$

Because wine is rarely sold on tap in the Soviet Union and vodka is
sold only in bottles, primarily half-liters, an important limitation
arises for the alcoholic because of the integer variables. His resources
are insufficient to satisfy this constraint, so he is obliged to join with
other alcoholics. Since all alcoholics have the same criteria of optimality, these criteria are additive; the limiting resources are equally
additive. After the formation of the criteria and the limiting resources,
the problem is reduced to the previous one. From the dual ratio of
this problem $\alpha_i = p_i \lambda$ or $\frac{\alpha_i}{p_i} = \lambda$, where λ is the Lagrangian multiplier, it is apparent that at the point of the optimum, the relation of
the alcohol content in the bottle to the price of the bottle for all kinds
of wine purchased, must be equal. This is in fact what the alcoholic does.

But the planners who established the prices for wine and vodka also understood this at one time; the price of vodka and the ordinary kinds of port were identical in terms of proof. It seems that the exception was "Upper-Volga Nalivka," much sought after by experienced alcoholics. Several years ago, the prices for vodka were raised and the prices for the popular types of port remained the same. At this point, a type of port called Solntsedar, "gift of the sun," appeared and it had the ratio $\frac{\alpha_i}{p_i}$ most favorable to the alcoholic. As a result of this, after solving the problem of linear programming, the alcoholics sharply increased their demand for port. In the provincial cities, because of the infrequent delivery of port, they began to buy it by the case. Because in the atmosphere around the alcoholic, wine and vodka quickly "go sour"--at least the Russian alcoholics are convinced of this--the use of alcoholic beverages increased still more. Thus the alcoholics disgraced the planners, who had shown their conservatism in the use of modern methods of science in establishing prices.

So that the reader does not get the impression that I am praising the inventiveness of the Soviet alcoholics and returning to the 1940s with the unrestrained praise of everything Russian, I would like to say a few words on behalf of the Western alcoholics as well. Apparently they have the honor of solving the second part of the problem of the efficient organization of collective drinking: how to fairly divide a bottle among drinkers when there is no measuring cup, but only the usual glasses. The solution to this problem "for two" is quite elegant: one of the participants pours and the other chooses. But how should it be "for three" (the most frequent number in the USSR), and in general for n participants? The generalization of this problem in the case of n participants was made by the remarkable Soviet mathematician, Dynkin.

2.   Allen, R.   Matematicheskai Economiia (Mathematical Economics) (Moscow: Foreign Literature Publisher, 1963), translated by E. Ershov, V. Mash, B. Mikhalevskii, and S. Shatalin.

3.   Actively supporting economic reform in the country, I. Birman had published a series of interesting articles in major newspapers, and he presented his doctoral dissertation as a book, Optimal Programming (Moscow: Ekonomika Publisher, 1968). As a dissertation, however, the book was open to debate. It was to a considerable degree a popularization, and a very successful one, of ideas of mathematical programming. In this respect it was primarily a textbook, but it also presented scholarly ideas. Textbooks also may be entered as doctoral dissertations if they bear a special stamp imprinted by the Ministry of Higher

and Secondary Specialized Education, which is difficult to obtain. Birman did not have such a stamp on his book, but referring to its scholarly parts and to the defense, as a formality in his case he insisted on
defending the dissertation.

Many reactionaries were members of the Higher Dissertation
Committee (VAK) for economic-mathematical methods of the Ministry
of Secondary and Higher Education, however. Their reactionarism was
reflected, for example, in the two-year long refusal to approve Victor
Volkonskii's doctoral dissertation because of insinuations by obscurant-
ists, such as Petr Maslov, of anti-Marxism. It, therefore, was better
not to give VAK the possibility for formal objections. It had taken
TSEMI a long time to approve the recently founded Council for the defense of doctoral dissertations, and VAK's rejection of a dissertation
might have damaged it. Moreover, Birman could have assembled his
scholarly works in the canonic form of a doctoral dissertation without
much effort.

Around the time of the Scholarly Council's discussion of the dissertation, Birman had a falling out with Vainshtein. Knowing Vainshtein,
I am sure that the reason was trifling, probably insufficient respect
shown him. Vainshtein had a sense of humor, but he was highly sen-
sitive to jokes aimed at him, and Birman was a cheerful type. Albert
L'vovich Vainshtein liked to sign papers "Al'b. L. Vainshtein," and
Birman's wife's name is Al'bina Feoktistovna Tret'iakova. At some
point, Birman wrote "Al'b. Tretiakova" next to "Al'b. Vainshtein."
This small incident, or others like it, might have caused Vainshtein's
negative attitude towards Birman.

4.   Iakov Gerchuk was one of the economists of the older generation
who actively helped the development of the economic-mathematical
school. When in exile in the Altai, he was among the first people to
react to Kantorovich's work on rational metal cutting. He tried to
implement these methods at the Rubtsov tractor factory in the 1940s.
Upon his return to Moscow in the 1950s, Gerchuk became actively involved in propagating economic-mathematical methods, but he could
add nothing new or creative in this field. Later he began to write works
devoted to the limitations of mathematical programming as a method of
research on economic phenomena. Although there is no question that
mathematical programming is a clearly limited means, Gerchuk's
arguments created unpleasantness. Even when he was severely ill
Gerchuk continued his critical activity.

5.   Upon meeting me later in the hall and seeing my unusually cool
attitude towards him, A. Vainshtein asked me if I was angry at him

for his speech at the council. I told him my opinion to his face, but that was face to face; it wasn't the opinion I had expressed at the council. For me, the incident of the Gerchuk-Vainshtein statement was educational. Not by nature a militant person, I understood that it was also impossible to be indifferent; it was a question of degree. For the future, I chose the following position for myself: I would always speak out when scholars are attacked for their views under the cover of political accusations in my presence. Since then, I have tried to follow this principle.

6. I. Kantorovich, The Best Use of Economic Resources (Cambridge, Mass.: Harvard University Press, 1965).

7. It may be that Lev Dudkin was the first in Soviet economic-mathematical literature to introduce the function of utility for the analysis of national-economic models. However, he did not connect its investigation with general theoretical problems, since his interest, for many years, had been in the sphere of practical application.

8. A. Lurie, "An Abstract Model of an Optimal Economic Process," Ekonomika i Matematicheskie Metody, 1(1966): pp. 12-30.
    A. Aganbegian, K. Bagrinovskii, "About the Problems Concerning the Optimal Development of the National Economy," Voprosy Ekonomiki, 10 (1967): pp. 116-122.

9. In the autumn of 1965 N. Fedorenko called me and said that a session of the Academy of Sciences was soon to take place, which would be devoted to the economic problems of technological progress. It was suggested that he give a speech, in the name of the institute, of course, on the problems of price formation. He asked me, together with a number of other workers, to prepare the speech. In the body of this speech, price was mathematically defined as a partial derivative of the objective function, given the corresponding constraints. Then the translation of this expression into economic language, which I have cited previously, was given.
    I remember what a commotion there was in the hall for several minutes when Fedorenko cited the definition of price. The audience did not expect such blasphemy. Gradually, however, the definition given in the speech became quite current. All this did not prevent Fedorenko from later emphasizing in other publications, although in a restrained form, his advocacy of the labor theory of value. Later the speech itself appeared in the journal Kommunist, in the form of an article by Fedorenko (see N. Fedorenko, "Prices and Optimal Planning,"

<u>Kommunist</u>, 8(1966) pp. 84-93. As far as I know, because of the editorial board, mention of the fact that the article was based on a speech prepared by a group of workers at TSEMI was removed.

Lurie said to me more than once that I had done a great thing, concluding that Fedorenko, if only through his own name, had promulgated this definition. Unfortunately, it never occurred to him how dangerous it is to strive for the development of science by such methods; the temperament of the fighter developed under Soviet conditions was the cause.

10. By an ironical twist of fate, at the end of the 1940s, Israel Bliumin signed several of his works under the pseudonym of Sonin. This same surname belonged to a Soviet economist, Michail Sonin, also of Jewish origin.

11. I. Bliumin, V. Shliapentokh, "About the Econometric Track in the Bourgeoise Political Economy," <u>Voprosy Ekonomiki</u>, 6(1959): pp. 105-113.

12. Above and beyond the general atmosphere of the Stalin regime, in which it was difficult and dangerous for an active young scholar to study history, Shliapentokh's Jewish origin also had its effect. It was aggravated still more by his heightened activity, his unusual surname, and his red hair. When Shliapentokh's son, who externally resembled his father, returned home from his first day at school after having been "educated" by his seven-year-old friends in class, he announced, "I don't want to be Jewish, red-headed, and Shliapentokh."

13. V. Shliapentokh, <u>Econometrics and Problems of Economic Growth</u> (Moscow: Mysl' Pub., 1966).

14. Around 1964, Shliapentokh went to work in the Siberian Academic Town. There he was finally given the opportunity to work on what interested him most--social problems. He expanded a large work on the sociology of the press. At the end of the 1960s, Shliapentokh moved to Moscow, to the then newly created Institute of Concrete Social Research of the Academy of Sciences. His interest centered on the methodology of sociological research, but he continued to be interested in mathematical economics. He tried to organize an investigation of consumer demand and took part in the discussion of questions on principles of modeling, in particular at the seminar at TSEMI in 1973 where he gave a speech on Kornai's book, <u>Anti-equilibrium</u>. In the spring of 1979, Shliapentokh emigrated to the United States.

15. A. Kolmogorov, "A Presentation on the First All-Union Scientific Conference on the Application of Mathematical Methods to Economics," General Problems of Application Mathematics in Economics and Planning (Moscow: "Nauka," 1961) pp. 185-188.

16. Some young historians came to economics because they were unable to apply their creative talents to history, one of the fields of Soviet science most rigorously controlled by the Party. The potential for creativity in history of one of these youngsters can be judged, for example, by the following fact. In the mid-1940s, during the tight conditions of the Stalin regime, two young historians, I Kantorovich and V. Shliapentokh, decided to create a theory explaining the interrelations between countries, which they termed "monads." The creation of this theory was stimulated by the formation in this period of the large Stalinist empire, which also involved China, Eastern European countries, and so on. The essence of this theory I will risk giving in its own terms.

It was assumed that the interrelations among "monads" that were close to each other in ideology involve a great number of points of contact and similar desires. These countries, however, would inevitably clash, and the monad system which included them would become unstable. Thus they predicted the fall of the socialist system, which, in truth, had been expected from the time of China's desertion. When Yugoslavia fell away from the socialist camp in 1948, Kantorovich, having heard the news on the radio, ran home at one o'clock in the morning, called Shliapentokh, awoke him, and shouted, "It's begun!"

I understand that for a Western individual this concept of two young Soviet historians seems trivial. However, one must remember that they created it while cut off from the Western world, under conditions in which they feared to discuss it with anyone.

17. Regarding this point, the following story may be interesting. It demonstrates one way in which the Soviet economists who were deprived of a serious mathematical education succeeded in establishing contacts with highly professional mathematicians.

I decided that in order to attract scholars to economics it was necessary in the first place to try to elicit respect from them. To this end, I decided to select a sphere of conversation with which everyone was well acquainted. Sex proved to be such a sphere. Questions of sex seem comprehensible to everyone, and at the same time discussions of them smack of acuity, especially in the Soviet Union where until recently it was not acceptable to speak on the subject at all.

A group of quite prominent mathematicians gathered one day at the

house of one of my friends and I was invited. Alone and surrounded by
many unknown mathematicians, I was uncomfortable. One of the guests,
a man with humanistic ideas and brilliant mathematical abilities, spoke
very condescendingly with me about something insignificant. And at
this point I decided that it was necessary to make myself respected.
Rushing into the general conversation at an appropriate moment, I
quite pretentiously announced that mathematicians, like all other
narrow specialists, were quite limited people, that they can be sur-
prised--a necessary demand for a scholar--only in their own sphere;
in other spheres they are ordinary mortals. As proof, I suggested
that they could not formulate just one nontrivial problem about sex, an
area in which everyone has approximately the same initial information.
"Moreover," I added, "even if I formulate such a problem and you
think that it is not trivial (I trust your conscience), then all the same
you will not be able to give a nontrivial answer to it." They thought
the question over and, of course, were not able to propose anything
immediately. Then I formulated the following question for them: "Why
do male primates have their testicles on the exterior, while the ovaries
of the female are hidden deep within the organism?" Both the question
and my answer to it were acknowledged to be nontrivial. I might add
that one of the participants in this conversation phoned me several
years later and said that in the just-published issue of the journal
Priroda (Nature) there was a letter from a reader which asked the
first part of my question.

I remember how the mathematician whom I have already mentioned
sat almost the entire evening in a corner of the room thinking of an
answer to my question. He did not give an answer, but he was an expert at thinking up nontrivial questions concerning "unnatural" systems,
i.e., from social life, to which I, as a person close to it, could not
give nontrivial answers. For example, the question: to whom are the
teams for saving drowning people subordinate in the USSR? I later
became very friendly with this mathematician who was a wonderful
person and a great scholar. Several of my other friends who are mathematicians, whom I jokingly called "my students in sex problems,"
later gave me questions about sex and produced nontrivial answers to
them. The best answers to my questions about sex were given by a
brilliant physicist, Mark Azbel.

18. Valentina Gaganova became famous at this time as a brigadier in
a weaving factory who had transferred from her advanced brigade to a
brigade which was falling behind. She was able to turn the laggardly
brigade into a progressive one. Gaganova's initiative received wide
publicity in the press, and she received the title of "Hero of Socialist

Labor. " This initiative was organized from above, as was the Stak-
hanovite movement as a whole and other initiatives, in the hope of increasing the effectiveness of production in an easy way. But there
were too few peredoviks (exemplary factory workers) in the country,
and even more to the point, too few of them wished to transfer to lag-
ging brigades with the concomitant pay cuts in order to exert a serious
influence on the growth of the effectiveness of production.

Gaganova's initiative was quickly forgotten, but the people immor-
talized it for posterity in the following couplet: "I'll dump a good guy
and I'll be a jerk's wife; 'That's Valentina Gaganova,' they'll say of
my life. "

19. P. Morse and G. Kimball, Methods of Operations Research
(Cambridge-New York, Massachusetts Institute of Technology and
Wiley Press: 1951).

20. Within autocratic systems, where the role of feudal structures is
great, titles acquire considerable significance, sometimes in rather
amusing ways. In the system of the Academy of Sciences, there is a
post of senior scientific-technical researcher, a job with a very long
name for an assistant to scientific personnel. When one of the senior
scientific-technical workers of the Institute of Economics went on a
business trip to the Baltic with his boss, a senior research worker,
the hotel gave preference to the assistant because he was not only a
senior research worker, but also a technical one.

21. Some of these leaders, feeling their own strength even in the
Stalinist period of mass purges of Jews by the central apparatus, were
able to defend the Jews. The director of the Central Statistical Administration V. Starovskii, did not allow Jews to be fired from the
Administration, where they occupied a series of leading positions. In
fact, the Statistical Administration at the beginning of the 1950s was
the only central union agency in which there was such a significant
percentage of Jews in leading jobs. Apparently Starovskii's ability to
be needed by the government--he held his job as head of the administration, where he worked from 1940 on through Stalin, Malenkov, Khrushchev, and Brezhnev--and the understanding that for this an appropriate
staff was necessary, gave him the opportunity to show independence in
deciding personnel questions too. I was told one of the secrets for
Starovskii's successes. He always tried to know in advance what the
leaders might need in the near future and prepared the necessary
material. When the material was demanded, for practical purposes
everything was already ready. In the mid-1940s, for example,

Starovskii was apparently called by Stalin with a request to answer a
series of questions concerning statistical data about the period of Ivan
the Terrible, since Stalin was very interested in Ivan the Terrible.
Through Alexander Poskrebyshev, the boss of Stalin's secretariat,
Starovskii had found out earlier about the leader's interest in this material, and when Stalin called, Starovskii said that he would soon have
the material ready. I do not remember exactly what time period was
mentioned to me, but in a very short time Starovskii gave Stalin the
answer, for which he received "Thank you, comrade Starovskii,"
great praise from Stalin.

22. The roots of anti-Semitism in Russia go very deep. The phenomenon has biological and social causes and they can be traced by comparing Russian attitudes toward the three nationalities living in the
territory of Russia: the Jews, the Tatars, and the Germans.

I want to mention at least three factors which determine anti-
Semitism. The first of them is the biological instinct to be cautious
toward an alien; the habits of the alien are unknown, and it is necessary
but not a sufficient condition for anti-Semitism. The Russians were
also cautious with the Tatars and Germans.

Another factor which determines anti-Semitism could be expressed
in the form of a coefficient of resistance, i.e., in the relationship
between the aggressiveness of the alien to obtain scarce goods and the
possibilities of the natives to defend these resources. The unfriendly,
but not malicious, attitude toward the Tatars, a significant portion of
whom live among the Russians, is apparently explained by the fact that
the Tatars en masse do not actively lay claim to scarce goods. In
Moscow there is a large percentage of Tatars among the janitors and
Muscovites take such work extremely unwillingly. But the coefficient
of resistance for the jewish people is very high.

One can also isolate such a factor as whether the alien is a guest
or a stranger. The Germans were quite aggressive guests, and due
to a higher cultural level, they obtained prominent positions in the
Tsarist government. For many of my Russian acquaintances, it was
strange to hear that the last ruling people of the house of Romanov had
considerable German heritage. At the same time, there was not the
same animosity toward the Germans as there was toward the Jews.
The Germans were guests in Russia, not strangers, and behind them
stood a great Germany to which they could always return. The Jews
came to Russia mainly after the partitions of Poland; there was no
other place for them to go. Emigration to America was for many of
them negated by the expense of the journey. The Jews who found
themselves in Russia were distinguished by a higher culture and level

of activity than the local population. I don't know whether the Jewish
people as a nation are genetically distinguished from other nationalities
in terms of activity and abilities, but the European Jews endured a
century of "unnatural selection" in the struggle with highly cultured
Europeans. In the case of European Jews, it is possible that the numbers of active, capable people increased in this struggle. In any event,
there was also a deviation in another direction: the percentage of
psychological illness among the Jews was higher than among the nationalities surrounding them.

The cited reasons for anti-Semitism in Russia, of course, are not
exhaustive. Religion and the creation of Israel were also important
reasons, but the previous reasons were sufficient for the rulers, under
difficult conditions, to try and maintain a social equilibrium by ex-
ploiting the unfriendliness of the population to Jews. These difficult
conditions always arise; such is the nature of the development of society.
These conditons arose under the Tsars, as evidenced by the pogroms.
These conditions arose also under Stalin, as evidenced by the planned
deportation of the Jews from the big cities. It seems true that in March
1953 Stalin was planning a mass exile of Jews to Siberia. This would
have been accompanied by a large propaganda campaign, which actually
had already begun in connection with the unmasking of the doctor-
murderers and the praise of the popular heroine, Lydia Timashuk.

In February 1953, the editor-in-chief of Pravda, Shepilov, assembled a large group of well-known Soviet Jews. Among them was academician, Trakhtenberg, a well-known economist and specialist on the
Western financial system. The editor-in-chief suggested that those
assembled sign a text addressed to Jews of the Soviet Union on the
necessity of going to Siberia. This necessity was argued as follows:
among the Jews, as the experience of postwar years demonstrated,
there were many renegades, enemies who had sold themselves to the
Jewish Joint Distribution Committee, a Western intelligence service.
In total accord with Marxist-Leninist theory, reasons for this phenomenon were pointed out, i. e., the lack of a working class and kolkhoz
peasantry among the Jews. The Soviet government wished to help the
Jews correct their mistakes and created appropriate conditions to form
a working class and a kolkhoz peasantry in the region of Siberia.

Needless to say, Trakhtenberg told his close friends that he refused
to sign this document.

23. The opinion is quite widespread that if young people can obtain
better material living conditions in the West, they they are potential
emigrants. This opinion is only partially correct; improvement in
living conditions does not, for many people, provide a good enough

reason to emigrate. Many young people are connected with parents and family who not only do not want to emigrate themselves but actively resist it. For many elderly people who have comfortable apartments, decent work or a pension, and friends, it seems outlandish to emigrate when the authorities do not directly urge it upon them. Another important consideration, of course, is the fear that if the children emigrate they might never see their parents again.

Furthermore, many young Jews in the USSR, as well as their parents, are well assimilated and devoid of the nationalistic and religious feelings which often contribute to the desire to emigrate. The high percentage of mixed marriages can serve as an indicator of assimilation.

It should be kept in mind that the intellectual portion of Jewish youth in the Soviet Union now knows about the difficulties which befell the Jews who emigrated to the West. In the first place, these difficulties involved a loss of their customary cultural environment.

What I have said about the difficulties for Jews in deciding to emigrate is supported by the fact that very few do despite conditions that make it statistically apparent that a Jew, not having security clearance and not being a prominent specialist in the sphere of natural sciences or art, can probably obtain permission to emigrate. Indeed, the existence of only statistical information, and not of any firm legal grounds, serves to preserve considerable fears on the part of would-be emigrees. The treatment by the Soviet authorities of the so-called "secret people" (people with security clearance who want to emigrate) is more arbitrary still. One may argue whether the government has a right to detain its secret people, but in any case I think it is true that explicit legal guidelines should exist for handling such special cases.

24. Although TSEMI was maligned among the academic institutes for its record on the emigration of Jews, at the end of 1972 the institute received an honorary certificate of the Central Committee of the CPSU, the Presidium of the Supreme Soviet of the USSR, and the Council of Ministers of the USSR as a winner in the All-Union Socialist Competition in honor of the fiftieth anniversary of the formation of the USSR. This certificate was received by only several thousand organizations in the country and in particular, by only two institutes of the USSR Academy of Sciences. But in 1976 the director of TSEMI had to pay for the high rate of emigration of the TSEMI scholars, but the price was reasonable: dismissal of a group of people from leading positions.

25. In recent years, members of the intelligentsia have joined the Party for precisely these reasons. Aspirations of people to increase

their security, to realize their desire for activity, and to see the world are natural. It is quite difficult to demand that people suppress these aspirations because it necessitates Party membership. The press into which people are squeezed has more power than the spiritual resistance of the ordinary person. And how are these spiritual powers to be increased?

I do not justify it, but I understand the many people who have joined the Party for these reasons; their behavior and their interests urge them to do this. I was patient with them. These people are still more attractive to me than those who fanatically joined the Party in the sincere belief that they could remake the world. Yet I am sorriest for the people who joined the Party in the late 1960s and early 1970s, sincerely convinced that if there were more decent people in the Party, they could succeed in doing much to change the situation in the country. On a local level, these people were sometimes right. For example, in the Party cells of some research institutes where there were a considerable number of decent Communists, the dissidents were not censored. However, Party bosses, understanding this, at meetings of the regional committees or city committees of the Party, examined the cases of the dissidents from such organizations.

The Party apparatus is formed according to its own principles, and the higher the level of the Party hierarchy, the closer the cultural level of the Party functionary is to the level of the highest leaders. It is not by chance that in the apparatus of the Central Committee of the CPSU, in positions beginning with the head of a section (a phase transition), there is not one intellectual. The intellectual's top capacity is deputy to the head of a section.

Those I cannot condone, however, are the people who join the Party when all their previous behavior has led others with whom they have been quite frank to believe that joining the Party was impossible for them. The deception of this group is unforgivable, the more unforgivable because these people are renegades; they enter an organization previously foreign to them, wishing to win trust from the Party through damage they do to their fellows.

It was precisely for this that the mathematician Iuli Finkelstein joined the Party in TSEMI at the end of the 1960s. His acquaintances knew him as a more or less capable mathematician, moving in an environment of critically minded people, a man who did not hide his sharply critical attitude toward his surroundings. It is true that Finkelstein demonstrated too great a desire to obtain the position as section head; but as there are also non-Party heads, this promotion was not connected with his possible entry into the Party. Suddenly I saw an announcement in the Institute about Finkelstein's acceptance

into the Party; it was a bolt out of the blue. This action was not in
accord with the man's past behavior. After joining the Party, Finkelstein took up public work with the zeal of a neophyte. The trouble here
was in how he fulfilled it. When one of the workers, under Finkelstein's
pressure, refused at the session of a political education (in those
divisions where it is organized, all workers must participate in these
sessions) to make a speech concerning acute current political events,
Finkelstein approached his refusal with the fundamentalism inherent
in a real Communist. There was a fuss in the institute, but the affair
was somehow settled, and the worker was not dismissed. Finkelstein,
however, was later forced to leave the division of mathematical programming. He was willingly accepted in another division where the
workers were more similar to him in spirit.

CHAPTER 3

1.   The Institute's journal Voprosy Ekonomiki (Problems of Economics),
received a particularly large number of such letters. The late Konstantin Baev who was on the staff of that journal once decided to get rid
of one of the more persistent writers in a rather witty way. In one of
his regular answers to this man, Baev began with some sentences concerning economics and connected to the ideas of the article's author.
Then he took at random a volume of the encyclodedia dictionary by
Brockhaus and Efron and copied a text on field mice from it. That
ended his correspondence with this particular individual.

2.   In the Soviet Union, in order to defend a candidate's dissertation,
two readers are required, and one of them must have a doctoral degree
(Doctor of Science); for a Doctor of Science defense, three readers are
needed and all three must have doctoral degrees.

3.   It was also not a good idea in works destined for publication by the
institute to refer to any publications positively indicating the name of
the author. Of course, the classics of Marxism-Leninism were exceptions to this rule. The high priests of economics continue even now
to write in this style. Later I ran up against this limitation on references when working on a book in 1959 on the economic effectiveness of
complex mechanization and automation in machine construction. Insofar as there were many references in the book to works of various
authors, difficulties arose with the administration in obtaining approval
for the book to go to press. The reason was explained as follows: if
tomorrow it turns out that the author whose work is referred to is an
enemy of the people, the book will have to be taken out of circulation.

This conversation took place in 1958, during the time of rehabilitation of hundreds of thousands of people imprisoned by Stalin for political reasons, and it was therefore possible to persuade the administration to include author references.

4.   I met Konstantin I. Klimenko on January 6, 1953. The reason for this meeting was the manuscript of my book on the organization of labor and wages, which I had given to the publishing house, Mashgiz, in the fall of 1952. The head of the economics division of Mashgiz, Teodor Saksaganskii, met me earlier. In 1950 I had come to him off the street, so to speak, at the offices of the journal Vestnik Mashino-stroeniia, where he was in charge of the economics department, and I proposed to write an article on the qualifications of workers in flow production on the basis of my experience at the Calibr factory's shop for flow production of micrometers.

The motivation for the article was my criticism of the widespread opinion among engineers that in flow production the workers' qualifications are lower. From experience working in the shop I had become convinced that this opinion of workers' qualifications in flow was not so simple. When the engineers stressed that in flow less qualified workers are needed, they were right for situations in which serial production is replaced by large series or mass production which usually accompanies flow, and if it is demanded that workers be strictly specialized for the given operation. These conditions have a practical significance, especially when it becomes necessary to expand production of some product quickly in a situation in which there is a shortage of qualified workers. However, in accordance with mastery and perfection of flow, it makes sense to raise both the breadth and depth of workers' qualifications. The worker's mastery of several continuous operations in a flow ensures flexibility in the case of illness, especially if the number of ill workers exceeds the size of the reserve group for execution of the given operation. The worker's combination of several functions, instead of using equipment adjusters, makes the worker more productive because there is no need to lose time waiting for the adjuster.

Saksaganskii suggested to me that for appearance sake the head of the micrometers shop, Nicolai Lesin, should also sign the article, and I agreed to this. My first journal publication, "Concerning Higher Qualifications for Workers on Production Lines," appeared in Vestnik mashinostroeniia, 9 (1950) pp. 62-65. Apparently someone from a higher up organization even praised the editors for this article. Therefore, when I came to see him with the manuscript of the book in 1962, Saksaganskii made an effort to help me. However, for him, a person

of Jewish origin, it was not without danger to help an unknown person
who was also a Jew and writing on problems which were then rather
controversial: the organization of and payment for work. To cor-
roborate his decision, he decided to send the summary of the book to
six specialists and as far as I remember, they were all Russians.
Despite the wave of anti-Semitism at that time, two of them sent back
positive reports. They were Nikolai Kabanov, the head of the labor
and salary department of the First State Bearings factory and the head
of the labor department of one of the machine construction ministries.
When the other reports did not come in, Saksaganskii advised me to
go to the reviewers myself, in particular to a representative of the
scholarly world whose opinion was important. This person was Konstantin Klimenko.

I did not know Klimenko personally, so I went to see him at the
Institute of Economics on a day when he had office hours. The office-
hour days are an interesting phenomenon. The humanities and social
science institutes of the Academy of Sciences do not have enough work
space for the staff. Technicians and administrators are assigned
space, but scientists often do not even have their own desks and must
use the desk of a technician. That is why each institute establishes
limited office hours for scientists. The bosses try to fight this system
of work, and ordinances from the Presidium of the USSR Academy of
Sciences appear regularly, demanding that labor discipline be increased
and everyone should work in his institute's building the whole week.
Since the space is not increased by these edicts, the commands cannot
be obeyed. In the mid-1960s, one of these ordinances was particularly
threatening. The immediate reason for it was apparently upset in the
academy because several scholars had signed petitions on behalf of
dissidents. In order to teach scholars not to interfere in politics, it
was decided to tie them more strictly to their places of work, but in
this situation the constant space limitations turned out to be decisive,
and everything in fact remained the same.

When I met Klimenko, he said that he had received my book for
review, but since he was not a specialist on incentives, it would be
better for me to find someone else in the institute to review it. I told
him I thought my work was closer to his. In my work I tried to analyze
the system of incentives as a function of the organization of labor and
the character of technology used. The latter aspect was among Klimenko's interests. Klimenko asked me to give him a brief review of
the content of my work. Having heard me out, he said that he liked
the ideas very much and asked me to call, come see him in a week at
his home, and he promised to write a review. A week later, on
January 13, I read in Pravda the note on the doctors' plot. I remember

that entire day well; I thought about my visit to Klimenko and wondered how the great Russian would receive me on that day. I still decided to phone, as I had nothing to lose and around 10:00 p.m., as he had asked, I called; he said I could come over.

Klimenko wrote an excellent review of my book. We did not discuss the Jewish question directly. We sat and talked for a long time, and Klimenko told me how Stalin had killed the famous Soviet general, V. Blucher, about mistakes in running the economy, and so on. For me, such conversation was a total revelation. I had known little of the events of 1937 and did not know of these mistakes. Moreover, such talks were not common in the Soviet Union, particularly with a stranger and on such an unusual day.

Because I lived in a suburb of Moscow I could only get home from where Klimenko lived on the commuter train since I did not have money for a taxi. At 12:30 a.m., feeling that I was going to miss the last train, I began to take my leave. Then Klimenko's wife, Elena, came out of the other room. (Klimenko lived in a private three-room apartment, an unusual phenomenon for those years.) Having been introduced, she asked how I felt about the day's news of the doctors' plot. I answered that every nation has its scoundrels, but that the people as a whole are not responsible for them. I sincerely believed that those doctors were guilty. What, then, was my amazement when Mrs. Klimenko said, "Really, young man! This is simply an ordinary Stalinist provocation!" Then Mr. Klimenko, in his Viking character, proclaimed that it was not for this that he had fought at the Samara barricades against the Black Hundreds when he was a schoolboy, not for this had he taken part in the revolution. Thus, we stood at the door until 1:30 a.m., and I walked home, arriving around 6:00 a.m. Later Konstantin Klimenko and I often remembered that evening. I said to him that he had done a lot for me when he helped with the publication of my books and obtaining a job at the Institute of Economics, but nothing could be compared with what he had done for me that evening to restore my human dignity.

5. At the end of the 1960s, working at TSEMI, Pliukhin defended a doctoral dissertation on the use of economic-mathematical methods in agriculture. In TSEMI, he joined the Communist Party and tried to take an active part in the social life of the institute. Several times Pliukhin's amoral behavior—outrageous behavior to the wife and two children he had left—was the subject of discussion at the institute's Party bureau. However, suddenly in 1972 he was named director of an institute dealing with the creation of an automated system of management in the medical industry. He seemed to have great potential, and I was told of his grandiose plans.

6.   Compared to the famous schemes of growth by Marx and Lenin,
I intended to introduce a different structure in the production process.
In the production of consumer goods links were observed between raw
materials and finished products; in the production of machinery, including maintenance and the manufacture of spare parts, the links
between raw materials and finished products were also examined. Of
course, there were versatile products that could be utilized both in the
production of consumer goods and machinery, but this factor was unimportant to working out the process.

7.   The basic subjects of my conversations with Faerman were various
problems in the general systems theory. We were both interested on
the whole in questions of cognition and the creation of an artificial intelligence. However, we understood that this interest could be satisfied to a certain extent if the principles of the construction of any one
complex system were understood. However, the difficulties in receiving initial information interfered with applying this to natural systems,
especially the biological system. From this point of view it seemed
that the process of cognition in economics was simpler than in natural
systems, because economics was a relatively recent artificial system
with a short and visible history; the groundwork in many respects lay
on the surface.
     All this predetermined our decision to attempt a mutual study of
the economic system in order to branch out to the investigation of
another system. I don't know what the outcome of Faerman's investigations will be, since he is still studying the economic system, but my
interest in recent years has fundamentally shifted toward general
systems theory.

8.   At that time obtaining a senior research scientist's job in the
Institue of Economics was difficult and its attainment was accompanied
by some sort of confused bureaucratic procedure. According to this
procedure, in order to hold the job of a senior researcher, it was
necessary to receive the title of senior researcher, but to receive
this title one had to hold the corresponding job.
     In any event, after overcoming the bureaucratic difficulties, in
1960 I was nominated for the job and title of senior researcher simultaneously. This nomination had to be officially confirmed by a resolution of the Presidium of the Academy of Sciences of the USSR. Moreover, its confirmation by the Economics Department of the Academy
of Sciences of the USSR was required first. I was summoned to meet
with the secretary of the Department, Bolgov, who was the author of
conservative works on the economics of agriculture and apparently

worked himself up to the academy as the assistant to the Politburo
member, Michail Suslov. Bolgov questioned me about my scientific
works and whether I was a member of the Trade Union. The latter
question was irrevelant because the Trade Unions didn't play an essential role in the Soviet Union. At the conclusion of the interview,
he said that the department could not recommend me, citing no reasons.
He kindly added that I could continue my work at the academy. The
members of the Bureau of the Economics Department--Plotnikov,
Nemchinov, and Khachaturov--who found out about this conversation
with Bolgov saw to it that the department recommended me for the title
and job of senior researcher. The appointment was confirmed by the
Presidium of the Academy of Sciences.

9.   B. Rakitskii, The Forms of the Management Systems of Enterprises (Moscow: Nauka, 1968).

10. L. Gatovskii, M. Sakov, "About the Principal Foundations of
Research in Economics," Kommunist, 15 (1960): pp. 79-90.

11. I. Bruk, "Computers for serving the National Economy," Kommunist, 7 (1957): pp. 124-127.

12. V. Belkin, I. Birman, "The Fear of the American Economists
Concerning Input-Output Tables," Voprosy Ekonomiki, 6 (1959):
pp. 105-113.

13. V. Belkin, Prices at a Single Level and the Economic Measurements at their Foundation (Moscow: Ekonomika, 1963).

14. L. Postyshev, "The Labor Theory of Value and Optimal Planning,"
Kommunist, 3 (1967): pp. 49-61.

15. I also know of other examples of victims of the Stalin regime
speaking with ecstasy of Stalin, and recalling their meetings with him.
Thus I was told about one Soviet philosopher whose last name I do not
remember but whom I will call Sh-v, for the sake of convention. In
the mid-1930s, Sh-v was deputy to the director of the Philosophy Institute of the Academy of Sciences. After the purge and destruction
of the personnel who worked for the Ministry for Foreign Affairs in
the mid-1930s, Sh-v was offered work there as the leader of the press
department. The position was a high one (it was to instruct the Soviet
Press on international events, etc.) and that is why this position belongs to Stalin's nomenclature. Soon one morning there was a call

from Molotov who had replaced M. Litvinov. Molotov said that Sh-v
was to meet with Stalin at 10:00 a.m. the same day, but Sh-v had no
car, and Molotov went off to the Kremlin without Sh-v. (Sh-v spoke
negatively of Molotov, and quite sharply.) With difficulty, Sh-v
managed to find a car, but he was late. When he came into Stalin's
reception room, Molotov was already there. The head of Stalin's
secretariat, Poskrebyshev, after hearing the reasons for Sh-v's
tardiness, began to scold Molotov, who at that time was the second
most powerful person in the state. Molotov excused himself before
Poskrebyshev and promised at once to provide Sh-v with a personal
car. Finally, Stalin received Sh-v. He exchanged greetings with him
and called him by name and patronymic although it is said that he did
this very rarely. In the course of the conversation, Stalin began to
clarify how Sh-v would write a textbook on Western European philosophy
and added that such a textbook was much needed. Turning to Molotov,
Stalin asked him to create conditions for Sh-v under which he could
continue work on the textbook. Sh-v had still other meetings with
Stalin and more than one conversation on the telephone, but this first
meeting, and the conversation about the textbook moved him for many
years. Although in 1940 during one of the purges of the people's
enemies, Sh-v was sent to a camp, he retained the warmest memories
of Stalin.

I have more than once encountered Stalinists to whom Stalin had
made a gift of his favor, and they lived well while he was alive and
after his death. The fact that these people retained their love for
Stalin is not surprising. What is surprising in the cited examples is
that people who became his victims retained their love for him, dicta-
ted by no means other than adherence to a specific ideology. To spec-
ulate about it, their love for Stalin may be explained by the fact that
in their subconscious, as in general for many people, love for a leader
plays a tremendous role--the biological instinct for obedience to the
leader and the will toward his preservation. If the leader expresses
his attention to a certain individual and distinguishes him, in other
words, singles him out, then this sharply improves his position in the
collective. Such signs of attention are necessary apparently to make
an impression. If it is bad later, then it is not the leader who is to
blame, but the circumstances.

16. For many years Mash collected a library of English literature. I
became acquainted with him through one of our common acquaintances,
the economist Georgi Mett, who took care of Mash's English library
w hen he went to the Far East. Mett was remarkable in that at the end
of the 1920s or the beginning of the 1930s he wrote a novel and Maksim

Gorkii liked the novel. The novel was already accepted for publication
or possibly even printed when Mett, after understanding at the last
moment the danger of publishing a novel, destroyed it. Many years
later, Mett worked on the organization of production at machine-
constructing enterprises, worked actively in the society of machine-
builders, and died in his bed in the 1960s.

17. R. Kaizer, Russia, The People and the Power (New York: Atheneum,
1976); H. Smith, The Russians (New York: Quadrangle, 1976).

18. It is quite a frequent phenomenon for a scholar with an initial mathematical or engineering education to become a Ph. D. or Doctor of
Economic Sciences. Such a tendency is quite natural because upon
entering the field of economics many mathematicians and engineers
began to study economic problems. This is quite easy for them because the economic-mathematical trend has only begun to be developed
in the Soviet Union. Furthermore, it is easier to write a dissertation
on economic sciences than on engineering or mathematics because it
is less exacting.

19. I will digress a little in order to compare Prudenskii with Olimpiada
Kozlova, an economist of his generation, and to demonstrate in this
comparison how oddly the ruling nucleus of the economic-mathematical
trend was formed. The fates of Kozlova and Prodenskii are in some
respects similar, although Kozlova was even less inclined toward
scholarly activity than Prudenskii.
     During the war, Kozlova was the secretary of the Party organiza-
tion at the Vladimir Ilich Factory in Moscow. Then she became the
secretary of one of the Moscow District Committees and the Moscow
City Committee of the Party. During the 1950s, she became the director of the Sergo Ordzhonikidze Moscow Engineering-Economics Institute, which she administered continuously for more than twenty
years. The story of Kozlova's doctoral dissertation, which was devoted to the growth of the cultural and professional working class in
the Soviet Union, provoked in its time not a little talk. Many humorous
stories were circulated about Kozlova's answers during the defense.
     Kozlova, however, was one of the first to respond promptly to the
development of mathematical methods and computers. She organized
the preparation of students in this direction and the research in a
special laboratory at the institute. I will not undertake to judge the
quality of the work executed by this institute on economic-mathematical
methods. In one of Kozlova's accounts of the work conducted at the
institute on the present trend, it was said that the institute had worked

out 617 algorithms for the solution of economic problems. Among the algorithms were those which provided the definition of the productivity of labor by means of dividing the gross product into the number of workers.

Kozlova was not elected a Corresponding Member of the Academy of Sciences. One time she was able to obtain the last vacancy in the Corresponding Members of the Academy of Sciences after the preliminary elections had taken place in the economics department, but the general meeting of the Academy of Sciences voted against her; someone obviously feared her as a competitor. Kozlova always blamed the Jews for her failures, and her anti-Semitism was widely known. One time she even had certain foundations for this since Genrikh Abramovich Kozlov, a Jew at least by blood who was the chairman of the Department of Political Economy of the Party school of the Central Committee of the CPSU, was elected a Corresponding Member in economics instead of Olimpiada Vasilievna Kozlova!

20. K. Valtukh, The Societal Utility of Products and the Labor Expenditures of Their Production (Moscow: Mysl', 1965).

21. V. Lumelski, "Aggregation of the Matrix of the Input-Output Tables by means of the Algorithm of Diagonalization of Communication Matrix," Avtomatica i Telemekhanika, 9 (1970): 69-72.

22. E. Braverman, "A Production Model with Unequilibrium Prices," Ekonomika i Matematicheskie Metody, 2 (1972): pp. 175-191; "A Model of the Mechanism of Modification of Prices in a Production Network," Ekonomika i Matematicheskie Metody, 2 (1973): pp. 218-230.

23. E. Braverman, Mathematical Models in Planning and Control in Economic Systems (Moscow: Nauka, 1976).

24. L. Rosonoer, "A Generalized Thermodynamic Approach to Resource Exchange and Allocation, I," Automation and Remote Control 5 (1973): pp. 781-795; II, 6 (1973): pp. 915-927; III, 8 (1973): pp. 1272-1289.

25. A. Malishevskii, "Natural Systems," Automatika i Telemekhanika, 11 (1973) pp. 42-57.

26. B. Razumikhin, Physical Models and the Methods of Theory of Equilibrium in Programming and Economics (Moscow: Nauka, 1975).

27. This state of affairs is characteristic not only of science but of art
as well. Thus, two new theaters, Sovremennik and Teatr na Taganke,
have achieved a great deal even within the stricture of Soviet censorship.
The attempts to revitalize Khudozhestvennyi Teatr have proved futile
in spite of the fact that its present director was at one time director
of Sovremennik. It, therefore, would seem that the most natural
source for the development of new ideas should proceed within the
framework of new organizations. Old organization eventually have to
die off and expediting their death is, of course, quite a delicate task.

CHAPTER 4

1. Other than the economists, of whom I will speak later, teachers
in related disciplines were also dismissed. Thus, one of the best
philosophy departments in the Soviet Union was broken up. Genrikh
Ezrin, a decent man who supported the new trends and who worked in
MINKH for more than 20 years, was removed from leadership. Other
qualified professors, e.g., Boguslavskii and A. Rakitov, were obliged
to leave with him.

2. See, for example, A. Birman, Some Problems of the Science
Concerning the Management of the National Economy (Moscow:
Ekonomika, 1965).

3. Turetskii had known and trusted me since 1946 at MGEI. Therefore, when we met by chance in 1963 on vacation in the boarding house,
Berezka, he revealed some of his knowledge to me. In a very capti-
vating manner he related the details of the Promparty trial. He knew
the facts from one of the participants in the trial, Sergei Pervushin,
who by that time had died. He saw the external side of the entire trial
in the Gosplan, where he then already occupied a prominent position.
The Promparty trial was organized by Stalin and his assistants in the
early 1930s, as is well known, in order to find those responsible for
the economic difficulties. The group of specialists was placed in a
special little house within the Butyrka Prison. There they were
assigned to write the program of the Promparty. The necessity for
taking the guilt upon himself in the interests of Russia and his prestige
were argued to Leonid Ramzin, the leader of the imaginary Promparty.
(This was during the heyday of the ideas of internationalism; only later
was the idea of love for Russia, the Motherland, introduced into the
ranks of official political doctrine.) But Ramzin would not listen to
these arguments, and the other members of Promparty would not
agree. Because of their obstinacy, all the Prompartians were taken

to the main building of the prison where their living conditions deteri-
orated, but this didn't sway them. Then they were led into the inner
court of Butyrka, and two of them were shot before the eyes of the
others. After this, the Prompartians decided to return to their little
house. Having assessed the programs and regulations of various
parties, they began to create the program of Promparty.

At the same time, a meeting was set up between G. Krzhizhanovskii,
the chairman of Gosplan, and Ramzin. Ramzin was warned that if he
even gave a hint at the meeting that all the accusations shown to him
were not true, it would be tantamount to breaking a promise! After the
meeting with Ramzin, Krzhizhanovskii collected a group of workers at
the Gosplan and told them about Ramzin's sabotage. It is difficult to
say whether Krzhizhanovskii believed in what had occurred or was just
using the arranged farce.

What is strange and extremely unusual about the Promparty affair
is the fact that several of its participants and its leader, Ramzin, were
freed even before the war, obtained work, and died in their beds. After
the trial, Pervushin worked in nonferrous metallurgy; he abandoned
general theoretical research. During the war, he called the attention
of the government to rare earth metals on the Kolsk peninsula and
moved to Moscow, where for many years he headed the economics
department of nonferrous industry in what was then called the Kalinin
Institute for Nonferrous Metals. Pervushin was a member of the expert commission of the Higher Certifying Commission. As Konstantin
Klimenko told me, he and Pervushin more than once helped people
presenting dissertations who were treated unjustly. Pervushin died
in the mid-1960s. Why Stalin spared the Prompartians remains a
mystery.

4. It was unpleasant for me to discover that in 1972 Itin talked about
the Jewish problem on television. As an economist he justified the
collection of "payment for training" from Jews emigrating from the
Soviet Union. I think that he was pressured as a Communist. The
situation in the institute, with the arrival of Mochalov as president,
was threatening for Itin. I have great respect for the heroes who
carry out noble acts under inhuman conditions, but I understand that
the overwhelming majority of people cannot be heroes. The system
must be blamed, if under threat of torture, prison, and exile, it
forces a man to commit amoral acts, but it seems to me possible to
demand a certain sense of citizenship from people not threatened by
torture, prison, and deprivation.

5.   S. Feld, The United Balance of Energy for the National Economy
(Moscow: Ekonomika, 1964).

6.   I will note that Pugachev is continuing this practice. I have been
told that after my emigration from the Soviet Union, Pugachev also
came out against his rival, Victor Danilov-Danilian, during the defense
of Danilian's dissertation. Pugachev called attention to the fact that
Danilov-Danilian had done nothing new in comparison with me. In order
to destroy someone else, he did not even fear to use the name of an
emigrant,and the word emigrant in theUSSR is a synonym for scoundrel,
enemy of the people, etc. !

7.   My course consisted of four basic parts. In part I, I covered the
methodology of the investigation of economic systems, including an
analysis of the connection between economics and other humanities
disciplines, as well as biology, technology, and mathematics.
    In the second part, I acquainted the students with the diverse
methods of mathematical description in economics. It is well known
that each method of description provokes a false association with a
certain type of system. The investigation of the possibility of the
transformation of one method of description into another allowed the
students to understand the invariants of different economic systems.
For details, see my book Studies in Soviet Economic Planning (White
Plains, N.Y.: M.E. Sharpe, 1978).
    In the third part of the course, one method of description was
applied to a number of economic categories (rent, wages, depreciation,
interest rate, etc.) and their connections were demonstrated in the
process of dynamic equilibrium.
    Finally, in the fourth part of the course, the mechanisms for ob-
taining dynamic equilibrium were analyzed. Here the evolution of
economic institutions was examined, as well as economic interpretation of several of the algorithms for achieving equilibrium, e.g., the
Dantzig-Wolf algorithm.

8.   With the students in the branch of economic cybernetics at MGU,
the lecturer sensed a reciprocal tie with the audience. Among the
sixty to seventy students who took the economic cybernetics class,
there were a considerable number of capable students. When one is
giving lectures, it is very important to feel that in the audience someone is not simply listening and taking notes, but is also able to think
over what has been said and to react to it, asking questions and throw-
ing out critical remarks.

While I was occupied with seniors and graduate students writing
papers for the course, I tried to select an unknown economic problem
that interested me and to absorb the students with the connected mathematical apparatus. Since the students had a greater knowledge of
mathematics than I, I asked them to tell me about the mathematical
apparatus of the problem being examined. In my turn, I tried to connect
the posing of the problem and the course of its analysis with economic
problems with which I had greater experience.

9.   My investigations in axiology were stimulated by the possibility of
finding several approaches to the substantiation of a moral and ethical
system. To do this, it is possible to use new methods of scientific
research on the functioning of systems under conditions of uncertainty.
The presence of significant knowledge of scientific methods among
contemporary youth encourages in this youth more rationalism, and in
many respects destroys youth's religiosity and receptivity to art, which
are the basic means of transmitting moral values.

In the next decades with mass education in civilized countries,
youth is coming into the arena of history so educated that it is easier
to fall victim to all sorts of Utopian fancies as a result of heightened
rationality. Therefore, it becomes a pressing need to use this rational
knowledge for the elaboration and realization of scientific approaches
to moral and ethical problems and to attract students to art through
this knowledge.

In telling the students about the functioning of systems under conditions of uncertainty in the quite precise language of chess (computer)
programs, I tried at the same time to show them the reflection of these
same problems in fiction. I wanted to bring to the students the ideas
of one of my Moscow friends that the Shakespeare of Hamlet, Macbeth,
Richard, and especially King Lear is the antithesis of Machiavelli,
that these works are a reflection of the argument of the great strategist
Shakespeare with the great tactician, Machiavelli.

I further wanted to bring to the students the elaborations of the
remarkable Soviet writers, Ju. Koriakin and N. Eidelman, who demonstrated how the problem of ends and means evolved from Pushkin's
"Queen of Spades" where Herman, in pursuing the end of obtaining from
the old woman the valuables for the good of his own kin, contributes to
her death; to the great novels of Dostoevski, especially Crime and
Punishment, where Raskolnikov kills the old woman, thinking of the
great ideals of mankind, and ultimately of his own glory. I wanted to
show the students in this connection the grandeur of the ideas of Lev
Tolstoy to demonstrate how he, even more than Dostoevski, realized
the value of the means in and of themselves. After posing the question

of the permissibility of the murder of a robber, Tolstoy pushed the problem of the means to the limit. With the inadmissibility of the murder of the robber, Tolstoy emphasized that murder, whether for the good of mankind, for self-defense, or for any other reason, still destroys the personality of the murderer.

Turning to the ethology of Konrad Lorenz, it might be said that at this time the destruction of the biological instinct against murdering one's own kind is taking place in the murderer. The teaching of the Indian sects which urge the acceptance of death from a killer--thus perished Bandaranaika, the Prime Minister of Ceylon--are remarkable from this standpoint. The borderline situations are significant in that they reveal the problem and allow new conclusions about behavior to be obtained. One of these conclusions is that people who have killed a robber must not be proud of themselves for this, or not so proud of themselves for this, but must mourn and repent because of the means adopted.

And strange as it may seem, I believe that my conversations with students about the reflection in classical literature of the problem of the ends and means were, in a certain sense, entirely in the spirit of the modern demands of those who have power. For countries that have passed through the stage of revolutionary enthusiasm and where the peoples have already succeeded in convincing themselves of the impossibility of realizing the bright ideals of revolution, the government must especially fear all sorts of revolutionary phrases and the actions following from them. Ilin's shot at Brezhnev, although Ilin was declared insane, was a threat. Apparently it is not by chance that Dostoevski's novel, The Possessed, considered for a long time an anti-Communist work, at present is not only published in the Soviet Union, but also receives complete official approval. It is not by chance that a second look is being taken at the attitude toward the members of the People's Will and Tsar Alexander II, to which Iuri Trifonov's novel, Impatience, bears witness; its title apparently is evoked by Natan Eidelman's wonderful book, Lunin. This novel was printed in the 1970s in the journal, Novy Mir, and came out later in a large edition in the State Publishing House of Political Literature in the series, Fiery Revolutionaries.

The above mentioned novels demonstrate that engaging in terrorist activities, even for the noblest of reasons, ultimately leads to the destruction of personality and the transformation of the people involved in these activities into tyrants.

CHAPTER 5

1. A former employee of TSEMI, Emmanual Belitskii, now outside
of the Soviet Union, had written an essay concerning some activivies
of this institute. It was printed by the Soviet and European Research
Center of the Hebrew University of Jerusalem and was distributed
among the Western scholars who were experts on the Soviet economy.
My own evaluation of TSEMI agrees with that of Belitskii's.

2. N. Kobrinskii, The Foundations of Economic Cybernetics (Moscow:
Ekonomika, 1969).

3. N. Kovalev, Computers in Planning (Moscow: Ekonomika, 1964)

4. This could be tested by the collaboration between V. Kossov, the
deputy chief of the Summary Section of the Gosplan, and V. Pugachev.
Kossov and Pugachev were pragmatists. In the moral sense they were
alike. Both of them were distinguished by the unscrupulousness they
employed for career achievements. I think that if they would have in-
stilled methods of optimal planning, they would have had a greater
chance for receiving great wealth, since it was known that several conservative members of the Politburo supported this direction.
      Kossov's and Pugachev's closest collaboration appears to be their
joint article, "The Multi-Stage System of the Optimization of the Calculations of Perspective Economic Plans," published in the journal,
Planovoe Khoziaistvo 10 (1974).
      Furthermore, in the same journal, 4 (1976), V. Kossov and F.
Kotov published a review of the book written by two TSEMI collaborators,
V. Danilov-Danilian and M. Zavelskii, The System of Optimal Planning
of Economy. This book, as well as other similar works published by
TSEMI workers, were subjected to severe criticism in this review.
V. Pugachev's work was the only exception, because they said that it
was "utilized in the Gosplan...for calculating the long-term plan. "

5. See Aron Katsenelinboigen, Studies in Soviet Economic Planning
(New York: M.E. Sharpe, 1978), especially Chapter 1.

6. See V. Lefebvre, The Structure of Awareness (Beverly Hills:
Sage Publications, 1977).

7. Problems in the Optimal Functioning of the Socialist Economy
(Moscow: Nauka, 1972).

8. Boris Mikhalevskii came from a well-known family of economists, and his grandfather, F. Mikhalevskii, was a Corresponding Member of the Academy of Sciences. Mikhalevskii knew languages, apparently the result of education at home, but the bulk of economists and mathematicians who joined the new trend, like the Soviet intelligentsia as a whole, do not know languages. Serious study of languages was typical of families in the old intelligentsia, but after the revolutionary purges of the 1920s and 1930s, there were extremely few of them left in the Soviet Union. The new intelligentsia has only just been formed, and it knows languages only from school, where there are thirty to forty pupils in a class studying languages and classes meet only twice a week. Furthermore, the languages are hardly ever practiced.

9. In the 1930s a special division was created in the NKVD, apparently headed by academician, Evgeni Zhukov, with responsibility for the translation of anything printed in the West that represented a special interest to the Soviet Union. In particular, a book about the organization of the security service in Germany was translated there, as was Moscow of 1937, by Lion Feikhtwanger.

10. In general, it is curious to note that the children of a number of famous traditional economists working in the Institute of Economics of the Academy of Sciences have traveled new paths in science, different from those of their fathers. The daughter of the Doctors of Economic Sciences A. Notkin and F. Lifshits graduated from the Division of Economic Cybernetics at Moscow State University and is working in TSEMI. The son of the Doctor of Economic Sciences, M. Sonin, after getting his Ph.D. in mathematics at MGU, went to work in TSEMI. Fedorenko's daughter began to study in the Division of Economic Cybernetics at MGU, but then transferred to the Division of World Economics.

11. A more detailed understanding of the work programs carried out by Iu. Leibkind and E. Maiminas is given in their article, "Complex Planning System," also signed by N. Fedorenko, A. Modin, S. Shatalin and O. Iun'; the article was published in the journal Ekonomika i Matematicheskie Metody, 3 (1972): pp. 323-341.

12. I wrote a positive review of Maiminas' book in the journal, Izvestiia Akademii Nauk, Seria Ekonomicheskaia 6 (1972): pp. 167-171, although I noted several conservative views of the author.

13. V. Shklovskii, Once Upon a Time (Moscow: Goslitizdat, 1964), p. 394.

CHAPTER 6

1. R. Ackoff, A Concept of Corporate Planning (New York: Wiley,
1970); R. Ackoff and F. Emery, On Purposeful Systems (New York:
Aldine, Atherton, 1972); H. Simon, Models of Man: Social and Rational
(New York: Wiley, 1957); R. Ackoff, Planning in Large Economic
Systems, translated into Russian by G. Rubal'skii (Moscow: Sovetskoe
Radio, 1972).

2. Ackoff, A Concept of Corporate Planning; R. Ackoff and F. Emery,
On Purposeful Systems, translated into Russian by G. Rubal'skii
(Moscow: Sovetskoe Radio, 1974).

3.   Ia. Kronrod, "Theoretical Problems of the Optimal Development
of the National Economy," Planovoe Khoziaistvo, 5 (1973), pp. 80-92;
A. Kats, "Belated Acknowledgements and Fruitless Borrowing,"
Planovoe Khoziaistvo 7 (1972), pp. 91-108, 9 (1972), pp. 107-127,
10 (1972), pp. 103-121; Iu. Belik, "Scientific Predition in Long Range
Planning," Planovoe Khoziaistvo 5 (1973), pp. 24-35.

4.   For example, in 1960, Evald Il'enkov published a philosophy book,
The Dialectics of the Abstract and Concrete in Marx's Kapital (Moscow:
Nauka, 1960). In its time, the book was a phenomenon in the scholarly
world, although it was in fact written from a Marxist position. It was
a work with an attempt at serious discussions, thus sharply distinguished from the accepted propagandistic literature. Il'enkov's book went
through many difficulties, however. It was already being printed, the
Italian Communists applied to Il'enkov for permission to have the
manuscript of the book for translation, and Il'enkov gave them the
manuscript. At this time in the Soviet Union, the case against Boris
Pasternak had begun with the particular accusation that the manuscript
of his book had been published in Italy. As Il'enkov's book had been
approved with great difficulty--Il'enkov also had a reputation as a free-
thinker--he became frightened that its appearance in Italy before its
appearance in the USSR could lead to unfortunate results. Il'enkov
rushed to announce to the Party organization of the Philosophy Institute
that he had committed such an unseemly act as the transfer of the
manuscript. The joy of the Party bosses at the institute was indes-
cribable; the institue had its own Pasternak. They fairly swaggered
around Il'enkov--he received, it seems, a strict reprimand as a member of the Party--the publication of the book was halted, the layout
was almost destroyed; but finally the book was published.
      Kronrod considered himself, and not without reason, the philosopher

of economics. Kronrod's destructive review, "Concerning the Mistaken Enlightenment of the Problems of the Marxist Economic Theory" of Il'enkov's book followed in the journal Voprosy Ekonomiki 2 (1961): pp. 143-146. In this review, Kronrod did not spare abuse and name-calling. Workers at the journal told me that in their opinion the published review, which had been edited by the staff, was the height of decency in contrast to the original version.

5.   An analogical position could have been observed in Soviet biology. It is well know that for a long time the monopoly in biology was in the hands of the late academician T. Lysenko, who was the bitterest enemy of the geneticists. After a long conflict, Lysenko was overthrown. Lysenko's enemy, the famous geneticist and academician Nicolai Dubinin, was victorious. Immediately, Dubinin began to introduce an Arachkeev-like regime in the genetics institute he headed, suppressing new ideas. Moreover, in the elections at the Academy of Sciences, Lysenko and Dubinin were often known to form alliances against scholars who did not agree with their opinions.

6.   Information Bulletin #9, The Scientific Council of Concrete Sociological Investigations of the Academy of Sciences of the USSR, Moscow, 1968.

7.   Nikolai Baibakov, "The Future Improvement of Planning--The Most Important National Economic Task," Planovoe Khoziaistvo 3 (1974): p. 12.

8.   J. Stalin, Economic Problems of Socialism in the USSR (New York: International Publisher, 1952).

9.   E. Liberman, "Concerning the Economic Levers for Fulfillment of the Plan by the Soviet Industry," Kommunist 1 (1959): pp. 88-97.

10. Ivan Shevtsov, In the Name of Father and Son (Moscow: Moskovskii Rabochii Publisher, 1970).

11. A. Kats, "Belated Acknowledgements and Fruitless Borrowings," Planovoe Khoziaistvo 7 (1972): pp. 91-108, 9 (1972): pp. 107-127, 10 (1972): pp. 103-121.

12. Iu. Belik, "Scientific Prediction in Long-Range Planning," Planovoe Khoziaistvo 5 (1973): pp. 24-35; and Ia. Kronrod, "Theoretical Problems of the Optimal Development of the National Economy," Planovoe Khoziaistvo 5 (1973): pp. 80-92.

13. I. Soloviev, "A Strange Position," Pravda, June 4, 1973, No. 155 (20029), p. 2.

14. I would like to point out that in the environment of the Soviet intelligentsia, consciousness of the intrinsic value of the means is growing. A remarkable specialist in the sphere of mathematical psychology, V. Lefebvr, was working in TSEMI. Lefebvr is a person of tremendous decency and brilliant talent, a man of his own convictions, who at the same time well understands the importance of the right of the members of the Soviet intelligentsia to think differently. Georgi Shchedrovitskii, who has done much for the establishment of a number of modern trends in Soviet philosophy, was in a certain sense Lefebvr's teacher. Then their paths diverged; their meetings at seminars or conferences were usually accompanied by hot and caustic arguments.

At the beginning of the 1970s, Shchedrovitskii wrote an article in Literaturnaia Gazeta about the impossibility of working on concrete sociological investigations until the necessary concepts were developed. This article concentrated on the importance of the scientific basis for concrete investigations, especially with the stormy flow of inquiries of dilettantes. At a time when conservative philosophers came out against sociology in every way, this article, with its extreme character, had an important negative effect.

The advocates of concrete sociological investigations decided to repulse Shchedrovitskii, using for this their own powerful patrons. In reply to Shchedrovitskii's article, a rejoinder appeared in Pravda in which Shchedrovitskii was accused of all sorts of mortal sins, right down to a deviation from dialectical materialism. Shchedrovitskii's dissidence--he had signed the collective letters in defense of the condemned dissidents--plus the rejoinder in Pravda did their job; he was dismissed from work. With great difficulty he later succeeded in finding some sort of temporary refuge. Such are the drawbacks of the renaissance of science in the Soviet Union.

After the appearance of the rejoinder in Pravda, Lefebvr wrote an article in Shchedrovitskii's defense and sent it to Literaturnaia Gazeta. Lefebvr did not share Shchedrovitskii's concept, but he well understood that it was impossible to defend the brightest ideals by shoddy means, as it was done by Pravda. Unfortunately, the state of his health, the result of living through the Leningrad blockade in his childhood, prevented Lefebvr from playing a more active political role. The conflict between the sharp sense of the injustice of life in the Soviet Union in a man with an intensified sense of citizenship and a fighter by nature, and the small opportunities he had for fighting because of the condition of his health, led to Lefebvr's decision to emigrate in 1974.

15. "The Actual Problems of Planning, " Planovoe Khoziaistvo 10 (1973): pp. 152-157.

16. A similar case in relation to a review in Pravda, although not of such magnitide, occurred in the mid-1960s. An article appeared in Pravda in which Pavel Bunich's doctoral dissertation was attacked. The Academic Council of the Moscow Institute of the National Economy, where the dissertation was defended, after discussing the article in Pravda, decided that the author of the article was basically incorrect. The Ministry of Higher and Secondary Specialized Education created a special commission to investigate the case mentioned in the article in Pravda. Among the commission members was the provost of the Moscow Institute of the National Economy, Alexander Birman. During the meeting of the commission, Birman unexpectedly turned to the author of the article in Pravda with a question that seemed stupid at first, "Had he read the dissertation which he criticized?" The author of the article replied that, of course, he had. Then Birman asked him where he read the dissertation. The author replied that it must have been in the library of the Moscow Institute of the National Economy; the dissertation was transferred to the library of the institute where the defense was to take place no later than ten days before defense. Then Birman took from his briefcase a reference from the library of the institute that showed that Bunich's dissertation had not been used; all readers are noted on the library card in the dissertation. In reply, the author of the article announced that he apparently had read the dissertation in the Lenin Library, the official location for copies of all defended dissertations. Then Birman took from his briefcase a statement from the Lenin Library, maintaining that the dissertation had not been received in the library. A scene of silence.... After such an unexpected development in the case, the decision of the commission was determined.

　　Pravda cannot write that it permitted a mistake printing the article against Bunich. Pravda, as an organ of the supreme power, is exempt from criticism, but it saves itself through self-criticism. The form of Pravda's applogy to Bunich was that after some time an article of his was published therein.

17. S. Trapenikov, "Economics--On the Level of Modern Problems, " Voprosy Ekonomiki 2 (1974): pp. 3-18.

18. P. Fedoseev, "Economics: Several Problems in Its Development," Voprosy Ekonomiki 2 (1974): pp. 60-64.

Index

About the Author

ARON KATSENELINBOIGEN was born in 1927 in the Soviet Union. He graduated from Moscow State Economic Institute in 1946 and obtained a Doctor of Sciences degree in Economics in 1966 from this institute. From 1956 to 1973 he worked in the USSR Academy of Sciences and was promoted to a head of the Department of Complex Systems at the Central Economic Mathematical Institute. From 1970 to 1973 Professor Katsenelinboigen taught mathematical economics at Moscow State University.

Since his emigration to the United States in 1973, Dr. Katsenelinboigen has been a visiting lecturer in the Department of Economics at the University of Pennsylvania, and in 1978 he joined the Social Sciences Systems Unit of this university as a research professor.

Dr. Katsenelinboigen is the author of seven books, the last of which was published in the United States under the title Studies in Soviet Economic Planning (White Plains, N.Y. : M.E. Sharpe, 1978). About 25 articles of the author have been published, but only in the western countries.

Dr. Katsenelinboigen's current research primarily concerns systems and values, creativity, creation of a potential of a system, and economic invariants.